For Mica and Conor

www.houghtonmifflinbooks.com

The text of this book is set in 11.5-point Souvenir Light.
Photo credits appear on page 260.

Library of Congress Cataloging-in-Publication Data
Schlosser, Eric.
Chew on this : everything you don't want to know about fast food
/ written by Eric Schlosser and Charles Wilson.
p. cm.
Includes index.
ISBN 0-618-71031-0 (hardcover)
1. Junk food—Juvenile literature. 2. Eating habits—Juvenile literature. 3. Fast food restaurants—
Juvenile literature. 4. Food industry and trade—Juvenile literature. I. Wilson, Charles, 1974– II. Title.
TX370.S35 2006
394.1'2—dc22
2005027527

ISBN-13: 978-0-618-71031-7
Printed in the United States of America
QUM 10 9 8 7 6 5 4 3 2

EVERYTHING YOU
DON'T WANT TO KNOW
ABOUT FAST FOOD

BY **ERIC SCHLOSSER** AND CHARLES WILSON

Houghton Mifflin ⌇ Boston

Contents

Introduction   7
The Pioneers   13
The Youngster Business   37
McJobs   63
The Secret of the Fries   92
Stop the Pop   128
Meat   156
Big   202
Your Way   234
Photo Credits   260
Notes   262
Acknowledgments   293
Index   297

Pull open the glass door and feel the rush of cool air. Step inside. Look at the backlit color pictures of food above the counter, look at the cardboard ads for the latest Disney movie, get in line, and place your order. Hand over some money. Put the change back in your pocket. Watch teenagers in blue-and-gold uniforms busy working in the kitchen. Moments later, grab the plastic tray with your food, find an empty table, and sit down. Unwrap the burger, squirt ketchup on the fries, stick the plastic straw through the hole in the lid of your drink. Pick up the burger and dig in.

The whole experience of eating at a fast-food restaurant has become so familiar, so routine, that we take it for granted. It has become just another habit, like brushing your teeth before bed. We do it without even thinking about it—and that's the problem.

Every day about one out of fourteen Americans eats at a McDonald's. Every month about nine out of ten American children visit one. McDonald's has become the most popular fast-food chain in the world—and by far the most powerful. In 1968 there were about 1,000 McDonald's restaurants, all of them in the United States. Now there are more than 31,000 McDonald's, selling Happy Meals in 120 countries, from Istanbul, Turkey, to Papeete, Tahiti. In the United States, McDonald's buys more processed beef, chicken, pork, apples, and potatoes than any other company. It spends more money on advertising and marketing than any other company that sells food. As a result, it is America's most famous food brand. The impact of McDonald's on the way we live today is truly mind-boggling. The Golden Arches are now more widely recognized than the Christian cross.

Despite McDonald's fame and all the money it spends on advertising, every day the vast majority of its customers don't plan to eat there. Most fast-food visits are impulsive. The decision to buy fast food is usually made at the last minute, without much thought. People generally don't leave the house in the morning saying, "I'm going to make sure to eat some fast food today." Most of the time, they're just walking down the sidewalk or driving down the road, not thinking about anything in particular. Maybe they're hungry; maybe they're not. Maybe they're in a hurry and don't have time to cook. And then they see a great big fast-food sign—the Golden Arches, the red-and-blue of a Domino's pizza box, the picture of Colonel Sanders— and they suddenly think, "Hey, I want some of that." So they stop to eat fast food. They do it because they feel like it. They just can't resist the impulse.

The point of this book is to take that strong impulse we all feel—our hunger for sweet, salty, fatty fast foods—and make you think about it. *Chew On This* will tell you where fast food comes from, who makes it, what's in it, and what happens when you eat it. This is a book about fast food and the world it has made.

Food is one of the most important things you'll ever buy. And yet most people never bother to think about their food and where it comes from. People spend a lot more time worrying about what kind of blue jeans to wear, what kind of video games to play, what kind of computers to buy. They compare the different models and styles, they talk to friends about the various options, they read as much as they can before making a choice. But those purchases don't really matter. When you get tired of old blue jeans, video games, and computers, you can just give them away or throw them out.

The food you eat enters your body and literally becomes part of you. It helps determine whether you'll be short or tall, weak or strong, thin or fat. It helps determine whether you will enjoy a long, healthy life or die young. Food is of fundamental importance. So why is it that most people don't think about fast food and don't know much about it?

The simple answer is this: the companies that sell fast food *don't want you to think about it*. They don't want you to know where it comes from and how it's made. They just want you to buy it.

Have you ever seen a fast-food ad that shows the factories

where French fries are made? Ever seen a fast-food ad that shows the slaughterhouses where cattle are turned into ground beef? Ever seen an ad that tells you what's really in your fast-food milk shake and why some strange-sounding chemicals make it taste so good? Ever seen an ad that shows overweight, unhealthy kids stuffing their faces with greasy fries at a fast-food restaurant? You probably haven't. But you've probably seen a lot of fast-food commercials that show thin, happy children having a lot of fun.

People have been eating since the beginning of time. But they've only been eating Chicken McNuggets since 1983. Fast food is a recent invention. During the past thirty years, fast food has spread from the United States to every corner of the globe. A business that began with a handful of little hot dog and hamburger stands in southern California now sells the all-American meal—a hamburger, French fries, and soda—just about everywhere. Fast food is now sold at restaurants and drive-throughs, at baseball stadiums, high schools, elementary schools, and universities, on cruise ships, trains, and airplanes, at Kmarts, Wal-Marts, and even the cafeterias of children's hospitals. In 1970, Americans spent about $6 billion on fast food. In 2005, they spent about $134 billion on fast food. Americans now spend more money on fast food than on college education, personal computers, computer software, or new cars. They spend more on fast food than on movies, books, magazines, newspapers, and recorded music—combined.

Fast food may look like the sort of food people have always eaten, but it's different. It's not the kind of food you can make in your kitchen from scratch. Fast food is something radically new. Indeed, the food we eat has changed more during the past thirty years than during the previous thirty thousand years.

In the pages that follow, you'll learn how the fast-food business got started. You'll learn how the fast-food chains try to get kids into their restaurants, how they treat kids working in their kitchens, how they make their food. And you'll learn what can happen when you eat too much of it. These are things you really need to know. Why? Because fast food is heavily advertised to kids and often prepared by workers who are kids themselves. This is an industry that both feeds and feeds off the young.

For the most part, fast food tastes pretty good. That's one of the main reasons people like to eat it. Fast food has been carefully designed to taste good. It's also inexpensive and convenient. But the Happy Meals, two-for-one deals, and free refills of soda give a false sense of how much fast food actually costs. The real price never appears on the menu.

Hundreds of millions of people eat fast food every day

without giving it much thought. They just unwrap their hamburgers and dig in. An hour or so later, when the burger's all gone and the wrapper's been tossed into the garbage, the whole meal has already been forgotten. Chew on this: people should know what lies beneath the shiny, happy surface of every fast-food restaurant. They should know what really lurks between those sesame seed buns. As the old saying goes: you are what you eat.

THE PIONEERS

Hamburger Charlie

The story of fast food begins in October 1885, near the small town of Seymour, Wisconsin. A friendly and outgoing fifteen-year-old boy named Charlie Nagreen was driving his family's ox cart down a dirt road amid wide-open fields. Charlie was going to Outagamie County's first annual fair, where he wanted to earn some extra money selling meatballs. What happened next was the unlikely origin of a delicious sandwich that would one day change the world.

As Charlie sold meatballs at the fair, he noticed that customers had trouble eating them and strolling at the same time. People were impatient. They wanted to visit Mr. John Bull's popular beehives (encased in glass), to see the fancy new harvesting machines, and to enjoy all the other thrilling attractions at the fair. They didn't want to waste time eating meatballs. Charlie suddenly had an idea: if he squashed the meatballs and put them between two slices of bread, people could walk and eat. And so Charlie invented the hamburger.

German immigrants lived in Charlie's hometown of Hortonville, Wisconsin, and he later claimed that the new sandwich was named after the German town of Hamburg, long famous for its ground-beef steaks. Charlie continued selling burgers at the Outagamie County Fair until 1951. By then he was an old man who liked to sing this rhyme while flipping burgers on the grill:

Hamburgers, hamburgers, hamburgers hot!
Onions in the middle, pickle on top.
Makes your lips go flippity flop.

Charlie had not only invented the hamburger but also composed one of the first advertising jingles for it.

A number of other cities—including New Haven, Connecticut; Akron, Ohio; and Hamburg, New York—now claim to be the true birthplace of America's favorite sandwich. But the residents of Seymour, Wisconsin, will have none of that. The signs that welcome people into Seymour let everybody know they're entering THE HOME OF THE HAMBURGER. And every August the town has a big parade in honor of Hamburger Charlie.

killer burgers

Despite Charlie's best efforts, burgers didn't become America's national dish overnight. For a long time after that 1885 Outagamie County Fair, hamburger meat had a bad reputation. Many people assumed that ground beef was dirty. According to one historian, during the early 1900s the hamburger was considered "a food for the poor," polluted and unsafe to eat. Restaurants generally didn't sell them. Burgers were served at lunch carts parked near factories, at circuses and carnivals. It was widely believed that ground beef was made from rotten old meat full of chemical preservatives. "The hamburger habit is just about as safe," one food critic warned, "as getting meat out of a garbage can."

The hamburger's reputation wasn't helped when murderers started using ground beef to kill people. In 1910, Alexander J. Moody, a wealthy baker from Chicago, died after somebody put poison in his burger. The police were never able to solve the case. One year later, a Chicago pie maker was poisoned the same way. Similar murder stories appeared in newspapers

ONE DEAD, SIX ARE ILL FROM POISONED DINNER

Paterson Man's Whole Household Affected, Possibly from Arsenic.

AGED WOMAN SOON SUCCUMBS

One Victim, Eating Only Beef, Is Affected as Are the Others—County Physician's Inquiry.

Death by hamburger, April 1904

across the United States. Ground beef seemed like the perfect food in which to hide a deadly poison.

The widespread fear of hamburgers caused a great deal of frustration among butchers. They liked to grind leftover pieces of beef into hamburger meat. They liked selling every scrap of meat in the store. They didn't want to waste any of it. But most customers preferred to buy solid pieces of steak. That way you could see exactly what you were buying—and feel confident there was nothing poisonous in it.

In 1925, when New Yorkers were asked to name their favorite meal, hamburger ranked nineteenth. Of the 180,000 people who voted for their favorites, just 2,912 voted for hamburger. It beat out gefilte fish (1,361 votes). But the burger lost big to corned beef and cabbage (23,061 votes) and roast loin of pork (5,411 votes). By a wide margin, most New Yorkers even preferred eating cow tongue and spinach (8,400 votes).

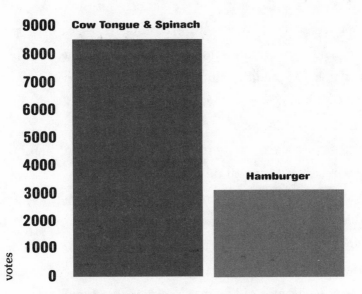

Preference for hamburger or cow tongue
and spinach among New Yorkers, 1925

Around this time Walt Anderson set out to defend the hamburger from its many critics. A former janitor and short-order cook, Walt loved burgers and opened a small restaurant in Wichita, Kansas, devoted to selling them. Walt grilled the burgers right in front of his customers, so they could see for themselves that the meat and the equipment were clean. The place was so successful that Walt found a business partner and started opening more hamburger restaurants, built in the shape of small white medieval forts. Walt called them White Castles, a name suggesting that the place was solid and the food was pure. White Castle restaurants claimed that their ground beef was delivered twice a day, to insure freshness, and supported an unusual experiment at the University of Minnesota. For thirteen weeks a medical student there consumed nothing but White Castle burgers and water. When the student not only survived the experiment but also seemed pretty healthy, people started to view hamburgers in a new light. Now hamburgers seemed wholesome, not deadly.

White Castle was popular among workingmen in the East and the Midwest, but it didn't attract many women or children. It didn't turn hamburgers into America's favorite sandwich or create the modern fast-food business. A pair of brothers in southern California did all that, along with a traveling salesman who for years had failed at just about everything he tried.

speedee service

Richard and Maurice (Mac) McDonald left New Hampshire in the 1930s, hoping to find jobs in southern California's movie business. For a while they built scenery at a Hollywood studio, saved their money, and then bought their own movie theater in Glendale, California. The theater was a flop, and the two brothers struggled to come up with ideas for how to make a living.

All around them, southern California was giving birth to a whole new way of life—and a new way of eating. Los Angeles was growing at the very moment when ordinary people could finally afford to buy cars. New roads were being built, and farmland was rapidly being turned into houses, shops, and parking lots. Between 1920 and 1940, the number of people in southern California almost tripled, as families from across the United States moved there to find work and enjoy the warm, sunny weather. By 1940 there were about a million cars in Los Angeles, more than anywhere else in the United States. Los Angeles soon became unlike any other city in the world, sprawling for miles and miles. It was a city of the future, designed to be traveled by car.

The new mood in southern California encouraged people to question how things had been done in the past and to come up with fresh ideas. Anything felt possible in a place that was changing so quickly. Cars gave people a sense of freedom, a feeling of control over their lives—and a love of speed. All the changes sweeping through Los Angeles seemed to preach the same basic message: faster is better. The world's first motel was built there (allowing you to park your car right in front of your room), as well as the first drive-through bank (allowing you to get money without getting out of your car). More importantly, a whole new kind of restaurant appeared.

"People with cars are so lazy they don't want to get out of them to eat!" said Jesse G. Kirby, the founder of a drive-in restaurant. When you parked at Kirby's Pig Stand, a waitress came to the car to take your order, then brought your food to the car. Los Angeles was soon full of Pig Stands and other restaurants just like them. In the rest of the United States, drive-in restaurants were usually open only during the summer. In Los Angeles, it felt like summer all year long. The drive-ins never had to close, and an exciting new business was born.

So many drive-in restaurants opened in southern California that they had to compete for attention. Restaurant owners often painted the drive-ins in loud colors and covered them in flashy neon lights, hoping to catch the eye of people driving past at high speed. The owners hired pretty girls to work as waitresses and came up with all sorts of memorable uniforms for them. The young waitresses, known as "carhops," were often

Carhops at the Chicken Villa

dressed up like cowgirls, cheerleaders, or Scottish girls in kilts. Carhops weren't paid by the hour. They earned money from tips and received a small share of the money their customers spent. The more food and drinks a customer ordered, the more money a carhop earned. As a result, carhops tended to be very nice to their customers and encouraged them to eat and drink a lot.

Drive-in restaurants soon became popular hangouts for teenage boys. Drive-ins seemed cool. They were something really new and different—a mix of pretty girls and cars and late-night food. Before long, the bright lights of drive-ins were beckoning customers at intersections all over Los Angeles. Eager to cash in on the new craze, Richard and Mac McDonald opened their own drive-in restaurant in 1937. Located in Pasadena, California, it had three carhops and sold mostly hot dogs. A few years later Richard and Mac moved the restaurant to a larger building in San Bernardino and opened the McDonald Brothers Burger Bar Drive-In. The new restaurant was right next to a high school, employed twenty carhops, and soon made the McDonald brothers rich.

By the end of the 1940s, however, the McDonald brothers had grown tired of the drive-in business. They were tired of constantly looking for new carhops and cooks as the old ones left for jobs that paid more money. They were tired of replacing the dishes, glassware, and silverware that their teenage customers often broke or stole. And they were tired of their teenage customers. The brothers thought about selling their restaurant. Instead, they decided to try something new.

Richard and Mac fired all their carhops in 1948. They closed the McDonald Brothers Burger Bar Drive-In, installed larger grills, and reopened three months later with a radical new system for preparing food. The system was designed to prepare food faster, lower the prices, and increase sales. The brothers got rid of most of the items on the menu. They got rid of everything that had to be eaten with a knife, spoon, or fork. They got rid of regular plates and glasses, replacing them with paper cups and paper plates. All the food on the new menu could be held in your hand and eaten while driving a car. The only sandwiches the new restaurant sold were hamburgers and cheeseburgers.

The McDonald brothers also changed how the work was done in the kitchen. Instead of having one skilled cook who knew how to prepare many kinds of food, they hired a few people to prepare the same thing again and again. Workers in the kitchen became like workers on a factory assembly line, repeating the same simple tasks all day. One person grilled the hamburgers; another person put them in buns and wrapped them in paper; another person made the milk shakes; another person cooked French fries. Skilled cooks were no longer necessary. Workers only needed to learn how to do one thing, not many things. People were easy to hire for these jobs, easy to fire, and unlikely to demand a big paycheck. Richard and Mac had turned their restaurant kitchen into a little factory for making cheap fast food.

All the hamburgers were sold with the same toppings: ketchup, onions, mustard, and two pickles. No substitutions were allowed. And since there were no carhops, nobody brought the food to your car. You had to get out of the car, wait in line, and get the food yourself. The McDonald brothers called this new arrangement the Speedee Service System. An ad of theirs later spelled out some of its benefits for restaurant owners: "Imagine—No Car Hops—No Waitresses—No Dishwashers— No Bus Boys—The McDonald System is Self-Service!"

Richard McDonald designed a new building for the restaurant, aiming to make it easy to spot from the road. Although Richard had no training as an architect, the building that he sketched became one of the most important and influential designs of the twentieth century. On two sides of the roof he put golden arches. They were lit by neon at night, and from a distance looked like the letter M. His design combined advertising with architecture and created one of the most famous corporate logos in the world.

The Speedee Service System, however, got off to a slow start. Customers drove up to the restaurant, sat in their cars, and waited to be served. They honked their horns and wondered what had happened to the carhops. People weren't used to waiting in line and getting their own food. Within a few weeks, however, customers learned the new routine and started to arrive in droves. But the McDonald brothers didn't want their restaurant to become a teenage hangout. They wanted to attract as many people as possible and worried that hiring young girls would attract the wrong crowd. So they employed only young men behind the counter. Families started to line up at the McDonald brothers' new restaurant. One historian described the lasting impact of their new self-service system: "Working-class families could finally afford to feed their kids restaurant food."

orphans, dropouts, and self-made men

The first McDonald's was so successful that other restaurant owners were soon visiting it, taking notes, and opening places just like it. "Our food was exactly the same as McDonald's," the founder of a rival fast-food chain later admitted. "If I had looked at McDonald's and saw someone flipping hamburgers while he was hanging by his feet, I would have copied it."

Carl Karcher drove to the new McDonald's from Anaheim, California, where he ran Carl's Drive-In Barbeque. After seeing the long lines of people waiting to eat McDonald's fifteen-cent burgers, he went home and opened his own self-service restaurant, naming it Carl's Jr. Keith G. Cramer, the owner of Keith's Drive-In Restaurant in Daytona Beach, Florida, heard about the McDonald brothers, flew to California, ate at their restaurant, returned home, and with his father-in-law opened the first

Insta-Burger King. Glen W. Bell, Jr., fought in World War II, came back to California, and ate at the new McDonald's. He decided to copy it and use the kitchen's assembly-line system to make Mexican food. The restaurant chain he founded came to be known as Taco Bell.

The people who started America's mighty fast-food companies weren't rich or famous. They didn't work for big banks or corporations. Most of them never even went to college. They were self-made men who worked hard and took risks in pursuit of their dreams. They were door-to-door salesmen, orphans, and high school dropouts. They were true entrepreneurs.

William Rosenberg dropped out of school at the age of fourteen, delivered telegrams for Western Union, drove an ice cream truck, worked as a door-to-door salesman, sold sandwiches and coffee to factory workers in Boston, and then opened a small doughnut shop. He named it Dunkin' Donuts. Dave Thomas started working in a restaurant at the age of twelve, left his adoptive father, took a room at the YMCA, dropped out of school at fifteen, served as a busboy and a cook, and later opened his own fast-food place in Columbus, Ohio, calling it Wendy's Old Fashioned Hamburgers Restaurant. Thomas S. Monaghan spent much of his childhood in a Catholic orphanage and a series of foster homes, barely graduated from high school, joined the Marines, and bought a pizzeria with his brother in Ypsilanti, Michigan, getting hold of the restaurant with a first payment of just $75. Eight months later his brother decided to quit, accepting a used Volkswagen Beetle for his share of the business—which was soon called Domino's Pizza. At the age of seventeen, Frederick DeLuca borrowed $1,000 from a family friend and opened a sandwich shop in Bridgeport, Connecticut. He named it Subway.

The story of Harland Sanders is perhaps the most remarkable. Sanders left school at the age of twelve, worked as a farmhand, a mule tender, and a railway fireman. At various times he worked as a lawyer without having a law degree and delivered babies without having a medical degree. He sold insurance door to door, sold Michelin tires, and operated a gas station in Corbin, Kentucky. He served home-cooked food at a small dining room table in the back of the gas station, later opened a popular restaurant and motel, and then had to sell them both to pay off debts. At the age of sixty-five, Sanders became a traveling salesman once again, offering restaurant owners the "secret recipe" for his fried chicken.

The first Kentucky Fried Chicken restaurant opened in 1952, near Salt Lake City, Utah. Lacking money to promote the restaurant, Sanders dressed up like a Kentucky colonel, wearing

Harland Sanders

a white suit and a black string tie. The outfit gained a lot of attention, and Sanders helped turn KFC into the largest fast-food chicken chain. His smiling face and Kentucky colonel out-fit now appear on restaurant signs and fried chicken buckets all over the world. But the truth is, Colonel Sanders never served in the military. He just liked to dress up like a colonel.

dog eat dog

Although the McDonald brothers were a big success in San Bernardino, if it weren't for a salesman named Ray Kroc, the rest of the world might never have heard of them or their hamburgers. Kroc was selling milk-shake mixers in 1954 when he first visited the McDonald's self-service restaurant. The brothers were two of his best customers. The milk-shake machine that Kroc sold was called a Multimixer. It could make five milk shakes at once. Kroc wondered why the McDonald brothers needed eight of these machines. That was a lot of milk shakes for one small burger joint. Over the years Kroc had visited a lot of restaurant kitchens, demonstrating all the special features of the Multimixer. But he'd never seen anything like the McDonald's Speedee Service System. Kroc looked at the new restaurant "through the eyes of a salesman" and dreamed about putting McDonald's at busy intersections across the United States.

Up until that day Kroc's life had been full of failure, missed opportunities, and disappointment. He'd grown up in Oak Park, Illinois, not far from Chicago, where his father worked for a telegram company. Kroc was a charming and funny young man. He set out to be a jazz musician, played in a band at nightclubs, and worked at a Chicago radio station. Unable to earn a good living as a musician, he became a traveling sales-man. He'd picked up a few tricks of the trade while briefly employed at his uncle's coffee shop. "That was where I learned you could influence people with a smile and with enthusiasm," Kroc later admitted, "and sell them a sundae when what they'd come for was a cup of coffee."

For years Kroc struggled to find the product that would earn him a fortune. At various times he sold coffee beans, sheet music, paper cups, Florida real estate, powdered instant drinks called Malt-A-Plenty and Shake-A-Plenty, a gadget that could dispense whipped cream or shaving cream, and square ice cream scoops. The main problem with square scoops of ice cream, he discov-ered, was that they slid off the plate when you tried to eat them. Despite one setback after another, Kroc kept at it, always con-vinced that success was waiting just around the corner. "If you believe in it, and you believe in it hard," he later said, "it's impos-sible to fail. I don't care what it is—you can get it!"

After meeting with the McDonald brothers, Kroc was eager to go into business with them and spread their Speedee Service System nationwide. Richard and Mac were less ambi-tious. They were already earning more than $100,000 a year

Ray Kroc

from their restaurant, a huge amount in those days. Nevertheless, Kroc convinced the brothers to let him open new McDonald's restaurants. Richard and Mac could stay at home while Kroc traveled around the country making them even richer. A contract was signed, and the three men became business partners.

After gaining the right to use the McDonald's name and the Speedee Service System, Kroc faced a big problem. He didn't have the money to open new restaurants across the United States. And banks wouldn't lend money to the high school dropouts and dreamers like him who were trying to create fast-food businesses. The banks thought it was too risky. So Kroc used a new type of franchising deal to get the money.

Under one of these deals, a local businessman would build a new McDonald's restaurant with his own money—and Kroc would tell him exactly how to run it. The profits from the restaurant would be shared. Franchising arrangements had been around for decades, but Kroc came up with one that proved extremely successful. Franchising became central to the growth not only of McDonald's but of the entire fast-food business. It allowed companies to open many restaurants without spending much money and gave local businessmen a chance to make a lot of money without having to figure out how to run a restaurant.

The key to a successful franchise can be described in a single word: sameness. Ray Kroc insisted that everything be the same at every one of the new McDonald's restaurants. The signs had to be the same. The buildings had to be the same. The menus had to be the same. And, most importantly, the food had to taste exactly the same. If the fries were lousy at one McDonald's, Kroc worried that it would hurt business at every McDonald's. He had little patience for McDonald's restaurant owners who tried to do things differently, who would not conform to his rules. "We have found out . . . that we cannot trust some people who are nonconformists," Kroc once said. "We will make conformists out of them in a hurry. The organization cannot trust the individual; the individual must trust the organization."

Kroc didn't look for wealthy people to put up the money for new McDonald's restaurants. He tried to find businessmen who would actually run the restaurants as well as own them—people willing to give up their former lives and devote themselves fully to McDonald's. These new owners had to start with just one restaurant. They would have to follow Kroc's orders. And if they behaved well, they would get the chance to open a second McDonald's. Most of all, Kroc demanded loyalty. He believed so completely in McDonald's that the company almost seemed to him like a new religion. Anyone who broke the rules was likely to be punished. And any other restaurant chain that tried to steal McDonald's customers was headed for trouble. Kroc had a harsh view of how to compete with fast-food rivals. "This is rat eat rat, dog eat dog," he argued. "I'll kill 'em, and

I'm going to kill 'em before they kill me. You're talking about the American way of survival of the fittest."

While Kroc traveled the country, spreading the word about the Speedee Service System, Richard and Mac relaxed in San Bernardino. Kroc began to resent the McDonald brothers, claiming that while he was doing all the hard work—"grinding it out, grunting and sweating like a galley slave"—they were sitting at home, reaping the rewards. His original agreement with the McDonalds gave them the right to block any changes to the Speedee Service System. The brothers had the final word in running the restaurants that carried their name, a fact that angered Kroc. In 1961, Kroc borrowed money to buy Richard and Mac's share of the company. The brothers each received about $1 million. That sounds like a lot of money. But as the company grew, so did the value of what they gave up. If Richard and Mac had kept their share of McDonald's instead of selling it to Ray Kroc, by the 1990s their income would have reached more than $180 million a year.

As part of the buyout deal, the McDonald brothers insisted on keeping their original restaurant in San Bernardino. Kroc let Richard and Mac keep that one restaurant, but forced them to change its name. "Eventually I opened a McDonald's across the street from that store, which they had renamed The Big M," Kroc later admitted, "and it ran them out of business."

more and more of the same

Led by McDonald's, the fast-food industry spread across the United States. The southern California way of life was no longer so unusual. The federal government was building the interstate highway system, encouraging people to travel by automobile. Other cities began to rely on cars instead of trains, and new suburbs grew throughout the country, just as they had in Los Angeles. Between 1960 and 1973, the number of McDonald's restaurants increased from 200 to almost 3,000. Gasoline shortages in 1973 gave the fast-food industry a brief scare, as many people worried that America's love affair with the automobile was about to end. When that crisis passed, McDonald's began to open restaurants in downtown city centers as well as in the suburbs. One by one, the founding fathers of the fast-food business sold their companies or retired. An industry that had started in the 1950s with a series of small, local fast-food chains became dominated in the 1980s by multinational corporations. Family-owned restaurants found it hard to compete with these giants and began to disappear.

The success of McDonald's had an enormous impact on other small businesses, too. Franchising deals seemed like an easy way to create new companies in everything from the auto parts business (Meineke Discount Mufflers) to the weight-control business (Jenny Craig International). Some companies grew through franchising, others by owning all their stores. The most important thing that many businesses copied from McDonald's was the total dedication to sameness. They started selling the same products the same way in hundreds of buildings that looked exactly the same. In 1969, Donald and Doris Fisher decided to open a store in San Francisco that would sell blue jeans the way that McDonald's, Burger King, and KFC sold fast food. They called their store the Gap. Thirty years later, there were more than 1,700 Gap, GapKids, and BabyGap stores in the United States. American cities and towns that once looked very different from one another—that once had mainly small, family-owned businesses—all began to look the same.

Hamburger Charlie could hardly have imagined, as he squished those meatballs between two pieces of bread at the Outagamie County Fair, how much change one sandwich could set in motion. Hamburgers eventually became a lot more popular than cow tongue and spinach. Altogether, Americans now eat about 13 billion hamburgers every year. If you put all those burgers in a straight line, they would circle the earth more than thirty-two times.

THE YOUNGSTER BUSINESS

In late August 2004, on the island of Singapore, John Pain asked a large gathering of businesspeople from Malaysia, China, Indonesia, and the Philippines to stand up. Then he asked them to raise their arms and form the shape of three letters, one after another.

"Give me a Y!" Pain yelled out.

"Y!" they yelled back. The auditorium was suddenly full of people looking like Y's.

"Give me a *U!*"

"*U!*"

"Give me an *M!*"

"*M!*"

"What's that spell?"

"*YUM!*"

"What's that spell?"

"*YUM! YUM! YUM!*"

It was strange to see adults behaving this way, especially at a business meeting in Southeast Asia. John Pain worked for KFC, and he was trying to get the crowd excited about Yum! Brands, Inc., the company that owns KFC, Pizza Hut, and Taco Bell. He was giving a speech about the "Top Ten Ways to Market to Asian Youths of Today" at the Youth Marketing Forum 2004 conference. Hundreds of businesspeople had paid thousands of dollars to learn the secrets of how to sell things to children. Sitting in the audience were representatives from McDonald's, Disney, Coca-Cola, Toyota, Nestlé, and MTV. A special workshop held the previous day had promised to help companies create "brand preference and loyalty" among children.

"It is all about establishing a relationship early," Paul Kurnit, the president of a marketing firm called KidShop, told the conference on opening day.

The relationship between big companies and small children

has changed enormously in the past thirty years. Until recently, just a handful of companies aimed their advertising at children, and they mainly sold breakfast cereal and toys. Today companies selling all kinds of products realize that kids have a lot of money to spend and a lot of influence on what their parents buy. Every year in the United States children are responsible for more than $500 billion worth of spending. Big companies want that money. And too often they are willing to manipulate kids in order to get it.

Two men played a central role in turning America's children into the targets of major advertisers: Ray Kroc and Walt Disney. The two had a great deal in common. They were both from Illinois. They were born a year apart, Kroc in 1901, Disney in 1902. They knew each other as young men, serving in the same ambulance corps during World War I. They both left Illinois to create whole new industries in southern California. And they both had a powerful desire to control things, make them orderly, and always keep them clean. Occasionally that trait led to odd behavior. Walt Disney sealed the windows of his animation studio shut so that employees couldn't change the indoor temperature. Ray Kroc was so worried about cleanliness at McDonald's that sometimes he'd scrub the holes in his mop wringer with a toothbrush.

Kroc and Disney shared a limitless faith in science and technology. They ran their companies in much the same way, making all the big decisions and letting other people handle the details. Walt Disney didn't write or draw any of the classic animated films that carried his name. Ray Kroc didn't come up with the recipes for any of McDonald's sandwiches. Both men, however, knew how to hire the right people. Although Disney gained success first, Kroc wound up having a greater lasting influence. His company eventually wielded more power over the American economy—and created a mascot, Ronald McDonald, who became even more famous than Mickey Mouse.

More importantly, Walt Disney and Ray Kroc were both terrific salesmen. Instead of simply marketing one thing to children, they created imaginative worlds for selling many things: Disneyland and McDonaldland. They carefully linked products to the feelings, ideas, and dreams of children. And their huge success encouraged other businesspeople to use the same tactics and pull the same tricks on kids around the globe.

synergy

Walt Disney served as a role model for Ray Kroc, selling Mickey Mouse films and toys worldwide while Kroc was struggling to sell square ice cream scoops. At the age of twenty-two, Disney had left the Midwest and opened his own movie studio in Los Angeles. He was famous before he turned thirty. His early success was based not only on the popularity of Mickey Mouse but also on his new method for making animated films. The Walt Disney Studio was called a "fun factory." Disney's artists were treated like workers on an assembly line. They weren't allowed to draw an entire scene. They were told to sketch and color small parts of a scene again and again. They were kept under strict control and told exactly what to do. "Hundreds of young people were being trained and fitted," Disney explained, "into a machine for the manufacture of entertainment."

Disney loved science and technology and mechanical gadgets. That love of science soon became part of the message in many Disney films. New ways of doing things, Disney seemed to be saying, were always better than the old ways. And buying things was a sure path to happiness. He called Disneyland "the happiest place on earth." At the Tomorrowland section of the park, you could find everything from space travel to the kitchen of the future, portrayed in the same cheery, optimistic tone. There was never a hint that some new products—and the scientific thinking behind them—could be harmful.

The future celebrated at Disneyland was one in which almost every aspect of American life had a corporate sponsor. Walt Disney was the most beloved children's entertainer in the world. Kids were eager to hear whatever he had to say—and big corporations were eager to link their advertising to Disney's message. General Dynamics, a company that built nuclear reactors, sponsored the Disney film *Our Friend the Atom,* which told children that nuclear reactors were safe. General Dynamics also sponsored the nuclear submarine ride at Disneyland. Monsanto, a company that made chemicals and plastics, sponsored Disneyland's House of the Future, which was made out of plastic. Richfield Oil, which sold gasoline, sponsored Autopia, a ride that let kids drive gas-burning automobiles.

Walt Disney also pioneered the marketing practice now known as synergy. The aim of synergy was to link many products together in the mind of a consumer and secretly advertise them all at once. When it worked, most people didn't even realize that they were seeing an ad. During the 1930s, Disney signed agreements with dozens of companies, allowing them to use pictures of Mickey Mouse on their products and in their advertising. The movie *Snow White* broke new ground: Disney had already signed seventy marketing deals before it even opened, using Snow White to sell toys, books, clothes, and snacks. Disney later used television to take the idea of synergy beyond anything that anyone had previously imagined. His first television broadcast, "One Hour in Wonderland," was basically an ad for the upcoming Disney movie *Alice in Wonderland.* His first television series, *Disneyland,* broadcast in 1954, provided weekly reports on the construction work at the amuse-

Walt Disney and the plans for Disneyland, 1954

ment park. Episodes of *Disneyland* advertised Disney films, books, and toys. Most of all, the TV show advertised Walt Disney himself, the living, breathing embodiment of the brand—the man who neatly tied all these products together into one fun, cheerful, friendly idea.

the hamburger-eatingest clown

During McDonald's tough early years, Ray Kroc could only dream of having his own TV show to sell hamburgers. He didn't have the money for that kind of marketing. But he believed passionately in McDonald's and had a bold idea about how to make it popular. Children would be the new restaurant chain's target customers. The McDonald brothers had aimed for a family crowd, and now Kroc improved and refined their marketing efforts. He'd picked the right moment. During the decade after World War II, the number of children in the United States had increased by 50 percent.

One of the first things Kroc did after going into business with the McDonald brothers was to write a letter to his old friend Walt Disney. The two hadn't seen each other in more than thirty years. "Dear Walt," the letter said. "I have very recently taken over the national franchise of the McDonald's system. I would like to inquire if there may be an opportunity for a McDonald's in your Disneyland Development." Kroc thought that opening a McDonald's at the new amusement park would make the restaurant an instant hit with small children. But McDonald's success didn't come that easily. Although Walt Disney wrote Kroc a polite reply, the proposal went nowhere. When Disneyland opened, it had a lot of restaurants. None of them were McDonald's.

Unable to share any of Disney's synergy, Kroc came up with other ways to spread the word about McDonald's. He understood that how you sold food was just as important as how the food tasted. He liked to tell people that he was really in show business, not the restaurant business. He decided to market McDonald's as a safe, clean, all-American place for kids. Aiming at children was, above all, a business decision. "A child who loves our TV commercials," Kroc later explained, "and brings her grandparents to a McDonald's gives us two more customers."

McDonald's first mascot was a cartoon character named Speedee, a winking little chef with a hamburger for a head. In 1957, Richard McDonald suggested handing out lollipops shaped like Speedee at orphanages, Girl Scout and Boy Scout meetings, and children's hospitals in order to profit from "this youngster business." Kroc thought it was a good idea, adding that Speedee pops should also be given away at schools, especially to children in kindergarten, first grade, and second grade. As a marketing tool, Speedee turned out to be a flop for McDonald's. The mascot used to sell Alka-Seltzer, a medicine for upset stomachs, was named Speedy, and McDonald's worried that some people might think there was a connection between the two brands. It wouldn't help McDonald's if people thought that eating the hamburgers advertised by Speedee might cause the stomach problems Speedy promised to cure.

McDonald's new mascot wasn't created by Ray Kroc or by anyone at corporate headquarters. In 1960, Oscar Goldstein, who owned a few McDonald's restaurants in Washington, D.C., decided to sponsor *Bozo's Circus,* a local TV show starring a lovable clown. As part of the deal, Bozo the Clown visited Goldstein's restaurants, attracting thousands of new customers. When the local TV station canceled *Bozo's Circus* in 1963, Goldstein hired Willard Scott, the actor who played Bozo, to help create a new clown who could make appearances at McDonald's. An advertising agency designed a new clown costume, Scott came up with the name Ronald McDonald—and a star was born.

The original Ronald McDonald looked very different from the one you see today. Willard Scott wore a tray holding a hamburger, a milk shake, and French fries on top of his head. He wore another tray just like it on his belt. And he wore a McDonald's paper cup over his nose.

During his first television ad, Ronald McDonald was introduced as "the world's newest, silliest, and hamburger-eatingest clown!" After searching for a moment, the camera found him sitting in a playroom watching TV. "Hey kids, isn't watching TV

Willard Scott as the original Ronald

fun?" he asked. "I like to do everything that boys and girls like to do, especially when it comes to eating those delicious McDonald's hamburgers!" Then he demonstrated the "magic tray" on his belt. Every time Ronald grabbed a hamburger from the tray, another one would instantly appear in its place.

The Ronald McDonald television ads were an immediate success, drawing parents and their children to the McDonald's restaurants in Washington, D.C. Two years later, Ray Kroc decided to introduce Ronald McDonald to children throughout the United States. Before the new TV ads were broadcast nationwide, Willard Scott was fired. He was considered too overweight to play Ronald. McDonald's wanted someone much thinner to sell its burgers, shakes, and fries. Although he was disappointed that someone else was hired to play Ronald, Scott later got a much better job, serving for years as the weatherman on NBC's *Today Show*.

The new Ronald McDonald ads featured a silent, slender clown who soared through the air on a flying hamburger. He often battled a villain named Mr. Muscle, who tried to steal his food. After defeating Mr. Muscle, Ronald would fly off to the next McDonald's. The ads were broadcast on Saturday mornings, when millions of American children were watching cartoons. McDonald's was the first fast-food chain to advertise during that time slot, and its ads soon made Ronald McDonald a household name. According to one survey, more than nine out of ten American kids know who Ronald McDonald is. There's only one make-believe character better-known than Ronald. His name is Santa Claus.

As McDonald's mascot became more popular, Kroc thought about creating an amusement park to compete with Disneyland.

Instead, McDonald's pursued a different approach. It built small Playlands and McDonaldlands at restaurants all over the United States. The fantasy world of McDonaldland borrowed a good deal from Walt Disney's Magic Kingdom. A former Disney set designer gave McDonaldland its distinctive look. The composers responsible for all the songs in Disney's *Mary Poppins* as well as the Disneyland song "It's a Small World After All" wrote the music for the first McDonaldland commercials. Ronald McDonald, Mayor McCheese, and the other characters in the ads made McDonald's seem like more than just another place to eat. The restaurant chain presented a series of pleasing images to kids: bright colors, a playground, a toy, a clown, a drink with a straw, pieces of food wrapped up like little presents. McDonald's soon loomed large in the imagination of small children, the target audience for the ads. Kroc eventually succeeded, like Walt Disney, at selling the promise of a good mood to children, along with their fries. It was called a Happy Meal. McDonaldland—with its hamburger patch, apple pie trees, and Filet-O-Fish fountain—had one crucial thing in common with Disneyland. Almost everything in it was for sale.

threatening nags

The success of McDonald's helped create a huge boom in children's advertising during the 1980s. Many working parents felt guilty about not spending enough time with their kids—and started spending more money on them. After ignoring children for years, companies began to study them carefully and encourage them to buy things. Today the major advertising agencies have children's divisions, and some marketing firms are entirely devoted to kids. The new children's advertising tries to increase not only how much stuff kids buy now but also how much they will buy in the future. Companies now plan cradle-to-grave advertising strategies, hoping that childhood fondness for a brand will lead to a lifetime of purchases. They have come to believe what Ray Kroc and Walt Disney realized long ago—that a person's "brand loyalty" may begin as early as the age of two. Indeed, researchers have found that children can often recognize a company logo, like the Golden Arches, before they can recognize their own name.

Most of the ads aimed at kids have one simple goal: getting kids to nag their parents. "It's not just getting kids to whine," a marketer once explained, "it's giving them a specific reason to ask for the product." Ads often try to turn children into little salespeople, since kids know their parents better than anyone else does. Advertisers want children to bug their parents and keep bugging them and bug them really well.

How and why children nag their parents is a subject now being studied intensely by ad agencies. James U. McNeal, a professor of marketing at Texas A&M University, says that kids use seven different nags to get what they want. In his book *Kids as Customers,* McNeal describes them:

1. A *pleading nag* is when a kid repeats the same words over and over again, like "Please? Please?" or "Mom, Mom, Mom."

2. A *persistent nag* is when a kid constantly asks for something, using phrases like "I'm gonna ask just one more time."

3. *Forceful nags* are really pushy and may include mild threats like "Well, then, I'll go and ask Dad."

4. *Demonstrative nags* are the riskiest, sometimes leading kids to have an all-out tantrum in a public place—to hold their breath, cry, and refuse to leave a store until they get what they want.

5. *Sugar-coated nags* promise love in return for a purchase and may rely on sweet, adorable comments like "You're the best dad in the world."

6. *Threatening nags* are the nastiest, with kids vowing to hate their parents forever or to run away from home if what they want isn't immediately bought.

7. *Pity nags* claim that a kid will be heartbroken or humiliated or teased by friends if a parent refuses to buy something.

All seven of these nags can be used at the same time, McNeal says, "but kids tend to stick to one or two of each that prove most effective . . . for their own parents."

brand stickiness

Before trying to control children's behavior, advertisers have to learn what kids like. Today's market researchers not only interview children in shopping malls, they also organize focus groups for children as young as two or three. At a focus group, kids are paid to sit around and discuss what they like to buy. The idea of creating a squeezable ketchup bottle came from kids in a focus group. Heinz earned millions of dollars from the idea; the kids who thought of it were paid a small amount. Advertisers study children's artwork, hire children to run focus groups, pay children to attend slumber parties and then ask them questions late into the night. Advertisers send researchers into homes, stores, fast-food restaurants, and other places where kids like to gather. They study the fantasy lives of young children, then apply the findings to advertisements and product designs.

For years children's clubs have been considered an effective way both to advertise and to collect information about kids. These clubs appeal to a child's need for friendship and belonging. Disney's Mickey Mouse Club, formed in 1930, was one of the trailblazers. During the 1980s and 1990s, many new children's clubs were started. Corporations used them to get the names, addresses, ZIP Codes, and personal comments of young customers. "Marketing messages sent through a club not only can be personalized," James U. McNeal says, "they can be tailored for kids of a certain age or geographical group."

A well-run children's club can be extremely good for business. The creation of a Burger King Kids Club in 1990 increased sales of Burger King Kids Meals by 300 percent. Children who joined the club received a newsletter full of games, articles about Burger King toys, and profiles of other club members. "Children are important because they not only represent a significant percentage of our customers," a Burger King spokesman said, "but they also have an incredible influence on what fast-food restaurant their parents will choose."

The Internet has become another useful way to collect all sorts of information about children. A government investigation of children's Web sites in March 1998 found that 89 percent requested personal information from kids. Only 1 percent of the Web sites asked children to get permission from their parents before supplying the information. A character on the McDonald's Web site told kids that Ronald McDonald was "the ultimate authority in everything." The site encouraged children to send Ronald an e-mail revealing their favorite menu item at McDonald's, their favorite book, their favorite sports team— and their name.

Fast-food Web sites no longer ask children to provide personal information without asking their parents. Doing that is now against the law. But the Web sites still use cartoon characters and games to promote certain foods. On Ronald McDonald's Web site in early 2006, the Hamburglar said his "favorite thing in the whole wide world is hamburgers." Grimace said, "My favorite drink is a milkshake. I think milkshakes are the best." And the Happy Meal McNugget Moonbounce Game gave you twenty points every time you dunked a smiling little McNugget into a tub of sauce.

The latest scientific research is also being used to make kids buy things. At the Youth Marketing Forum 2004 conference in Singapore, Karen Tan, representing Coca-Cola, discussed how to make children remember a company's ads and create "brand stickiness." According to Tan, research has found that one way to make a lasting imprint on a child's mind is to run the same advertisement over and over again. Repeating the same ad for a product is more effective than running a variety of different ads. The more times a child sees exactly the same ad, the more likely it is that he or she will remember the product. Although the marketing research behind these repetitive ads may be new, the basic idea has been around for a long time. It's called brainwashing.

Jens Rasmussen, a representative from the lollipop maker Chupa Chups, revealed in Singapore that his company is sponsoring brain research at the Barcelona Institute of Technology. The research is called "NeuroMarketing." Scientists at the institute are now using equipment to study the magnetic activity of people's brains as they watch commercials. When people feel strongly about a brand, it sets off a response in a specific part of their brain. Rasmussen said that Chupa Chups hopes someday to use NeuroMarketing as a way of "creating loyal customers." The company is spending a lot of money and relying on a lot of high-tech equipment to make sure that kids will buy more lollipops.

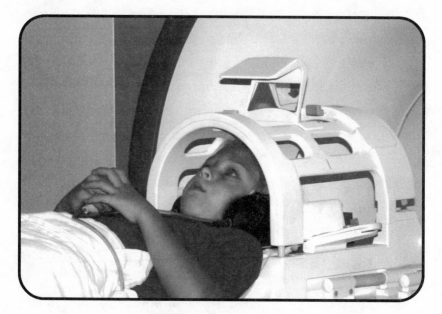

NeuroMarketing research

On the final evening of the Singapore marketing conference, its sponsors used an old-fashioned method of gaining information from children. Half a dozen kids, aged ten to fourteen, were brought onstage to be interviewed. As businesspeople in the audience asked questions, Camilla, the fourteen-year-old host of an Asia–Pacific Nickelodeon show called *Whacked!*, held a microphone so the kids could answer. The businesspeople fired one question after another at the children: What do you want your parents to buy you? What's your favorite brand of clothes? What kind of cell phone do you have? What's cool right now? What do you want to be famous for?

The kids onstage seemed shy and unsure of what to say. They were being asked some very personal questions in front of hundreds of strangers. Whenever one of them mentioned the name of a company with executives at the conference, people in the audience would suddenly start cheering—and the kid would look surprised, not fully understanding the reason for the applause. When asked what they liked to eat or drink, several kids said that they loved the fried chicken at KFC and the French fries at McDonald's.

Elias, a skinny twelve-year-old with big glasses who'd been quietly fidgeting, finally worked up the courage to speak. "My mom doesn't like me to drink Coke," he said. "She says it's bad for my teeth."

Nobody cheered for Elias. The room fell silent for a moment, and then there was some nervous laughter. Coca-Cola executives were sitting in the audience. Everyone ignored the boy's comment, and an advertising executive sitting onstage quickly changed the subject. It was as though Elias hadn't said anything at all.

toys, toys, toys

Despite the growing importance of the Internet, television remains the main place you'll find ads targeting kids. For years people have debated whether it's right or wrong to produce such ads for young children. Many studies have found that young children often can't tell the difference between a TV show and a TV commercial. They can't understand the real purpose of ads and trust that everything an ad says is true. The idea of banning children's ads is supported by many parents, teachers, and pediatricians. But it is strongly opposed by toy companies, television networks, and major advertising agencies. They earn a lot of money producing ads, broadcasting ads, or selling products with these ads.

Far from being banned, TV advertising aimed at kids is now broadcast twenty-four hours a day on some channels. The average American child now spends about twenty-five hours a week watching television. That adds up to more than one and a half months, nonstop, of TV every year. And that does not include the time spent in front of a screen watching videos, playing video games, or using a computer. Aside from going to school, American children now spend more time watching television than doing anything else except sleeping.

During the course of a year, the typical American child watches more than 40,000 TV commercials. About 20,000 of those ads are for junk food: soda, candy, breakfast cereals, and fast food. That means children now see a junk-food ad every five minutes while watching TV—and see about three hours of junk-food ads every week. American kids aren't learning about food in the classroom. They're being told what to eat by the same junk-food ads repeating again and again.

Although the fast-food chains now spend more than $3 billion every year on television advertising, their marketing efforts aimed at children don't stop there. McDonald's has opened more than eight thousand playgrounds at its restaurants in the United States. Burger King has built more than two thousand. A manufacturer of these "playlands" explains why fast-food chains build them: "Playlands bring in children, who bring in parents, who bring in money." As American cities and towns spend less money on parks and playgrounds, fast-food restaurants have become a gathering place for families. The seesaws, slides, and pits full of plastic balls have been successful at luring small children. Another form of advertising, however, has proven even more effective. "The key to attracting kids," one marketing publication says, "is toys, toys, toys."

The fast-food chains now work closely with America's leading toy makers, giving away small toys with children's meals and selling larger ones at their restaurants. As part of its Happy Meals program, McDonald's has worked with Fisher-Price to give away "Toddler Toys" aimed at kids aged one to three. One of the Fisher-Price toys was a tiny doll of a McDonald's worker holding a milk shake. Both McDonald's and Burger King have given away Teletubbies dolls. Teletubbies are aimed at children too young to speak.

Children's meals often come with different versions of the same toy, so that kids will nag their parents to keep going back to the restaurant to get a complete set. For many hard-working parents, buying a children's meal that includes a free Hot Wheels car, a Simpsons talking watch, or a Butt-Ugly Martians doll seems like an easy way to make their kids happy. For the fast-food chains, the toys are an easy way to make money. Giving away the right toy can easily double or triple the weekly sales of children's meals. And for every additional child, one or two additional adults are usually being dragged into the restaurant to eat.

"McDonald's is in some ways a toy company, not a food company," says one retired fast-food executive. Indeed, McDonald's is perhaps the largest toy company in the world. It sells or gives away more than 1.5 billion toys every year. Almost one out of every three new toys given to American kids each year comes from McDonald's or another fast-food chain.

McDonald's buys its Happy Meal toys from manufacturers in countries where the prices are low. On the bottom of these toys you often find the phrase "Made in China." Too often the lives of the workers who make Happy Meal toys are anything but happy. In 2000 a reporter for the *South China Morning Post* visited a factory near Hong Kong. The factory made Snoopy, Winnie the Pooh, and Hello Kitty toys for McDonald's Happy Meals. Some of the workers there said they were fourteen years old and often worked sixteen hours a day—twice the number of hours in a typical American workday. Their wages were less than twenty cents an hour—an amount almost thirty times less than the lowest amount you can pay an American worker. They slept in small rooms crammed with eight bunk beds without mattresses.

At first McDonald's said it had seen no evidence that such poor conditions existed at the factory, but later it admitted that some things were wrong there. A few months later, a newspaper found that another factory in China that made Happy Meal toys was mistreating its workers. They were working seventeen hours a day—and being paid less than ten cents an hour. McDonald's now tries to ensure that children aren't employed to make its toys. But the company hasn't done much to increase the wages of the workers at Chinese toy factories. Low wages are one of the things that keep Happy Meal toys so cheap.

One of the most successful promotions in the history of advertising was the Ty Teenie Beanie Baby giveaway at McDonald's in 1997. At the time, McDonald's sold about 10 million Happy Meals in a typical week. Over the course of ten days in April 1997, by including a Teenie Beanie Baby with each purchase, McDonald's sold about 100 million Happy Meals.

Happy Meals are normally sold to kids between the ages of three and nine—which means four Teenie Beanie Baby Happy Meals were bought for every single

Full of beans

American child in that age group. Not all of those Happy Meals were purchased for children. Many adult collectors bought the meals, kept the stuffed toys, and threw away the food.

The desire for young customers has led the fast-food chains to join forces not only with toy companies but also with sports leagues and Hollywood studios. McDonald's has staged promotions with the National Basketball Association and the Olympics. Pizza Hut, Taco Bell, and KFC have advertised with college teams. Wendy's has linked with the National Hockey League. Burger King and Nickelodeon, Denny's and Major League Baseball, McDonald's and the Fox Kids Network, have all formed partnerships that mix ads for fast food with children's entertainment.

Bozo's first appearance at a McDonald's restaurant in 1960 unleashed a children's marketing trend that has swept the world. Amid all the cross-promotions, giveaways, and huggable mascots, it has become almost impossible to separate children's entertainment from fast-food advertising. And the industry is proud of that fact. After being criticized for offering hip-hop stars money to mention Big Macs in their songs, a McDonald's spokesman recently argued that there is nothing wrong with advertising to kids that way. "We believe that the McDonald's brand is so omnipresent already in America," the spokesman said, "that having it in music, having it in TV, having it in movies, is no more intrusive than anything else children experience these days."

In May 1996, the Walt Disney Company signed a ten-year deal with the McDonald's Corporation. The life's work of Walt Disney and Ray Kroc had come full circle, uniting in perfect synergy. The two companies that led the way in aiming ads at children decided to work together. Disney agreed to promote its films at McDonald's restaurants, and McDonald's started to sell hamburgers and French fries at Disney's theme parks. The basic thinking behind McDonaldland and Disneyland, never far apart, finally became one. Now you can buy a Happy Meal at the Happiest Place on Earth.

MCJOBS

Martinsburg a century ago

For almost two hundred years, Martinsburg, West Virginia, was a sleepy little community at the northern tip of the Shenandoah Valley. The town was founded in 1778 and named after Thomas Bryan Martin, an officer during the Revolutionary War. The first settlers came there on horseback along the Cumberland Trail, an important trade route in the early nineteenth century, and cleared the land for farming. The land was perfect for growing apple trees, and soon more apples were being grown in the Martinsburg area than almost anywhere else in the world. A number of Civil War battles were fought in the area, but on the whole, life in Martinsburg was peaceful and calm, year after year. A railroad passed through the city center, and a few factories were built nearby.

As workers moved into houses downtown, small businesses opened to serve them. At J. C. McCrory Co. 5 and 10 Cent Store you could buy socks and pants; at John W. Dean Co. you could find children's shoes; H. L. Doll and Co. was a popular hardware store; and the Alice Govnice Confectionery on South Queen Street was the place to go for ice cream, candy, and chocolate. All of these stores were owned by people who lived in Martinsburg, and farmers from throughout the county came into town to do their shopping. The Tip Top Restaurant at 119 North Queen Street sold a mean corned beef hash, with meat from nearby farms. The town didn't have a single McDonald's, Burger King, Wendy's, or KFC. And yet, somehow, people still managed to eat.

In the mid-1960s, a twenty-six-mile stretch of Interstate 81 opened on the western edge of Martinsburg. The new four-lane highway changed the town forever, connecting it to two big cities about an hour and a half's drive away: Washington, D.C., and Baltimore, Maryland. Life in Martinsburg soon began shifting west, toward Interstate 81, as though pulled by an irresistible force. The automobile now determined where and how people lived. All along the interstate, fast-food restaurants and chain stores started to open. Family-owned, historic businesses downtown closed. And Martinsburg started to look just like any other sprawling American suburb.

You could pick just about any city in the United States and see how fast food and the automobile have changed it over the past few decades. The kind of suburban development that was once found only in Los Angeles has spread across the country. And with it has come a feeling of sameness—and a loss of what was once special, unique, and memorable about these places.

Today Martinsburg no longer has the feeling of a sleepy little town. The number of people living in the area has more than doubled since 1970. Martinsburg now sits in one of the fastest-growing counties in the United States. Many of the new residents moved there from Baltimore or Washington, D.C., hoping to escape city life and enjoy being in the countryside. But so many people have arrived that the countryside is quickly vanishing. When you drive outside Martinsburg, you see piles of apple trees beside the road, dug up at their roots, making way for new housing developments. In 1942 there were about 3 million apple and peach trees in the area; today there are about 300,000. The last remaining farmers are selling their land to real estate developers, and new neighborhoods with names like Quail Ridge and Sycamore Village cover the rolling hills.

Fields where apple orchards once stretched as far as the eye could see now lie buried beneath thousands of nearly identical two-story houses.

"The strip" in Martinsburg

After the highway opened, most of the family-run stores in downtown Martinsburg closed. People now do most of their shopping on a mile-long strip near Interstate 81, a stretch of land that used to be part of two farms. During the 1980s the land was sold to a real estate developer for $350,000. Over the next twenty years the developer earned more than $30 million selling pieces of the land and bringing in chain stores from out of state. Today the hotels, motels, restaurants, and stores along the strip are exactly the same ones you find all over the United States: Days Inn, Holiday Inn, OfficeMax, and Wal-Mart;

Hampton Inn and J. C. Penney, Waffle House and Outback Steakhouse. The neon lights along the strip, the rush-hour traffic, the acres of pavement, and the boxy soulless buildings create the sort of feeling that songwriter Joni Mitchell once described: "They paved paradise and put up a parking lot."

In 1970, Martinsburg had six fast-food restaurants; today it has more than forty. The fast-food chains profit from the new suburban sprawl, encourage more sprawl, and help determine what the sprawl looks like. They build large signs to attract motorists and try to draw as many cars as possible into their parking lots. They love traffic, lots of it, and put new restaurants at intersections where traffic is likely to increase, where development is just getting started. Fast-food restaurants often serve as the first wave of sprawl, rolling into a new area and then starting a flood of identical stores. Whenever a new McDonald's opens, other fast-food restaurants soon open nearby, convinced that it must be a good location.

The McDonald's Corporation has perfected the art of choosing the best places for new restaurants. In the early days Ray Kroc flew in a small airplane looking for schools, so that he could open new restaurants near them. "When you're up a thousand feet in the air," Kroc once told a journalist, "you can see the schools and the traffic patterns . . . and you put that all together, now you're not looking at a town, you're looking at a

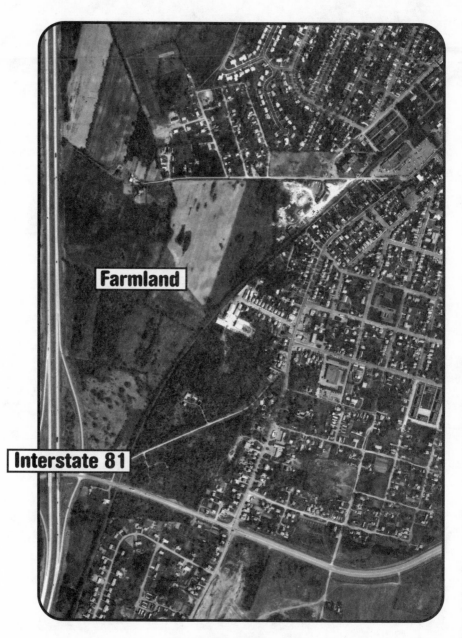

Western Martinsburg, 1974

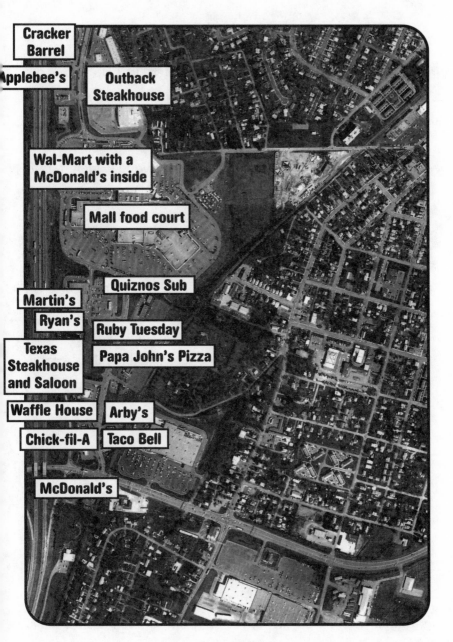

Western Martinsburg, today

market." McDonald's later used helicopters to help figure out how suburbs were growing, looking for cheap land along new highways and roads. The company sought places where lots of cars would drive past and children would live nearby. During the 1980s, McDonald's became one of the world's largest purchasers of satellite photographs taken from outer space, using them to get an even better view of local neighborhoods. What might seem confusing to someone on the ground—the relationship between one street and another, the distance between one highway off-ramp and another—looked clear in photos taken miles above the earth. Soon other companies started buying satellite photographs, and a technology that was originally invented to help the U.S. military spy on its enemies became one more tool to help fast-food chains sell more hamburgers.

just add hot water

Danielle Brent is a seventeen-year-old senior at Martinsburg High School. On Saturday mornings the alarm in her cell phone goes off at five-thirty. It's still dark outside as she stumbles into the bathroom, takes a shower, puts on her makeup, and gets into her McDonald's uniform. Her father stays in bed, but her mom always comes downstairs to the kitchen and says goodbye before Danielle leaves for work. Sometimes it's really cold in the morning, and it takes a while for the engine of the family's old Nissan Maxima to start cranking out heat. There are a lot of things Danielle would rather be doing early Saturday morning—such as sleeping. But like thousands of other American kids her age, she gets up and goes to work at a fast-food restaurant.

It's a ten-minute drive to McDonald's, and by the time Danielle gets there, the manager and a few workers are already unloading paper cups and wrappers from the storage area.

Danielle Brent

They're also removing the frozen pancakes, frozen bacon, frozen McGriddle biscuits, and frozen McMuffins from the freezer. Occasionally they're all so busy that they don't even notice that Danielle's arrived, and she has to bang loudly on the back door until the manager lets her in.

Fast-food chains often put attractive girls behind the counter to deal with customers, and that's where Danielle works. The first thing she does at the restaurant is log on to the cash register, punching the last four digits of her Social Security number into the touchscreen. Then she grabs a cup of coffee to clear her head before the doors open and customers start pouring in. She usually doesn't feel awake until ten or eleven o'clock, about halfway through her shift. But that grogginess never gets in the way of her job. Danielle thinks she could operate the cash register, as well as most of the other fancy machines, in her sleep.

Up and down the Interstate 81 strip, teenagers like Danielle run the fast-food restaurants of Martinsburg. The same is true throughout the rest of the country. No other industry has a workforce so dominated by teens. Teenagers open the fast-food outlets in the morning, close them at night, and keep them going at all hours in between. Even the managers and assistant managers are sometimes in their teens. Unlike Olympic gymnastics—a sport at which teenagers tend to be better than adults—the work in a fast-food kitchen doesn't require young workers. Instead of relying on a small, stable, well-paid, and well-trained workforce, the fast-food industry seeks out part-time, unskilled workers who are willing to accept low pay. Teenagers have long been the perfect candidates for these jobs. They usually don't have a family to support. And their youthful inexperience makes them easier to control than adults.

The labor practices of the fast-food industry have their origins in the assembly-line systems that were adopted by American factories in the early twentieth century. Although the

Ford assembly line, 1913

McDonald brothers never studied how to manage a factory, they understood the basic thinking and applied it to the Speedee Service System. Ever since then, the system they developed has been widely used and carefully improved. The kind of thinking behind the assembly line remains at its core. As a result, the fast-food industry has changed the way millions of Americans work and turned restaurant kitchens into little food factories.

At Burger King restaurants, frozen hamburger patties are placed on a conveyor belt and come out of a broiler ninety seconds later fully cooked. The ovens at Pizza Hut and at Domino's often use conveyor belts. The ovens at McDonald's look like commercial laundry presses, with big steel hoods that swing down and grill hamburgers on both sides at once. The burgers, chicken, French fries, and buns are all frozen when they arrive at a McDonald's. The shakes and sodas begin as syrup. At Taco Bell restaurants, the food is "assembled," not prepared. The avocado dip isn't freshly made by workers in the kitchen; it's made at a gigantic factory in Michoacán, Mexico, then frozen and shipped to the United States. The meat at Taco Bell arrives frozen and precooked in vacuum-sealed plastic bags. The beans are dehydrated and look like brownish corn-flakes. The cooking process is fairly simple. "Everything's 'add water,'" a Taco Bell employee says. "Just add hot water."

Although Richard and Mac McDonald introduced the

Speedee Service System, it was a McDonald's executive named Fred Turner who perfected it. In 1958, Turner wrote a training manual for the company that was seventy-five pages long. It was a book of instructions that described how almost everything had to be done. Hamburgers were always to be placed on the grill in six neat rows; French fries had to be exactly 0.28 inches thick. Today the McDonald's manual has ten times the number of pages and weighs about four pounds. Known within the company as "the Bible," it tells workers exactly how various appliances should be used, how each item on the menu should look, and how customers should be greeted. Cooking instructions are not only printed in this manual, they are often designed into the machines. A McDonald's kitchen is full of buzzers and flashing lights that tell workers what to do.

At some fast-food restaurants, computerized cash registers give commands. Once an order has been placed, buttons light up and suggest other menu items that could be added. Workers at the counter are encouraged to increase the size of an order by recommending special value deals, dessert, a larger soda. While doing so, they are told to be upbeat and friendly toward customers. "Smile with a greeting and make a positive first impression," a Burger King training manual suggests. "Show them you are GLAD TO SEE THEM. Include eye contact with the cheerful greeting."

The strict rules at fast-food restaurants help to create food that always tastes the same. They help workers fill orders quickly. And they give fast-food companies an enormous amount of power over workers. When all the knowledge is built into the operating system and the machines in the kitchen, a restaurant no longer needs skilled workers. It just needs people who are willing to do as they're told. Workers who lack skills can be hired cheaply. Instead of celebrating individual talent, the system seeks workers who are interchangeable. It seeks workers who can easily be hired, fired, and replaced.

long hours, low pay

Fast-food workers are the largest group of low-income workers in the United States. Moreover, the rate at which fast-food workers quit or are fired is among the highest in the American economy. When you have a good job, you don't want to leave it. A person who loves his or her job generally tries to do it for as long as possible. Many people, such as teachers, have the same job for as long as twenty or thirty years. The typical fast-food worker quits or is fired after only three or four months.

One of the reasons fast-food workers leave their jobs so often is that the pay is so low. Almost seventy years ago the U.S.

government established a minimum wage in order to make sure that employers couldn't force people to work for nothing (or next to nothing). The minimum wage is the lowest amount of money that an employer is legally allowed to pay a person for each hour of work. Most American industries pay their workers a lot more than the bare minimum. The fast-food industry, on the other hand, pays the minimum wage to more of its workers than any other industry in the United States. As a result, keeping that minimum wage low has always been part of the fast-food industry's business plan. Whenever members of Congress try to raise the minimum wage (which in 2006 is only $5.15 an hour), the fast-food industry always fights hard against any increase. And it almost always wins. Between 1968 and 1990, the years in which the fast-food chains grew at the fastest rate, the real value of the minimum wage fell by almost half. The real value of the U.S. minimum wage is lower today than it was fifty years ago. The fast-food chains earn large profits as wages fall, because it costs them less money to hire workers.

Many jobs in the United States provide good wages, health insurance, vacation pay, and all sorts of other nice benefits. But fast-food jobs generally don't. About nine out of every ten fast-food workers are crew members. They prepare the food in the kitchen, take orders behind the counter, and sweep the floors. They are usually paid a low hourly wage, receive no health insurance, and have little control over their working hours. Crew members are employed "at will." That means if business is slow, they're sent home early. And if the restaurant's busy, they're kept longer than usual. A typical McDonald's or Burger King restaurant has about sixty crew members. They work an average of thirty hours a week. By hiring a large number of inexpensive workers and sending them home when things are slow, the fast-food chains are able to keep their labor costs low.

Fast-food jobs can teach basic skills, such as getting to work on time and learning how to work with other people. A handful of fast-food workers are paid a regular salary. Each restaurant usually has four or five managers and assistant managers. They tend to earn about $25,000 a year—about $11,000 less than the average full-time worker earns in the United States. They receive health insurance and may get a chance to climb up the ladder to better, higher-paying jobs in the company. But they also have to work long hours. Spending forty hours a week on the job is the norm in the United States. Some fast-food assistant managers work as many as sixty or seventy hours a week. And the job offers little opportunity for independent decision-making. The computer programs, training manuals, and equipment in the kitchen decide how just about everything is done. Fast-food managers do have the power to hire, fire, and arrange the daily schedule. Much of their time is spent trying to persuade crew members to work hard and have "team spirit." It's not an easy job, and managers often leave after just a year or two.

The long hours, low pay, lack of health insurance, and strict rules that must always be obeyed have given fast-food jobs a bad reputation. Indeed, any job that's boring and doesn't pay well and doesn't teach important skills is now known as a "McJob." According to the *Oxford English Dictionary*, the *American Heritage Dictionary*, and the *Merriam-Webster Dictionary*, a McJob is a job that's low-paying and offers little opportunity to get ahead. McDonald's isn't happy about that dictionary definition and has publicly complained that it isn't fair to the company. But the dictionaries insist that's what the word actually means. A McJob is a job that doesn't promise much of a future.

too much work

Almost every fast-food restaurant in Martinsburg has a sign that says NOW HIRING. The fast-food companies have become victims of their own success, as one business after another tries to steal their teenaged workers. It used to be that fast-food restaurants were the only places that would hire young people. Now teenagers work behind the front desk at hotels and make phone calls for telemarketing firms. In Martinsburg a lot of teens try to get jobs parking cars at a local racetrack and casino, where they can earn $8.50 an hour. Other kids are eager to find jobs as salespeople in the clothing and shoe stores at the Martinsburg Mall, where they can often get discounts on merchandise and visit with friends who are shopping. The least popular jobs are the ones at fast-food restaurants.

When Danielle was a little girl, she loved to eat at McDonald's. Sometimes she'd even eat breakfast, lunch, and dinner there. When she was sixteen, a friend suggested that she apply for a job at the McDonald's near Interstate 81. The friend already worked there, classmates of theirs always ate there, and working behind the counter sounded like fun. Danielle soon realized that the job was different from what she'd expected. Some of the customers were rude. Workers in the kitchen didn't always wash their hands and didn't care if the food got dirty as a result.

Her friend soon quit the job, but Danielle can't afford to do that. She needs the money. A number of kids at school tease her for working so hard at a job that pays so little. Kids who break the law and sell drugs at her high school earn more money in a couple of hours than Danielle earns at McDonald's in a couple of weeks. Danielle refuses to have anything to do with drugs. She knows too many people who've gotten in trouble that way. Although Danielle doesn't like her job at McDonald's; it's honest work.

Danielle, like many other high school students today, is under enormous pressure to earn money. Not very long ago, even in poor families, the father would work and the mother would stay home to raise the children. Nowadays both parents often have to work—and their teenage children have to work, too. The kids leave high school in the afternoon and go straight to their jobs. Sometimes they work to buy clothes or computers. Most of the time they work to pay for their cars.

When kids go to work, they're not at school, they're not playing sports, and they're not doing their homework. If the job is boring and doesn't teach any skills, it can make them dislike having a job and doubt that honest work will ever get them anywhere. Studies have found that kids who work twenty hours or less a week during the school year usually benefit from the experience and gain self-confidence from their jobs. But kids who work more than twenty hours a week are much more likely to cut classes and drop out of high school.

Danielle worries about the amount of time she's spending at McDonald's. Sometimes she's there on school nights until two in the morning. "At school, I'm really tired, and I can't do my homework a lot," she admits. In many states it's against the law for children under the age of eighteen to work after eleven o'clock on a school night. In West Virginia, however, it's perfectly legal for sixteen- or seventeen-year-old kids to work very long hours. Sadi Lambert, a friend of Danielle's, used to have a job at a McDonald's in Martinsburg. She also worked at a local convenience store. During her senior year in high school, Sadi worked every day after school, from two in the afternoon until ten o'clock at night. On Saturdays she worked at the convenience store from six in the morning until two in the afternoon, then at McDonald's until ten at night. On Sundays she went to church in the morning and then worked at the convenience store in the afternoon. She worked seven days a week.

Sadi Lambert

One Saturday when she was sixteen, Sadi worked from eight o'clock in the morning until four in the afternoon at McDonald's. Just as she was getting ready to leave, the manager asked her to stay and work for a few more hours. Some of the other crew members had failed to show up. When a new manager arrived at seven o'clock, he asked if Sadi would keep working. The restaurant still didn't have enough crew members. She said okay. At eleven o'clock the manager asked her to help close the restaurant. Sadi finally left the McDonald's at half past three in the morning.

The next day, when Sadi showed up for her shift at McDonald's, one of the managers gave her a thank-you present. After all, she had just worked for nineteen and a half hours straight, without any sleep and with only a half-hour break. The gift was a bag of candy.

mcunions

In the summer of 1998, Pascal McDuff sent job applications to ten different McDonald's near his home in Montreal, Canada. Pascal was fifteen years old and excited about the idea of working at McDonald's. His parents had taken him there about once a month, as a special treat, when he was growing up. Pascal went for an interview with a manager at the McDonald's on

Peel Street. The two-story restaurant was in the heart of down-town Montreal and had a cheery, modern look, with lots of shiny steel and glass. The manager told him that McDonald's treated its workers well and paid well if they worked hard. Pascal got the job, started working there during the summer, and later worked there at night after school. He was asked to do all sorts of tasks in the kitchen. He pulled frozen hamburger patties from the freezer and tossed them on the grill. He placed the cooked patties on buns. He pushed the button that squirted the Big Mac sauce onto them. He carried trash out to the Dumpster, cleaned the big vats that hold cooking oil, filled the ketchup bins, mopped the floors. And he took pride in doing the job well.

The managers complimented Pascal on his hard work. Whenever they phoned him to say that a crew member had failed to show up, he would get on the bus and go to the restaurant to help out. Five months after being hired, Pascal was named "Employee of the Month" at the Peel Street McDonald's. Not long afterward, he received a work evaluation from his managers. A work evaluation is like a report card for workers, who get one of four different grades: "doesn't meet standards," "good work," "excellent work," and "exceptional work." Pascal was surprised to find that the grade he got was "good work." He felt hurt and thought that after all the hard effort, he deserved better.

Pascal started talking to other crew members at the restaurant and got the impression that some of the people who worked the hardest had also received low grades. It didn't make any sense. And then Pascal realized that a worker's pay increase was tied directly to his or her grade in the evaluation. By keeping grades low, the restaurant could keep wages low. His "good work" grade brought a pay increase of only ten cents an hour. Pascal worked thirty hours a week at the restaurant, which meant his pay raise would give him just an extra three dollars a week—barely enough to buy a Big Mac. It wasn't the money that upset him; it was the way the Peel Street McDonald's seemed to treat its workers with disrespect. A manager he liked suddenly left, and a new manager kept high school kids on the job until midnight, even when they had exams the next day. People who seemed to deserve promotions didn't get them. Pascal thought that something had to be done to help these workers.

One day in the summer of 2000 Pascal left the restaurant with his friend Maxime Cromp. Both of them worked at the Peel Street McDonald's; Pascal had been there for two years. As the two friends rode the subway home, discussing all the restaurant's problems, Maxime suggested that maybe they should start a labor union. "Yeah," Pascal replied. "That would be interesting."

A labor union is a group of workers who join together to gain better wages and working conditions. When a single worker tries to negotiate with a boss, he or she may feel weak and powerless. Why should a boss listen to one person, who can easily be fired? But when workers form a labor union and speak to their boss as a strong, united group, they have a much better chance of success. Labor unions have been formed in the United States since the early 1800s, but they didn't gain much power until the early twentieth century. Unions played a leading role in protecting workers from abuse and in getting them good wages. Before the rise of labor unions, children were put to work in dangerous factories; companies forced people to work six or seven days a week; women and minorities faced discrimination on the job; and workers rarely received health insurance or retirement benefits. The basic idea behind a labor union is that ordinary workers not only deserve respect but also deserve a fair share of the profits earned from their hard work.

In 1960 about one out of every three American workers belonged to a labor union. Today only one out of eight belongs to a union. Over the past few decades labor unions have lost a great deal of their strength. Some union leaders became corrupt, stealing money from workers and giving unions a bad reputation. More importantly, a number of companies decided they didn't like unions and did everything they could to get rid of them. When company executives deal with a union, they have to find ways to bargain, negotiate, and compromise. When there's no union, these executives have tremendous control over how they pay and treat their workers.

In June 2000, Pascal and Maxime secretly met with a representative of the Canadian Confederation of National Trade Unions (CNTU). They were afraid that if McDonald's found out they were trying to start a union, they might get fired. The CNTU representative warned that it was very difficult to organize fast-food workers. Crew members are often young, poor, and unlikely to work at any fast-food restaurant for long—not a good combination, when a union organizer needs to convince them to stick together and bravely fight for their rights. In order to form a union, an organizer had to persuade half the workers at the restaurant to sign a card saying they wanted to join. It would be a big challenge. Nevertheless, Pascal and Maxime said they wanted to go ahead with it. The CNTU was impressed and offered to help.

For the next few weeks Pascal quietly spoke to other crew members about the working conditions and the pay at the restaurant. Most of the workers seemed unhappy with how the place was being run. At first Pascal didn't mention the idea of a union. But once he felt confident that there would be support for one, he and Maxime began to hand out union cards.

According to the labor laws, the cards couldn't be signed on the job. So the two of them met with other crew members after work, standing at the entrance to the subway, sitting in Maxime's car, visiting people at their houses. It wasn't difficult to persuade workers to sign a card. Within a few days about three quarters had agreed to form a union. They were excited to be working together for a common cause.

Pascal and Maxime thought they'd managed to obtain all the necessary signatures without any of the managers finding out. They were wrong. One of the crew members had warned a manager that they were forming a union. The crew member was rewarded with a promotion. And then, just two days after Pascal and Maxime gave the government all the signatures they needed to start a union, the Peel Street McDonald's suddenly hired twenty-four new crew members. By adding so many workers at once, the owner of the restaurant hoped to block the union. If those twenty-four were included in the count, Pascal and Maxime wouldn't have cards from half the workforce.

With help from the CNTU, Pascal and Maxime challenged the restaurant owner in court, arguing that hiring all those workers at the last minute was an attempt to prevent a fair count of the vote. They won the case, and in November 2000, crew members at the Peel Street McDonald's joined a union—the only union at a McDonald's in North America. The owner of

Pascal and Maxime fighting for a union

the McDonald's immediately appealed the decision. Pascal and Maxime held rallies outside the restaurant, seeking public support for the workers. "I can't understand how a company making billions of dollars can't share it with the youths who help make it rich," Pascal said at one of these rallies.

McDonald's, however, had not given up the fight. Rumors were spread among the crew members that their union fees would go straight into Pascal's bank account—which wasn't true. Workers were promised free meals if they'd consider leaving the union. Fliers criticizing the union were distributed; they featured a drawing of Pascal with money falling from his pockets. Instead of encouraging cooperation and solidarity, the company pitted one young worker against another. Meanwhile, the legal battle continued in court. The Quebec labor commissioner promised to decide in May 2001 whether the union's victory at the Peel Street McDonald's should be upheld. A month before that ruling, the owner of the restaurant announced that it would be shut down. He claimed that the rent for the building had grown too expensive and that the restaurant's closing had nothing to do with the union. The union victory was upheld by the labor commissioner—but a few weeks later the owner of the Peel Street McDonald's shut the restaurant down.

McDonald's has about 1,400 restaurants in Canada, and it opens about 75 new ones there every year. The odds against a McDonald's restaurant in Canada going out of business—based on the chain's failure rate since the early 1990s—are about 300 to 1. It's an amazing coincidence that a McDonald's in Canada where workers voted to join a union suddenly went out of business. "Did somebody say McUnion?" a newspaper editorial later asked. "Not if they want to keep their McJob."

Pascal McDuff earned a degree in political science at the University of Montreal and now hopes to become a journalist. He wants to write books and articles that show people what's happening in the world, that tell them the truth. He has no regrets about spending a year trying to help the workers at

McDonald's. They put up a good fight for a good cause. Ever since the Peel Street restaurant closed, instead of working with the union, he refuses to eat at McDonald's. "They hurt me and they hurt other people," Pascal says, "and it's hard for me to give them any money."

THE SECRET OF THE FRIES

J. R. Simplot

Ray Kroc loved French fries. "The French fry [was] . . . almost sacrosanct for me," Kroc said, "its preparation a ritual to be followed religiously." The success of Richard and Mac McDonald's original hamburger stand had been based as much on the quality of their fries as on the taste of their burgers. The McDonald brothers had come up with an excellent system for making crisp, tasty French fries, one that was later improved by the restaurant chain. Every morning fresh russet Burbank potatoes were washed, skinned, and thinly sliced in the back of the kitchen. McDonald's used special fryers to keep the oil temperature above 325 degrees. As the fast-food chain expanded, it became more difficult—and yet all the more important—to maintain the quality of the fries. Kroc wanted to make sure that the French fries tasted exactly the same at hundreds of different locations. Using fresh potatoes peeled by hand created a risk that the fries might taste better at one McDonald's than another. Kroc couldn't bear that thought.

In 1965, Ray Kroc met with J. R. Simplot, Idaho's great potato baron. Simplot had an idea for McDonald's: switch to frozen French fries. He had good reason to propose such an idea. He was the biggest potato grower and shipper in the United States—and his company had spent years trying to develop the perfect frozen French fry. Simplot wanted Americans to eat more potatoes and hoped that frozen fries would become incredibly popular. Although Thomas Jefferson had brought the Parisian recipe for *pommes frites* to the United States in 1802, French fries didn't become well known until the 1920s. Americans traditionally ate their potatoes boiled, mashed, or baked. French fries were widely introduced in the United States by World War I veterans who had eaten them in Europe and by the drive-in restaurants that opened in southern

California during the 1930s and 1940s. Fries could be served without a fork or a knife, and they were easy to eat behind the wheel. But with all the peeling and slicing and frying, they were extremely time-consuming to prepare. The frozen fry promised to end all that hassle.

At first J. R. Simplot hoped that busy housewives would keep bags of frozen fries in their freezers. During the 1950s he assembled a team of chemists to find a way to freeze fries without ruining their taste or reducing their crunchiness. Americans were eating more fries than ever before, and the russet Burbank, with its large size and high starch content, seemed like the ideal potato for frying. Simplot wanted to create a frozen fry that was inexpensive and that tasted just as good as a fresh one. His chemists experimented with different methods for freezing and reheating French fries. They suffered a number of setbacks— such as learning the hard way that when you try to cook French fries in a potato chip fryer, the fries just sink to the bottom and burn. One day the chief chemist walked into Simplot's office with some frozen fries that had just been reheated. Simplot tasted them, realized that the manufacturing problems had been solved, and said, "That's a helluva thing."

J. R. Simplot received the first patent for frozen French fries. But sales were disappointing. Although the frozen fries were precooked and could be baked in an oven, they tasted better when reheated in hot oil. Busy housewives didn't always have the time to do that. Simplot needed to find restaurant owners who already had fryers in their kitchens, who had full-time workers to run the fryers, and who would recognize the tremendous potential of his frozen fries.

Simplot's meeting with Ray Kroc went well. The idea of switching to frozen French fries appealed to Kroc, as a way to make sure the fries tasted the same everywhere and as a way to cut costs in the kitchen. At the time McDonald's bought fresh potatoes from about 175 local suppliers, and crew members spent a great deal of their time peeling and slicing potatoes. Simplot offered to build a new factory solely for the manufacture of frozen French fries for McDonald's. Kroc agreed to try Simplot's fries but made no long-term promises. The deal was sealed with a handshake.

McDonald's began to sell J. R. Simplot's frozen French fries in 1966. Customers didn't notice any difference. And the reduced cost of using frozen potatoes instead of fresh ones made French fries one of the most profitable items on the menu—much more profitable than hamburgers. Simplot quickly became the main supplier of French fries to McDonald's. At the time, McDonald's had about 725 restaurants in the United States. Within a decade, it had more than 3,000. Simplot sold his frozen fries to other restaurant chains, helping the fast-food industry grow.

The success of the frozen fry also changed the nation's eating habits. Americans have always eaten more potatoes than any other food except dairy products and wheat flour. In 1960 the typical American ate eighty-one pounds of fresh potatoes and about four pounds of frozen French fries. Today the typical American eats about forty-nine pounds of fresh potatoes—and about thirty pounds of frozen French fries. Close to 90 percent of those fries are purchased at fast-food restaurants. Before J. R. Simplot figured out how to freeze them and McDonald's widely advertised them, French fries were a special treat. Now they're eaten all the time by adults, teenagers, even very young children. A study recently found that one out of every five American toddlers eats French fries every day.

Thanks mainly to the frozen French fry, J. R. Simplot—who dropped out of school in the eighth grade—is now one of the richest men in the United States. He is also one of America's biggest landowners. "I've been a land hog all my life," Simplot says, laughing. His company now has 85,000 acres of irrigated farmland, and he personally owns more than twice that amount of ranch land. He owns much of downtown Boise, Idaho, and a big hillside house that overlooks the city. At home he flies a gigantic American flag on a flagpole that's more than a hundred feet high. In addition to the land he owns, Simplot rents more than 2 million acres from the federal government. His ZX Ranch in southern Oregon is the largest cattle ranch in the United States. It's 65 miles wide and 163 miles long. Altogether, J. R. Simplot controls an area of land that is larger than the state of Delaware.

The farmers in Idaho who grow the potatoes haven't done nearly as well. There used to be hundreds of small companies that bought potatoes, and farmers were able to wait and see who would offer the best price. But the fast-food chains (and their desire for huge amounts of fries that taste exactly the same) have made a handful of fry companies extremely powerful. The small companies have either gone out of business or been bought out. Today three companies control about 80 percent of the American market for frozen French fries. And if potato farmers don't like the price being offered by those three companies, then they're out of luck.

This new system is good for the fast-food chains. They can buy frozen fries for about thirty cents a pound, reheat them in oil, and then sell them to customers for about six dollars a pound. The fast-food chains sell French fries for prices about twenty times higher than what they paid for them. No wonder Ray Kroc loved French fries. The farmer who planted the potatoes, carefully tended them, and harvested them doesn't get such a good deal. Out of every dollar-fifty that you spend on a large order of French fries at a fast-food restaurant, maybe two cents goes to the farmer.

Over the past twenty-five years, Idaho has lost about half its potato farmers. Family farms are giving way to corporate farms that stretch for thousands of acres. These corporate farms may be controlled by executives living in distant cities or states. Instead of being farmed by a family that has lived on it for generations, the land becomes just another asset of a corporation. It can be bought or sold or turned into a shopping mall without any consideration besides what's most profitable in the short term. The independent family farmers who helped found the United States, who came to symbolize its freedom and democracy, are rapidly disappearing. Powerful corporations are taking their place, either owning the land or controlling the farmers who work it.

factory fries

Although the J. R. Simplot Company supplies the majority of the fries that McDonald's sells in the United States, two other fry companies are now larger: McCain, a Canadian firm that became the number-two fry company in the United States in 1997, and Lamb Weston, the world's biggest producer of frozen French fries. The Lamb Weston factory in American Falls, Idaho, makes French fries for McDonald's and other fast-food chains. It's the sort of place that Walt Disney would have adored. It uses the latest science and technology to achieve better living through frozen food. You can hardly believe how many fries this one factory produces. It goes through about 4 million pounds of potatoes every day.

Lamb Weston was founded in 1950 by F. Gilbert Lamb, the inventor of a crucial piece of French fry–making technology. The Lamb Water Gun Knife uses a high-pressure hose to shoot potatoes at a speed of 117 feet per second through a grid of sharpened steel blades, thereby creating perfectly sliced French fries. After coming up with the idea, Gil Lamb tested the first Water Gun Knife in a company parking lot, shooting potatoes out of a fire hose. Lamb Weston now manufactures more than 130 different kinds of French fries, including Steak House Fries, CrissCut Fries, Hi-Fries, Mor-Fries, Flamethrower Fries, TaterBabies, and Taterboy Curley QQQ Fries.

In order to make that many fries, the Lamb Weston factory keeps potatoes in seven gigantic storage buildings. Each building can hold a mound of potatoes that's 20 feet deep, 100 feet wide, and almost as long as two football fields. The buildings are cool and dark, kept year-round at a steady 46 degrees. In the dim light, the potatoes look like grains of sand on a beach.

Outside, tractor-trailers arrive from the fields, carrying potatoes that have just been harvested. The trucks dump their loads onto spinning rods that take the larger potatoes into the building and let the small potatoes, dirt, and rocks fall to the ground. The rods lead to a rock trap, a tank of water in which the potatoes float and the remaining rocks sink to the bottom. The plant uses streams of water to float potatoes gently this way and that way, guiding different sizes out of different containers, then flushing them into a three-foot-deep stream that runs underneath the cement floor. The inside of the factory is gray, massive, and well lit, with huge pipes running along walls, steel catwalks, workers in hardhats, and plenty of loud machinery. If little potatoes weren't bobbing and floating past, you might think this was a place that manufactured jet engines or automobiles.

Conveyor belts take the wet, clean potatoes into a machine that blasts them with steam for twelve seconds, boils the water under their skins, and explodes the skins off. Then the potatoes are pumped into a tank and shot through a Lamb Water Gun Knife. They emerge as shoestring fries. Four video cameras scrutinize them from different angles, looking for flaws. When a French fry with a dark spot is detected, an optical sorting machine shoots a single burst of compressed air that knocks the bad fry off the production line. The fry drops onto a separate conveyor belt, which carries it to a machine with tiny automated knives that precisely remove the dark spot. And then the fry is returned to the main production line.

Sprays of hot water cook the fries, gusts of hot air dry them, and 25,000 pounds of boiling oil fry them to a slight crisp. Air cooled by compressed ammonia gas quickly freezes them, a computerized sorting machine divides them into six-pound batches, and a device that spins like a merry-go-round aligns the French fries so they all point in the same direction. The fries are sealed in brown bags, then the bags are loaded by machines into cardboard boxes and the boxes are stacked by machines onto wooden pallets. Forklifts driven by human beings carry the pallets to a freezer for storage. Inside that freezer there are millions of pounds of French fries, most of them destined for McDonald's, the boxes stacked as high as a three-story building, the stacks extending for roughly 40 yards. Every day about a dozen railway cars and about two dozen tractor-trailers pull up to the freezer, load up with French fries, and depart for McDonald's restaurants in Boise, Idaho; Phoenix, Arizona; Salt Lake City, Utah; Denver, Colorado; and points in between.

Near the freezer is a laboratory where men and women in white coats analyze French fries day and night, measuring their sugar content, their starch content, their color. Because potatoes contain different amounts of sugar at different times of the year, Lamb Weston adds sugar to the fries during the fall and leaches sugar out of them in the spring. The goal is to maintain a uniform taste and appearance throughout the year. Every half-hour, a new batch of fries is cooked in fryers identical to those installed in fast-food kitchens. The fries on the plate look out of place in this laboratory setting, this wild food factory with its computer screens, digital readouts, shiny steel platforms, and evacuation plans in case of ammonia gas leaks. The place may seem strange, but the French fries taste delicious—crisp and golden brown, made from potatoes that were in the ground that morning.

smells

McDonald's French fries are made at the same factories that make fries for the other fast-food chains. But there's something special about the taste of McDonald's French fries. Just about everyone, including some famous food critics, loves the taste of McDonald's fries. Their special taste doesn't come from the kind of potatoes that McDonald's buys, the technology that processes them, or the restaurant equipment that fries them. Other chains buy their fries from the same large processing companies, use russet Burbanks, and have similar fryers in their restaurant kitchens. The taste of a French fry is largely determined by the cooking oil. For decades, McDonald's cooked its French fries in a mixture of about 7 percent soybean oil and 93 percent beef fat. The mix gave the fries their unique flavor—and more saturated beef fat than a McDonald's hamburger.

When doctors and nutritionists argued that all that beef fat made the fries unhealthy, McDonald's responded to the criticism by switching to vegetable oil in 1990. The switch presented the company with an enormous challenge: how to make fries that taste slightly like beef without cooking them in beef fat. A look at the ingredients used in the preparation of McDonald's French fries reveals how the problem was solved. Toward the end of the list is a seemingly innocent yet oddly mysterious phrase: "natural flavor." The potatoes and the cooking oil at McDonald's both contain "natural flavor." And it's made out of beef. That fact helps to explain not only why the fries taste so good but also why most fast food—indeed, most of the food Americans eat today—tastes the way it does.

Open your refrigerator, your freezer, your kitchen cupboards, and look at the labels on your food. You'll find "natural flavor" or "artificial flavor" in just about every list of ingredients. The similarities between these two kinds of flavoring are far more important than their differences. Both are manmade additives that give most processed food its taste. When people buy food for the first time, it's usually because of how the food or its packaging looks. After that first purchase, it's the taste that makes them want to buy the food again.

Americans now spend more than $1 trillion on food every year—and more than 90 percent of that money is spent on processed food. But the canning, freezing, and dehydrating techniques used to process food destroy most of its flavor. Since the end of World War II, a vast industry has arisen in the United States to make processed food taste good. Without this flavor industry, today's fast-food industry could not exist. The names of the leading American fast-food chains and their best-selling menu items have become famous worldwide. But few people can name the companies that manufacture fast food's taste.

The flavor industry is highly secretive. Its leading companies will not disclose the formulas of their flavor compounds or the names of their clients. These secrets help protect the reputations of beloved brands. The fast-food chains would like people to think that the taste of their food comes from the cooking in their restaurant kitchens, not from distant factories run by other firms.

The heart of the flavor industry lies between Exit 4 and Exit 19 of the New Jersey Turnpike, a part of the state dotted with oil refineries and chemical plants. More than fifty companies manufacture flavors along that stretch of the New Jersey Turnpike. Indeed, the state produces about two thirds of the flavor additives sold in the United States.

International Flavors & Fragrances (IFF), one of the world's largest flavor companies, has a manufacturing facility off Exit 8A in Dayton, New Jersey. A tour of the IFF plant is the closest thing in real life to visiting Willy Wonka's chocolate factory. Wonderful smells drift through the hallways, men and women in neat white lab coats cheerfully go about their work, and hundreds of little glass bottles sit on laboratory tables and shelves. The bottles contain powerful but fragile flavor chemicals. The long chemical names on the little white labels seem like a strange foreign language. The chemicals are mixed and poured and turned into new substances, just like magic potions.

The IFF plant in Dayton makes the flavor not only of fast food but of many other products that Americans eat or drink every day. The IFF snack and savory lab is responsible for the flavor of potato chips, corn chips, breads, crackers, breakfast cereals, and pet food. The confectionery lab devises the flavor for ice cream, cookies, candies, toothpastes, mouthwashes, and antacids. The beverage lab is full of brightly colored liquids in clear bottles. It creates the flavor for popular soft drinks, sports drinks, bottled teas, and wine coolers, for all-natural juice drinks, organic soy drinks, and malt liquors.

In addition to being one of the world's largest flavor companies, IFF manufactures the smell of many of the best-selling fine perfumes in the United States. It also makes the smell of household products such as deodorant, dishwashing detergent, bath soap, shampoo, furniture polish, and floor wax. All of these aromas are made through the same basic process: mixing different chemicals to create a particular smell. The scientific principles behind the smell of your toothpaste are the same as those behind the taste of your TV dinner.

tasty

The aroma of a food can be responsible for as much as 90 percent of its taste. Scientists now believe that human beings acquired the sense of taste as a way to avoid being poisoned. Edible plants generally taste sweet; deadly ones, bitter. Taste is supposed to help us tell the difference between food that's good for us and food that's not. The taste buds on our tongues can detect the presence of a dozen or so basic tastes. Some of the more common tastes are sweet, sour, bitter, pungent, burning, warm, salty, astringent, metallic, and umami (a taste discovered by Japanese researchers, a rich and full sense of deliciousness triggered by foods such as meat, shellfish, mushrooms, potatoes, and seaweed). Although our taste buds can detect about a dozen basic flavors, our noses are far more sensitive. When your nose isn't clogged or stuffy, you can smell thousands of different chemical aromas. Indeed, whenever you eat something, the flavor you taste is mainly the smell of gases being released from what you've just put in your mouth.

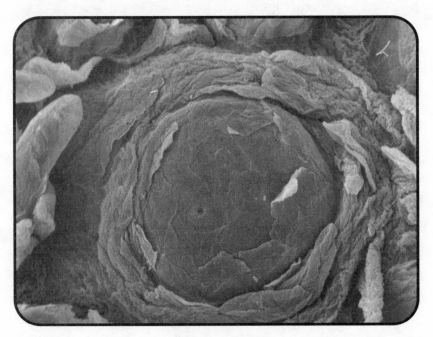

A human taste bud

The act of drinking, sucking, or chewing a substance releases its gases. They flow out of your mouth and up your nostrils, or up the passageway in the back of your mouth, to a thin layer of nerve cells called the olfactory epithelium. It's located at the base of the nose, right between your eyes. The brain combines the complex smell signals from your epithelium with the simple taste signals from your tongue. Based on those messages, the brain assigns a flavor to what's in your mouth and decides whether it's a food you want to eat—or spit out.

Babies like sweet tastes and reject bitter ones. We know this because scientists have put different flavors inside the mouths of infants and then studied the reactions on their face. A person's eating habits are largely formed in the first few years of his or her life. "It's during childhood that you learn to eat what foods you like," says Julie Mennella, a scientist at the Monell Chemical Senses Center in Philadelphia. Children can learn to enjoy hot and spicy food, bland health food, or fast food, depending on what the people around them eat.

Some of the latest research suggests that your taste in food can be formed even before you're born. The fluid in a mother's womb may carry the flavors of whatever she's been eating, and that fluid is often swallowed by the fetus growing in there. Julie Mennella conducted an experiment on how tastes are formed, studying mothers who drank carrot juice while they were pregnant or breastfeeding. She compared babies whose mothers drank carrot juice with those whose mothers didn't. All of the babies were given cereal mixed with water and then cereal mixed with carrot juice. The babies who had learned the taste of carrot juice from their mothers—either from breast milk or from amniotic fluid—liked the carrot juice/cereal combination much more than the other babies did. You probably have to be fed carrot juice at an early age (before you're old enough to say no) in order to want it on your cereal.

In another experiment, Mennella proved that babies can learn to like formula that tastes disgusting, if they drink it at a very young age. When babies who had been raised on sweet-tasting formula were given the disgusting one, they often reacted as though someone had put rotten garbage in their mouth. Meanwhile, babies who had been given the disgusting formula all their lives were happy to drink away.

 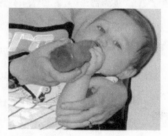

Babies reacting differently to a formula that tastes disgusting

Our sense of smell still isn't fully understood. Unlike hearing or sight, it is greatly affected by what a person is thinking. The mind filters out most of the chemical aromas that surround us, focusing on some and ignoring others. People can grow accustomed to bad smells or good smells. They can stop noticing smells that once seemed overpowering. Aroma and memory are somehow linked. A smell can suddenly bring back a long-forgotten moment. The flavors of childhood foods seem to leave a strong mark on us, and as adults we often return to them, without always knowing why. These "comfort foods" become a source of pleasure and reassurance—a fact that fast-food chains work hard to promote. Fond childhood memories of Happy Meals can lead to the yearning to eat at McDonald's many years later. The taste of fast food is no accident. It is carefully designed to be remembered all your life.

those strawberry shakes

The human craving for flavor has always been an important force in history. For thousands of years, royal empires have been built, unexplored lands have been crossed, great religions have been forever changed by the spice trade. In 1492, Christopher Columbus set sail for India to find seasoning; instead, he discovered America. Today the influence of flavor in the world marketplace is no less remarkable. The rise and fall of corporate empires—of soft-drink companies, snack-food companies, and fast-food chains—is often determined by the way their products taste.

The flavor industry emerged in the mid-nineteenth century, when processed foods began to be manufactured on a large scale. Food companies needed flavor additives to replace the aromas lost during processing. They soon turned to perfume companies, which had years of experience working with essential oils and creating memorable smells. The great perfume houses of England, France, and the Netherlands produced many of the first flavor additives. In the early part of the twentieth century, Germany's powerful chemical industry gave it an advantage in flavor production. Legend has it that a German scientist unexpectedly discovered one of the first artificial flavors, methyl anthranilate, while mixing chemicals in his laboratory. Suddenly the lab was filled with the sweet smell of grapes. Methyl anthranilate later became the chief flavor additive in grape Kool-Aid.

After World War II, much of the perfume industry shifted from Europe to the United States, settling in New York City, near the headquarters of the leading fashion designers. The flavor industry came with it but later moved to New Jersey, where larger factories could be built. At first manmade flavor additives were used mainly in baked goods, candies, and sodas. And then, during the mid-1950s, sales of processed food began to soar. The invention of fancy equipment that can detect gases at low levels, such as gas chromatographs, increased the number of flavors that could be manufactured. By the mid-1960s the American flavor industry was churning out compounds to supply the taste of Pop-Tarts, Hamburger Helper, BacO-Bits, Tab, Tang, Filet-O-Fish sandwiches, and literally thousands of other products.

Today the industry's latest gadgets—headspace vapor analyzers and high-tech spectrometers—can create a detailed map of a food's flavor chemicals. They can detect aromas present in amounts as low as one part per billion. The human nose, however, is more sensitive than any of these machines. A nose can detect aromas present in quantities of a few parts per trillion—an amount equal to about 0.000000000003 percent. Some aromas are more complicated than others. For example, the smell of coffee and the smell of cooked meat are produced by a mixture of gases from as many as a thousand different chemicals. The quality that people seek most of all in a food—its flavor—is usually present in an amount too small to measure in ounces or teaspoons or any other traditional recipe unit. The chemical that provides the main flavor of bell pepper, for example, can be tasted in amounts as low as 0.02 parts per billion. A single drop of this chemical is enough to make all the water in five swimming pools taste like bell pepper.

On the label of a processed food, the list of ingredients

describes what's in the food. At the top of the list are the ingredients used in the largest amounts, and at the bottom those used in the smallest amounts. The flavor additive usually comes last, or second to last, on the list. As a result, the flavor of a processed food often costs less than its packaging. Soft drinks contain a larger amount of flavor additives than most products. The flavor in a twelve-ounce can of Coke costs about half a cent.

The U.S. government does not require flavor companies to list the ingredients of their additives. This allows the companies to preserve the secrecy of their flavor formulas. It also hides the fact that flavor additives often contain more ingredients than the foods being given some taste. The phrase "artificial strawberry flavor" offers little hint of the scientific wizardry that can make a highly processed food taste like a strawberry.

For example, if you wanted to make a strawberry milk shake at home, here's all you'd need: ice, cream, strawberries, sugar, and a touch of vanilla.

Now take a look at the ingredients you might find in a fast-food strawberry milk shake: milkfat and nonfat milk, sugar, sweet whey, high fructose corn syrup, guar gum, mono- and diglycerides, cellulose gum, sodium phosphate, carageenan, citric acid, red food coloring #40, and artificial strawberry flavor.

And what does that artificial strawberry flavor contain? Just these few yummy chemicals: amyl acetate, amyl butyrate, amyl valerate, anethol, anisyl formate, benzyl acetate, benzyl isobutyrate, butyric acid, cinnamyl isobutyrate, cinnamyl valerate, cognac essential oil, diacetyl, dipropyl ketone, ethyl butyrate, ethyl cinnamate, ethyl heptanoate, ethyl heptylate, ethyl lactate, ethyl methylphenylglycidate, ethyl nitrate, ethyl propionate, ethyl valerate, heliotropin, hydroxyphrenyl-2-butanone (10% solution in alcohol), α-ionone, isobutyl anthranilate, isobutyl butyrate, lemon essential oil, maltol, 4-methylacetophenone, methyl anthranilate, methyl benzoate, methyl cinnamate, methyl heptine carbonate, methyl naphthyl ketone, methyl salicylate, mint essential oil, neroli essential oil, nerolin, neryl isobutyrate, orris butter, phenethyl alcohol, rose, rum ether, γ–undecalactone, vanillin, and solvent.

Although flavor additives are usually made by combining dozens of chemicals, a single one often supplies the strongest aroma. Smelled alone, that chemical gives a real sense of the food. Ethyl-2-methyl butyrate, for example, smells just like an apple. Today's highly processed foods are like a blank white canvas before you start painting it. Whatever chemicals you add will give them specific tastes. Adding methyl-2-pyridyl-ketone, for example, makes something taste like popcorn.

Adding ethyl-3-hydroxybutanoate makes it taste like marshmallow. The possibilities are almost endless. You could make the pages of this book taste like chocolate. By adding the right chemicals, processed foods can be made to taste like just about anything. Without changing their appearance or nutritional value, foods could even be made with aroma chemicals such as hexanal (the smell of freshly cut grass) or 3-methyl butanoic acid (the smell of body odor).

Artificial flavors were especially popular during the 1960s and 1970s. For the past twenty years food companies have tried hard to use only "natural flavors" in their products. These are made entirely from natural sources—from herbs, spices, fruits, vegetables, beef, chicken, yeast, bark, roots, and so on. Consumers prefer to see natural flavors on a label, out of a belief that they are healthier. But the difference between artificial flavors and natural flavors is much less simple than it sounds. Both kinds are manufactured at the same factories. The difference between them is based more on how the flavor additive has been made than on what it actually contains. Natural flavors and artificial flavors sometimes contain exactly the same chemicals, produced through different methods. Amyl acetate, for example, supplies the strong aroma of banana flavor. When you make amyl acetate from bananas, it is a natural flavor. When you make amyl acetate by mixing vinegar with amyl alcohol and sulfuric acid, it is an artificial flavor. Either way, it smells just like a banana.

kid testers

The small group of scientists who create most of the flavor in most of the food now consumed in the United States are called flavorists. Their work draws on research from a wide range of subjects: biology, psychology, physiology, and organic chemistry. A flavorist is a chemist with a trained nose and a poetic outlook. Flavors are created by blending many chemicals in tiny amounts. Although the mixtures are based on hard scientific principles, they also reflect a good deal of imagination and creativity. One flavorist compares his work to composing music, suggesting that a well-made flavor additive will always have the right "notes." The taste of a food can be changed enormously by tiny changes in the flavoring mix. "A little odor goes a long way," another flavorist says.

In order to give a processed food the right taste, a flavorist must always consider the food's "mouthfeel"—the combination of textures that you notice as you eat it. The mouthfeel can be adjusted through the use of different fats, gums, and starches. The chemicals that give food its smell can be studied easily with the right equipment, but mouthfeel is much harder to measure.

How do you measure the crispness of a French fry? A complex machine—the Universal TA.XT2 Texture Analyzer, produced by the Texture Technologies Corporation—tries to figure out the mouthfeel of a food using twenty-five separate probes. It is basically a mechanical mouth. It measures all the things that can give a food the right mouthfeel: the bounce, creep, breaking point, density, crunchiness, chewiness, gumminess, lumpiness, rubberiness, springiness, slipperiness, smoothness, softness, wetness, juiciness, spreadability, springback, and tackiness.

As marketing to children has become more and more important to processed-food companies and fast-food chains, flavorists have increased their efforts to discover what children like. The flavor companies constantly run "taste tests" for kids. These aren't the kind of taste tests you might get in your grandma's kitchen, when she's making brownies and asks you to lick the spoon. At flavor factories and flavor company offices, children are often placed in small booths, separated by plastic dividers. Researchers wearing white lab coats and plastic gloves slip samples of pizza, ice cream, flavored potato chips, and all sorts of other foods through small wooden doors. The kids taste the samples and then tell the researchers which ones taste best.

Some children feel uncomfortable sitting in the little booths. Whenever possible, IFF does its testing in a room that

Taste testing

feels more like a classroom. During one of those tests, at an IFF plant in Union Beach, New Jersey, a dozen kids between eight and twelve years old recently sat at a table with brand-new Fujitsu computers. Perched on black swivel chairs, some of the kids were so little that their heads could barely be seen above the table. A few rocked nervously from side to side. IFF promised to pay each one of them $10 to taste yogurts, and they talked excitedly about what to do with the money. The researchers were hidden behind a one-way mirror, able to watch the children without being seen.

The kids entered their "taster identification number" into the computer and then tasted a sample of yogurt. The computer asked them questions about the look of the yogurt as well as some questions that Goldilocks might have answered: Is the flavor too strong? Or too weak? Or just right? Once the children finished a sample, they drank a sip of water, took a bite of a cracker, and raised a blue card with a number on it to get another sample. Two women scurried around the room carrying small plastic cups filled with bright pink and blue yogurt.

The kids had fun answering the questions and eating the yogurt. But they seemed unaware of the nationwide impact this taste test could have. The answers they punched into their computers might convince IFF to use one set of flavors instead of another. In that room in Union Beach, a dozen local New Jersey kids were helping to decide the taste of yogurt that children might soon be eating all over the United States.

During the past two decades, the flavor industry's role in

food production has become so influential that many children now like manmade flavors more than real ones. Fresh fruits and vegetables often have complicated, unpredictable flavors that combine bitterness with sweetness. When flavorists create additives for adult foods, they try to imitate nature as closely as possible. When flavorists create additives for kids' foods, they usually get rid of the bitterness and increase the sweetness. Children's flavors are often twice as sweet as those made for adults. "Children's expectation of a strawberry is completely different," says a flavorist at IFF. "They want something that is strong and that has something like bubble-gum notes."

The use of strong, unusual flavors is now one of the most popular trends in kids' food. Doggie Man bubble gum tastes like a hot dog. Bubblicious Twisted Tornado gum is supposed to taste like whatever a tornado tastes like (without the dust). There are pepperoni pizza–flavored potato chips, cotton candy–flavored ice cream, and piña colada milk drinks. One candy manufacturer, inspired by the Harry Potter books, now sells jellybeans that are supposed to taste like earthworms, dirt, vomit, and boogers. Of course they don't taste exactly like those things. In real life, those things taste horrible. Although IFF could create candy that tastes just like barf, the company doesn't think it's a good idea. "We could do it very easily," an IFF executive says, "but I don't think that would be acceptable."

the bugs in your candy

The color additives in processed foods are present in even smaller amounts than the flavor additives. Many of New Jersey's flavor companies also manufacture these color additives, which are used to make processed foods look good. Food coloring serves much the same purpose as women's makeup, and it's often made from the same basic ingredients. Titanium dioxide, for example, is a mineral with many different uses. It can give candies, frosting, and icing their bright white colors. It is used as a coloring in makeup. And it is also commonly used in white house paints. So you can use titanium dioxide to ice your cake—or paint your house. At Burger King, Wendy's, and McDonald's, color additives can be found in many of the sodas, salad dressings, cookies, chicken dishes, and even sandwich buns.

One of the most widely used color additives comes from an unexpected source. Cochineal extract (also known as carmine or carminic acid) is made from the dead bodies of small bugs harvested mainly in Peru and the Canary Islands. The female *Dactylopius coccus costa* likes to feed on cactus pads, and color from the cactus gathers in her body and her eggs. The little bugs are collected, dried, and ground into a coloring additive. It takes about 70,000 of the insects to make a pound of carmine, which is used to make processed foods look pink, red, or purple. Dannon strawberry yogurt gets its color from carmine, as do many candies, frozen fruit bars, fruit fillings, and Ocean Spray pink grapefruit juice drink.

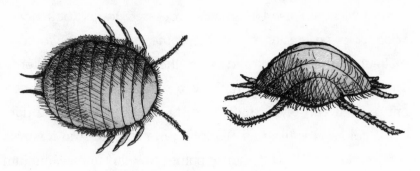

Dactylopius coccus costa

Studies have found that the color of a food can influence the way people think it tastes. Brightly colored foods seem to taste better than bland-looking foods, even when their flavors are exactly the same. The color additives in children's foods have become increasingly bold. According to IFF, kids are now drawn to outrageous colors and foods that change color in your mouth. Foods that are strawberry-flavored no longer need to be pink; grape-flavored foods don't need to be purple. Bright blue and green colorings are quite popular, regardless of the food's flavor. Boys are more likely than girls to try foods that are strangely colored (like purple French fries and purple ketchup) or foods that do strange things in your mouth (like Mega Warheads, which turn your tongue blue).

The popularity of unnatural colors, however, has led to accidental poisonings. Some laundry detergents and window-washing fluids are the same bright blue color as drinks such as Frost Gatorade. Small children have tried to drink these toxic liquids, thinking they will taste delicious. For thousands of years people could judge the safety of a food by its color. Foods that were dangerous or had gone bad often didn't look right. If your red meat turned green or blue, you'd probably decide not to eat it. The widespread use of bold food colorings has made it harder to see if something's wrong with your food. And some poisonous liquids, deliberately given unnatural colors so that nobody will drink them, now remind toddlers of their favorite drinks.

The U.S. government claims that the color and flavor additives widely used in processed foods are safe. That may not always be the case. Carmine can cause allergic reactions in some people. Tartrazine, a yellow food coloring, can cause hyperactivity, headaches, rashes, and an increased risk of asthma in some children. It has been banned in Norway, Finland, and Austria but is still used by food companies in the United States and Great Britain. Tartrazine can be found in British and

American sodas, candies, chewing gum, Jell-O, and butter-scotch pudding mixes, among other things.

A number of scientists now worry that eating so many different chemicals in processed foods may not be good for young children. A study conducted in 2004 at the University of Southampton in England looked at the behavior of 277 children who were three to four years old. Over a series of weeks the researchers gave each child either a fruit drink or a drink made with artificial colors and flavors that tasted exactly the same. The kids never knew which drink they were getting. They seemed much more hyperactive when they had the drink full of artificial ingredients than when they had the fruit juice. Each of the widely used chemical additives may be safe to eat by itself. But the safety of eating a large combination of additives at every meal remains unknown. "We assume that because these things do not make us drop dead, they're safe," says Dr. Vyvyan Howard, a leading expert on toxic substances at the University of Liverpool in England. "It's not true. In my opinion, I would recommend that kids just stay away from them."

poop on ronald

Even when a flavor additive is perfectly safe, it may be something that you don't want to eat. In 2001, Hitesh Shah contacted

McDonald's to find out if their French fries really did have beef in them. Shah was a Los Angeles software designer, a regular customer at McDonald's, a vegetarian, and a devout Jain. His religion, Jainism, strictly forbids eating any meat and wearing any clothing made from animal products. Jain monks and Jain nuns cover their mouths with cloth so that they will never accidentally swallow or breathe in any insects.

For years McDonald's had said that its French fries were cooked in pure vegetable oil and could be eaten by vegetarians. Shah had heard that there was beef in the fries—and he was very upset when McDonald's sent him an e-mail admitting that "a minuscule amount" of beef was indeed used for "flavor enhancement." Shah realized that every time he'd eaten French fries at McDonald's, he'd broken one of the basic rules of his religion.

Jain nuns

Shah forwarded the McDonald's e-mail to Viji Sundarama, a reporter at *India-West,* a California weekly newspaper with a large number of Hindu readers. Unlike Jains, Hindus are allowed to eat meat. But they must never eat beef. Hinduism teaches that cows are holy animals, and cows cannot legally be killed in India. Sundarama investigated McDonald's use of beef flavoring and wrote an article for *India-West* called "Where's the Beef? It's in Your French Fries." After reading the article, Harish Bharti, a Seattle attorney, angrily filed a lawsuit against McDonald's, claiming that the fast-food chain had misled people. "Eating a cow for a Hindu," Bharti later explained, "would be like eating your own mother."

When news of the lawsuit reached India, a crowd of five hundred Hindus marched to a McDonald's restaurant in a suburb of Bombay and destroyed it. At a McDonald's in Bombay, a crowd smeared cow poop on a statue of Ronald McDonald. In New Delhi, protesters staged a demonstration in front of McDonald's Indian headquarters. The sense of outrage that these Hindus felt seemed justified. They thought that McDonald's had shown disrespect to their religion by adding beef to the French fries in India. They assumed that the fries in India were being made the same way as the fries in the United States—a reasonable assumption. "If you visit McDonald's anywhere in the world, the great taste of our famous French fries and Big Mac is the same," a McDonald's Web site declared. But that wasn't always true. McDonald's didn't use any beef flavoring in India. Nor did it add beef to the fries in Great Britain, a country with a large Hindu population. Without telling anyone, McDonald's was quietly using different French fry recipes in different countries. In India and Great Britain, it didn't use any beef. In the United States, it used beef flavoring. And in Canada, Japan, Mexico, and Australia, McDonald's still made French fries the old-fashioned way, cooking them in beef fat.

McDonald's apologized to vegetarians in the United States, settled the lawsuit filed by Harish Bharti, and as part of the settlement donated $10 million to Hindu and vegetarian groups. The apology led other restaurant chains to admit that they were also using animal products to make their French fries taste better. At Denny's and Church's Chicken, the fries were flavored with beef. At Burger King the fries were flavored with chicken. Fries that taste like chicken may sound gross, but they're not as gross as some of the fries made in France. At restaurants over there, in the nation that invented French fries, they're sometimes cooked with horse fat. *Bon appétit!*

STOP THE POP

Kasigluk, Alaska

It takes a lot of work to get hamburgers, French fries, and Cokes to the school in Kasigluk, Alaska. The nearest highway is 400 miles away. There are no cows in Kasigluk. Or potatoes, for that matter. The village sits on the banks of the Johnson River, near the Bering Sea. During the summer, wild grasses stretch to the horizon. When the wind blows, the tall grasses make a peaceful rustling sound. About 540 people live in Kasigluk, give or take a few. During the winter, when the river becomes solid ice, they often travel on snowmobiles. And they have to bundle up. The village is so far north that on some days the sun comes out for just three hours and the temperature drops to 50 degrees below zero.

The people who live in Kasigluk are Yupiks, members of an Eskimo tribe that was among the last to encounter the modern world. For generations the lives of the Yupiks revolved around the land and the rivers, the gathering of food and the celebration of family life. Until about fifty years ago, Yupiks obtained almost all of their food by hunting, fishing, and harvesting wild fruits and vegetables. Children were taught at an early age to pick berries, catch small birds, trap rabbits, and collect water from melted snow. Many of the fish caught during the summer months would be dried and saved for the long winter.

It was a hard life. But the Yupik culture also had a great beauty tied to the seasons, the landscape, and most of all the rituals of hunting and gathering. The Yupiks had a name for the darkest part of the winter, when the sun would hardly ever appear: *Cauyarvik*. It meant "the time for drumming," and the coldest days of the year would be filled with village festivals, music, and dancing. People wrote songs and poetry, made masks and entertained one another during the *Cauyarvik*. They believed that all the souls of human beings were connected, even to the souls of animals. Seals that were captured were thought to have presented themselves as a gift to hunters who had behaved honorably.

In 1959, Alaska became the forty-ninth state of the United States and outsiders increasingly settled in the town of Bethel, twenty-five miles southeast of Kasigluk. A new airport opened in Bethel that same year, making it easier to fly in food and supplies from distant cities. Now that Kasigluk was part of the United States, Yupik children were required to attend school for nine months of the year, sitting in classrooms for much of the day. Instead of gathering food with their families, many children from Kasigluk were now sent away to boarding schools run by the U.S. Bureau of Indian Affairs. Few of the teachers were Eskimos, and the classes were taught entirely in English. A child caught speaking Yupik in school might have his or her mouth washed out with soap.

The Yupik elders had warned the children that they must be *upterrlainarluta,* which means "always getting ready," especially for the unexpected. One thing that the young Yupiks could not prepare for, however, was how quickly life would change in their village. The arrival of new people, new customs, and new laws from the outside world brought many conveniences. But it also threatened the heart of the Yupik culture: the unique rituals and reverence surrounding food.

Today most of the families in Kasigluk have cable television. They have a lot of spare time to watch TV. About half of the village's adults are unemployed. The opening of large commercial fisheries nearby has made it harder for Yupiks to catch fish in the Johnson River. Instead of picking berries and trapping rabbits, the village children can be found watching Nickelodeon, MTV, and reruns of *Friends*. They see ads for Burger King and McDonald's, even though many of them have never seen a real fast-food restaurant. The TV shows and commercials all seem to be preaching the same message: This is what you need to look like, this is what you need to buy, this is what you need to think, in order to be happy, pretty, popular, cool. The village elders still speak Yupik and want their children to respect tradition, while the images on TV promise the same American dream to everyone, everywhere.

Kasigluk now has its own school, the Akula Elitnaurvik School, attended by one hundred students from kindergarten through twelfth grade. The classes are taught in English, and the food served in the cafeteria wouldn't seem out of place in Des Moines, Iowa: hamburgers and French fries, macaroni and cheese. Much of the food has been donated or sold at a reduced price by the U.S. Department of Agriculture (USDA). Soda is sold at after-school events. The Akula Elitnaurvik School has its own warehouse, which can stock up to a year's worth of processed foods. Once a month, the school used to have a Native Food Day, and students would be served local dishes such as reindeer. Native Food Day was recently discontinued, and so at school the kids now eat nothing but food produced thousands of miles away. How do you get hamburgers, French fries, and Cokes to the school in Kasigluk? Like just about everything else, you get them there by cargo plane.

Three or four times a year, a plane carrying about a ton of frozen food heads to Kasigluk. It flies above the Kuskokwim and Johnson rivers, above a wildlife refuge that's home to rare birds (like the emperor goose) and rare animals (like the vegetarian muskox). It flies above an arctic wilderness that looks endless, that seems so ancient and pure you can almost forget, for a moment, the frozen hamburger patties and frozen pizzas that have come along for the ride.

mcschools

Throughout the United States, the menus in school cafeterias have come to resemble the menus at fast-food restaurants. The same kinds of foods are being offered at both places—increasingly, by the same companies. For years Ray Kroc liked to put new McDonald's restaurants near schools, but it wasn't until December 1976 that the first McDonald's opened *inside* a school. It was a high school in Benton, Arkansas, and to mark the occasion a gigantic portrait of Ronald McDonald was hung on the cafeteria wall. Students there could hardly believe their good luck. McDonald's viewed the opening in a high school cafeteria as an experiment. "We don't know if there will or won't be any others to follow," said a McDonald's spokesman. "It's an interesting thing and we're watching it."

Thirty years later, about 19,000 public schools—one of every five in the United States—sell branded fast food in the cafeteria. Pizza Hut, McDonald's, and Subway now serve fast food at elementary schools. The fast-food chains view school locations as just one more place to make money. Why have school officials, who are supposed to be concerned about the health of their students, invited these companies into their cafeterias? The answer also has to do with money. As communities have reduced spending on education, schools have scrambled to find enough money for teachers, classrooms, desks, computers, athletic programs, textbooks, and cafeteria workers. Selling food that kids like to eat has seemed to be an easier way to get money than convincing their parents to pay higher taxes. A number of school officials are even proud of the decision to sell fast food. "We want to be more like the fast-food places where these kids are hanging out," a Colorado school administrator told the *Denver Post*. "We want kids to think that school lunch is a cool thing, that we're 'with it.'"

Some schools sell exclusive cafeteria rights to a single fast-food chain. For example, in San Lorenzo, California, the school district signed a contract that makes Burger King the only fast-food restaurant at Arroyo High School. Student workers at Arroyo High wear red Burger King uniforms and caps while selling Whoppers. Even the garbage cans there have Burger King logos. "I don't think it's healthy," a ninth-grader told a reporter, "but I eat it because it tastes good." Other schools invite different fast-food chains into their cafeterias on different days of the week. On Tuesdays, it may be Subway; on Wednesdays, McDonald's.

Some kids have become so used to eating fast food and junk food at school that they get angry when it's taken away. Several years ago at a high school in Rhode Island, when administrators decided to take French fries off the lunch menu, students boycotted the cafeteria. A week later the fries were back. In 2004, when administrators in Starr County, Texas, removed sugary cereals and cookies from school meals and reduced the amount of fat and sugar in other foods, a group of students protested with signs that said, NO MORE DIET and WE WANT TO EAT COOL STUFF—PIZZA, NACHOS, BURRITOS, CHEESE FRIES. Half of the boys and one third of the girls in Starr County elementary schools are overweight.

Gibson City-Melvin-Sibley Unit #5 High School Lunch Menu for October 2004

Sun	Mon	Tue	Wed	Thu	Fri	Sat
					1 11:40 Dismissal NO LUNCH	2
3	4 Hot chicken/bun or Sloppy joe/bun	5 SUBWAY or Hot dogs w/toppings for lunch combo	6 McDonald's	7 Pizza Hut	8 NO LUNCH Teachers' Institute	9
10	11 NO LUNCH NO SCHOOL COLUMBUS DAY	12 SUBWAY or Chicken-fried steak/bun for lunch combo	13 McDonald's	14 Pizza Hut	15 Tacos w/toppings	16
17	18 Lasagna w/garlic bread	19 SUBWAY or BBQ chicken/bun for lunch combo	20 McDonald's	21 Pizza Hut	22 Potato bar w/toppings	23 Menu is subject to change.
24	25 Beef & noodles w/rolls	26 SUBWAY or Pork fritter/bun for lunch combo	27 McDonald's	28 Pizza Hut	29 Ribs/bun	30 Milk is offered daily.
31				Menu available for download at www.gcms.k12.il.us		

A "cool" and "with it" school lunch menu

the bitter cry of children

Hungry kids, 1909

A hundred years ago, the first school lunch programs weren't created to make money. They were started because American children too often didn't get enough to eat. In 1906, John Spargo's book *The Bitter Cry of Children* revealed that 2 million schoolchildren in the United States were so poor that they frequently went hungry. Most schools didn't serve lunch, and kids either went home for a meal or didn't eat. When a school did have a cafeteria, it was usually run by volunteer workers serving limited amounts of donated food. Spargo argued that hungry children could hardly be expected to pay attention in class and that spending money to educate kids without spending money to feed them was "an absolute waste." A couple of years later the first government school lunch program was started in New York City. Dr. William H. Maxwell persuaded the city board of education to offer a school lunch program in every school "whereby the pupils may obtain simple wholesome food at cost price."

During the 1930s, President Franklin D. Roosevelt decided that the federal government should help feed poor children. Roosevelt instructed the USDA to buy food from farmers and ship it to schools. The new program helped farmers by giving them money during the Great Depression, and it met the needs of poor children. The federal government hired people to work in school cafeterias.

By 1946 the national school lunch program was serving meals to 6.7 million children. That year Congress passed the National School Lunch Act, which expanded the program and announced that its goal was "to safeguard the health and well-being of the nation's children."

As the years passed, the needs of children became less important than the needs of companies hoping to sell them things. Soda, candy, and fast-food companies approached school officials and asked if they could put their products inside schools. The U.S. government worried that selling junk food and soda violated the spirit of the National School Lunch Act. In 1977 the USDA blocked the sale of "foods of minimal nutritional value" in schools. The National Soft Drink Association and other food companies didn't like that rule and filed a lawsuit against the USDA. At first the junk-food and soda companies lost in court. But they wouldn't give up, and in 1983 a federal judge ruled that sodas and junk foods *could* be sold in schools, with some restrictions.

Today, 43 percent of elementary schools, 74 percent of middle schools, and 98 percent of high schools have soda machines, candy machines, snack bars, or stores that serve foods high in sugar, fat, and salt. Many schools depend on money from the sale of soda and junk food to pay for uniforms for their sports teams, trips for their marching band, and other activities. The junk food competes with the food being offered by the National School Lunch Program. Given a choice between junk food and food supplied by the U.S. government, many kids go for the junk.

Jade Alexander is a thirteen-year-old eighth-grader who attends a public school in New York City. Her eating habits seem typical these days. Jade usually eats a twenty-five-cent bag of potato chips for breakfast. She thinks that the lunches served at her school are "nasty" and won't eat them. Instead she buys food at the school store right next to the cafeteria. "I love eating out of the school store," she says. "They have this thing called ketchup chips—potato chips with ketchup flavor on them. The store also has Bee honey-barbecue chips, and they have Combos, Fruit Roll-Ups, candy, and cookies." Since the food she buys at the school store isn't filling, Jade often meets her friends at KFC, McDonald's, Burger King, or Wendy's after school.

In the Brooklyn neighborhood where Jade lives, there aren't many restaurants that sell healthy food but there's no shortage of fast food. The Popeyes near her house has bullet-proof glass to protect the workers, and trays of food are passed through a revolving plastic door. Jade struggles with weight and knows that her problem, like her diet, is becoming typical. "Our school," she says, "it's mainly fat kids." That may sound like an exaggeration, but Jade's comment isn't far from the truth. More than 40 percent of the children in New York City public schools are now overweight, and almost 25 percent are obese (extremely overweight). In the city that created America's first school lunch program because poor kids were too hungry, many now have too much to eat.

the coke dude

While some companies want to enter the schools in order to

make money selling products, other companies look at schools as a good place to recruit future customers. Sometimes a company can do both. Children spend about 7 hours a day, 150 days a year, in school. When kids are in school, they're away from their parents. They have to listen in class. They have to do as they're told. They're a perfect, captive audience for corporate advertising. Many companies now send schools "educational" materials to be handed out in the classroom. Children have to be careful about believing everything in these materials. Kellogg's "Kids Get Going with Breakfast" program, aimed at third- and fourth-graders, said that cereals are low in fat—"Go ahead and enjoy them!" It failed to mention that many of Kellogg's cereals are also high in sugar.

The schools most likely to accept free educational materials are those with the least amount of money to buy books or pay their teachers good salaries. Channel One is a commercial television network aimed at schoolchildren. It gives free televisions to classrooms. There's only one catch: students must watch two minutes of ads on these free TVs every day. Poor schools often can't resist the offer of this equipment, even if it means forcing children to see ads. In a struggling Minnesota school district, General Mills gave $250 a month to ten elementary-school teachers. In return the teachers agreed to cover their cars in a vinyl wrap advertising a breakfast cereal named after a type of candy: Reese's Puffs. General Mills called the teachers "freelance brand managers."

A number of fast-food companies have created programs that link doing well at school with getting to eat at one of their restaurants. The Pizza Hut "Book It!" program offers a free Personal Pan Pizza to kids in kindergarten through sixth grade who read certain amounts each month. Pizza Hut expanded the program not too long ago to include preschoolers at 36,000 child-care facilities nationwide. McDonald's has programs that reward good grades with free food. These fast-food programs seem to be well-meaning efforts that encourage kids to work hard at school—until you look closely. They are also clever marketing schemes. A small child who visits Pizza Hut to get a free pizza almost always comes with parents or grandparents, and maybe a brother or sister or two. They all have to pay for their own food. What seems like a good prize is also a good way to draw people to your restaurant. More than 20 million elementary school students are now enrolled in Pizza Hut's "Book It!" program.

Over the past ten years soda companies have launched major advertising campaigns in American schools. Adults are now drinking less soda, and persuading kids to drink more is one way to increase sales. "Influencing elementary school students is very important to soft drink marketers," an industry newspaper explained, "because children are still establishing their tastes and habits." Eight-year-olds were considered the ideal customers, since they had about sixty-five years of buying sodas ahead of them. "Entering the schools makes perfect sense," the industry paper concluded.

The fast-food chains are also happy when children drink more soda. The chicken nuggets, hamburgers, and other sandwiches at fast-food restaurants usually are the least profitable things on the menu. Selling French fries is profitable— and selling soda is incredibly profitable. "We at McDonald's are thankful," a top executive once said, "that people like drinks with their sandwiches." Today McDonald's sells more Coca-Cola than anyone else in the world. The fast-food chains buy Coca-Cola syrup for about $4.25 a gallon. They add the syrup to bubbly water and serve it in a paper cup. A medium Coke that sells for $1.29 contains about nine cents' worth of syrup. Buying a large Coke for $1.49 instead, as the worker behind the counter always suggests, will add another three cents' worth of syrup—and another seventeen cents in pure profit. You can earn a lot of money selling sugar and water in a paper cup.

Thanks in large part to the marketing efforts of the fast-food chains, Americans now drink about twice as much soda as they did thirty years ago. In 1975 the typical American drank about twenty-seven gallons of soda a year. Today the typical American drinks about fifty-four gallons of soda a year. That's about 575 twelve-ounce cans of soda per person every year. And for every person who doesn't drink any soda, there's somebody who drinks more than a thousand cans a year. In 1978 the typical teenage boy in the United States drank about seven ounces of soda every day; today the typical teenage boy drinks nearly three times that amount, getting almost 10 percent of his daily calories from soft drinks. The amount of soda that teenage girls drink has doubled during the same period of time, reaching an average of twelve ounces a day. Many teenage boys now drink five or more cans of soda a day. Each can contains the equivalent of about ten teaspoons of sugar.

Even though soda tastes good, it isn't a good drink for kids to have all the time. Some critics call it "liquid candy." Coke, Pepsi, Mountain Dew, and Dr Pepper contain caffeine—a drug that can make kids irritable, give them headaches, and disturb their sleep. More importantly, soda is often a substitute for healthier drinks, such as milk. Thirty years ago, teenage boys in the United States drank twice as much milk as soda. Today they drink twice as much soda as milk. Drinking too much soda as a child may lead to calcium loss and a greater likelihood of broken bones. Even toddlers are now drinking soda. About 20 percent of American children between the ages of one and two drink soda every day.

School districts across the United States have been signing profitable deals with soda companies. In return for allowing kids to buy soda, the schools often get a share of the money. These deals, however, don't always work out as planned, forcing teachers to behave like soda salespeople. In 1998, at the beginning of the school year, School District 11 in Colorado Springs, Colorado, realized that its agreement with Coca-Cola wasn't raising as much money as expected. The district had promised to sell at least 70,000 cases of Coca-Cola products a year, but in the previous year had managed to sell only 21,000 at its elementary, middle, and high schools. John Bushey, an administrator at District 11, warned principals that their sales were falling short. He sent them a letter with a few ideas about how to solve the problem.

Allow students to take Coke products into the classrooms, Bushey recommended. Move Coke machines to places where students could use them all day. "Location, location, location is the key," he wrote. If the school principals felt uncomfortable about allowing kids to drink Coca-Cola during class, Bushey suggested letting them drink the fruit juices, teas, and bottled waters also sold in the Coke machines. At the end of the letter, Mr. Bushey signed his name and then identified himself as "the Coke Dude."

toothless

Kristina Clark of Glennallen, Alaska, is a twelve-year-old Blackfoot and Athabascan Native American who loves playing basketball, soccer, kickball, and football. She wanted to join the wrestling team, but the coach at her school wouldn't let her wrestle boys. Kristina thought that wasn't fair, and she let the coach know it. When she has strong feelings, she speaks her mind. And she has very strong feelings about junk food and soda pop. Several members of her family drink four to five cans of soda a day. Like many other Native Americans and Eskimos today, they've lost almost all their teeth.

Kristina has researched the subject and can tell you that during the 19th century you could travel far and wide in Alaska and never meet an Eskimo with a single cavity in his or her teeth. Vilhjalmur Stefansson, an explorer who traveled throughout Alaska in 1906, took a hundred Eskimo skulls to New York City so that researchers could examine their teeth. All of the skulls were carefully inspected at the American Museum of Natural History, Stefansson wrote, "but no sign of tooth decay has yet been discovered." The skulls belonged to Eskimos who had died before Americans visited Alaska. But Stefansson worried about the future of some Mackenzie River Eskimos he'd met. "Toothache and tooth decay were appearing," the explorer noted, "but only in the mouths of those who [liked] the new foods secured from the Yankee whalers."

Kristina Clark

Today many Eskimos are toothless, thanks largely to their new diet. It's not uncommon to meet Eskimos who drink half a dozen cans of pop every day. The sweet taste of the soda is only one part of its appeal. In remote rural areas, good drinking water is often hard to find. In villages without decent plumbing, people still have to get water from wells or from melted snow, and that water often doesn't taste very good. At many stores soda is cheaper than bottled water.

Coca-Cola executives are well aware of the large demand for soda in Alaska. In recent years Coke has thought up some imaginative ways of advertising to Eskimo children. In 2000, the Coca-Cola Company and a local bottler in Alaska decided to paint airplanes that regularly flew from the town of Bethel into dozens of Eskimo villages on Alaska's west coast. The planes were covered with enormous Coke and Sprite logos. They delivered mail, soda, and supplies to Kasigluk and other villages in the Yukon Delta National Wildlife Refuge. The Coke planes were a strange sight, with their brightly painted soda ads, flying over 22 million acres of wilderness. The year after Coke painted the planes, it paid Trajan Langdon—the first Alaskan player in the National Basketball Association and a hero to many Eskimo children—to fly into Yupik villages. Langdon arrived in Coke planes, visited children at schools, and gave out free T-shirts.

Trajan Langdon

"Young people in the small villages and towns of the Alaska bush often don't have the same opportunities as their big-city counterparts," Coca-Cola said in a press release announcing the visits. "They seldom come into contact with anyone outside their small town. So when a group of people flies into the bush bearing gifts and an NBA star, it's quite the local event."

Coke failed to mention that these Eskimo villages also don't have dentists. Edwin Allgair, a dentist who moved from Ohio to Alaska in 1998, travels every so often to Kasigluk and other Yupik villages, providing dental care to the children. He remembers visiting a village store one day in a community of about 160 people. Forty of them were children. It was a Monday, and the store had just received a stack of sodas four feet tall and four feet across. When he visited the store again on Friday, the sodas were almost gone. The owner of the store told him he had another shipment coming in a few days.

Dr. Allgair quickly did some math in his head. He calculated that to finish off that much soda in a week, every single person in the village would have to drink three to five cans a day. He figured that the owner of the village store earned about $20,000 a year just from selling soda. It's no coincidence, Dr. Allgair says, that many teenagers in the village have lost all their permanent teeth before they're sixteen.

Another problem that Dr. Allgair finds in Yupik villages is called "baby bottle syndrome." When mothers put soda or other sugary drinks in baby bottles, their children often fall asleep with the bottle in their mouth, creating a breeding ground for tooth decay. Baby bottle syndrome often causes the upper teeth to rot away into black nubs.

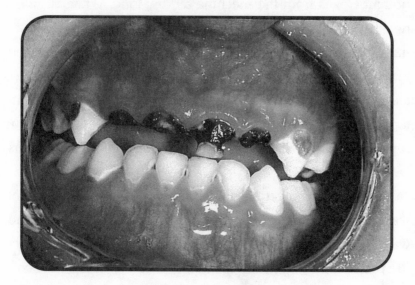

Baby bottle syndrome

Kristina Clark was upset by the dental problems she saw at Glennallen Elementary School. She says it made her angry to see "little kids with their teeth all black, drinking Pepsi and Coca-Cola all the time." She didn't want kids to suffer from bad teeth the way members of her family did. But she didn't know what to do about it.

In 2002, when Kristina was a fifth-grader, she started thinking about the soda machine down the hallway from the cafeteria at her school. It was supposed to be turned off during lunch periods, but nobody at the school bothered to do so. Kids bought Cokes from the machine all day long. While visiting a health clinic with her mother, Kristina learned a lot about the harmful effects of drinking too much soda. That night she went home and made a poster, including some of the facts she'd learned at the clinic. The next day Kristina went to school and taped the poster to the front of the Coke machine. Across the top of her poster she wrote a simple message in bold letters: "Stop the Pop."

The poster stayed up for about two weeks. Then Kristina walked past the machine one day and noticed that the poster was gone, tape and all. Nobody told her why. When she asked the principal at Glennallen Elementary if the school would consider getting rid of the soda machine, the principal listened to her and then didn't do a thing.

don't blame us

The power that fast-food companies and soda companies now wield inside schools has led many critics to believe that changing the law may be the only way to kick these companies out. In 2003, Mary Kapsner, a state representative from Bethel, felt uneasy whenever she saw the Coke planes take off from the local airport. Mary was thirty years old at the time— and had been elected to office at the age of twenty-four. Her mother was Yupik and her father was from Nebraska. She'd grown up loving traditional Eskimo foods and still kept dried salmon strips in her refrigerator as a snack. She wasn't happy about how good eating habits, practiced for centuries, were quickly slipping away. When she heard that many high schools in Alaska were inviting fast-food chains into their cafeterias, she became even more worried that local Yupik foods might vanish forever.

Mary Kapsner

Mary's husband, Jonathan, was a bush pilot who had come to Alaska from Minnesota. They had two kids. Jonathan told her that he was often hired to fly into Yupik villages carrying nothing but soda pop. Mary talked to people at the local hospital and dental clinic who described what soda was doing to the health of Eskimos. She decided to use her power as a state legislator to prevent schools from selling too much soda. The same companies that distributed Coca-Cola in Alaska also distributed alcohol, and she worried that kids who were now drinking six-packs of soda every day would soon be drinking six-packs of beer. Although these social problems were enormous, Mary decided to start with a small change. She pushed for a new state law that would forbid public schools to sell soda between eight in the morning and five in the evening.

Mary knew that some schools needed money from the machines to pay for uniforms and student travel. She promised that if her bill passed in the state legislature, she'd help to find other ways to give schools the money they needed. Her bill required that soda machines be turned off only during school hours. Coke and Pepsi could still be sold at sports events or after school.

Nevertheless, Mary's plan was swiftly opposed by the Grocery Manufacturers of America, the world's largest association of food and soda companies. The industry group sent a letter to leading members of the Alaska legislature, arguing that it was wrong to single out soda as the main cause of tooth decay. "Many factors contribute to the formation of dental cavities," the group wrote, "including diet, the level of oral hygiene, and access to professional dental care." Despite the friendly tone, the underlying message of the letter was clear: Don't blame soda for bad teeth. Blame yourself.

Mary didn't buy that argument. "Professional dental care" was hard to get in Eskimo villages, because they were remote and few dentists wanted to live in them. Teaching children to brush their teeth was part of the solution, she felt—but the soda companies had a big responsibility, too. After all, they were flying Coke, Sprite, and Trajan Langdon into these villages, not toothpaste, toothbrushes, and world-famous dentists.

Alaskan distributors of soda visited Mary's office in Juneau. They said her plan was a bad idea. "Why are you singling us out?" they asked. Their complaint made Mary wonder if she should go after the junk-food and fast-food companies, too. The legislature never passed her soda bill. In the meantime some local dentists and health officials painted a Dumpster in the center of Bethel, expressing their view on the matter:

Dumpster in Bethel

the power of one

At Glennallen Elementary, Kristina Clark recently sat at a student council meeting with her hand raised as high as it could go. She hadn't given up the fight against soda at her school. A new principal named Michael Johnson had been appointed, and she felt a little more hopeful. He used to be her fourth-grade teacher, and he always took her opinions seriously. Kristina was ready to tell the five other kids on the student council why the soda machine should be removed from the school. She'd done some more research and outlined a few talking points. At first she thought that nobody was calling on her because they didn't like what she was going to say.

When Kristina finally got her turn to speak, she calmly listed the problems that drinking too much soda can cause. Once she finished, the student council voted. The choices were (1) to keep nothing but soda in the machine, (2) to replace half the soda with fruit juice and bottled water, or (3) to get rid of all the soda. Everyone voted to replace half the soda with fruit juice and bottled water—except Kristina, of course. She was terribly disappointed and thought that kids would keep buying the soda anyway.

As Thanksgiving approached, the new principal thought long and hard about the arguments that Kristina had made about soda, about the courage it took for someone so young to speak out, about how she'd defended her beliefs when other kids disagreed. Mr. Johnson was impressed. Not long afterward, Kristina walked down the hallway and looked at the spot where her "Stop the Pop" sign had once been. The soda machine was gone.

MEAT

Emily, Ann, and Maggie Hanna

Emily Hanna grew up on a cattle ranch about twenty miles south of Colorado Springs, Colorado. Her father, Kirk Hanna, was handsome enough to be a cowboy in a Hollywood movie. He liked to take Emily along as he did chores on the ranch—even when she was a little baby. He'd carry her in a little sheepskin pouch and tie the pouch to a nearby fence post, then get to work. Emily and her sister, Maggie, who's two years older, were taught from an early age to work hard, to be fearless and independent. Sometimes Kirk would take them out on a four-wheeler, a small farm vehicle without a roof and with fat tires designed to drive off-road. Emily and Maggie would stand in the back and hold on tight to their father's shirt collar as he bounced the four-wheeler across the ranch. They'd ask him to drive faster. And whenever Kirk had to go round up some cattle, he'd stop the four-wheeler, tell the girls to get off, and leave them in the middle of the prairie, all alone. For half an hour or more, little Emily and Maggie would stay there, patiently waiting for their dad to return, surrounded by thousands of acres of open land, with the Rocky Mountains looming to the west and grasslands rolling eastward as far as the eye could see.

Emily's father died unexpectedly in 1998, and her mother, Ann, had to decide whether to keep the ranch or sell it. Ann had grown up in the suburbs of Chicago. She knew a lot about riding and training horses, but not as much about running a cattle ranch. That had always been Kirk's job. It soon became clear that the girls loved the ranch and didn't want to sell it—and neither did Ann. So the three of them took over the Hanna Ranch, with help from a new foreman named Jim and from Uncle Jay, who owned the ranch next door. Emily was seven years old; Maggie was nine. The girls had always done chores on the ranch. Now they had a lot more to do. They learned how to drive a four-wheeler and move cattle from one pasture to another. They learned how to throw a lasso and sort cattle in the corral. They took care of abandoned calves, feeding them milk from baby bottles and rubbing their sides at night to keep them warm.

Life was never dull on the ranch. No two days were ever the same, and all sorts of unexpected things happened. One afternoon Emily and Maggie got off the school bus and suddenly had to save the life of a pregnant cow. The ranch foreman was out of town, and their mother wasn't much use. A few days earlier Ann's horse had spooked, knocked her down, and busted her leg. Now she told the girls to change into their work clothes and get into the pasture as fast as they could. A cow was out there, lying on the ground away from the rest of the herd, starting to give birth but having trouble. If the girls couldn't help quickly, within a couple of hours both the cow and its calf would probably die. It was a freezing day in the middle of February, with temperatures way below zero. Emily was ten at the time; Maggie had just turned twelve. Each of them jumped on a four-wheeler and zoomed into the pasture.

The cow was acting crazy. It was snorting, feeling confused and in pain. Two of the calf's legs were already sticking out and dangling in the air, but the rest of its body was somehow stuck. Emily and Maggie calmly persuaded the cow to get up and head into the corral while they drove behind it on their four-wheelers, and then nervously watched as a neighbor helped pull the calf out safely. The mother cow and her baby survived.

Ann was proud of her girls. In all their years on the ranch, she'd never heard them say, "No, Mom, we can't do that." They just went out and did it.

Cattle on a Colorado prairie

Today the Hanna Ranch has about three hundred head of cattle. It also has horses, about half a dozen dogs that Ann rescued after other people abandoned them, and a variety of wildlife: deer, antelope, quail, wild turkeys, coyotes. Every so often one of the coyotes will attack a cow when it's lying on the ground giving birth and eat the calf. But most of the time the cattle spend their days and nights peacefully on the prairie, munching grass. Emily is fourteen now, a freshman in high school—and a fourth-generation rancher—who sometimes starts the morning by feeding the horses, feeding the dogs, and cleaning cattle pens before the school bus arrives. Despite all the hard work, she loves living on the ranch. "To me, this is real life," she says. Birth, death, happiness, loss, gorgeous sunsets, winter storms, the sweetness of animals, the power of nature—on the ranch she has seen them all. "You learn how to handle pressure," Emily explains. "When something's broken, you've got to try and fix it."

beef trust

Ranchers and cowboys have always been symbols of the American West. Some historians have praised them as national heroes, the living embodiment of freedom and self-reliance. Others have condemned them for harming the environment and driving Native Americans off the land. There's one fact about ranchers that can't be denied, however: more of them are being driven off the land today than at any other time since the Great Depression of the 1930s.

Ranchers now face a long list of economic problems: rising land prices, pressure from real estate developers, competition from overseas producers, health scares about beef. On top of all that, the growth of the fast-food industry has helped transform the way cattle are raised, slaughtered, and processed. Today McDonald's is America's largest purchaser of beef. In 1968, McDonald's bought fresh ground beef from 175 local companies. A few years later, McDonald's reduced the number of beef suppliers to five. It started to buy frozen ground beef that could be manufactured on a large scale with a uniform taste. As the chain grew, McDonald's wanted its hamburgers to taste exactly the same everywhere. Much like the French fry industry, the meatpacking industry has been completely changed to serve the fast-food companies. Many ranchers now argue that a few large corporations have gained a stranglehold on the market, using unfair tactics to force down the price of cattle.

A century ago, American ranchers confronted a similar problem. Every major industry was controlled by corporate groups known as trusts. There was a sugar trust, a steel trust, a tobacco trust—and a beef trust. The beef trust set the prices offered for cattle. Ranchers who spoke up against this monopoly power were often shut out of the market, unable to sell their cattle at any price. In 1917, at the height of the beef trust, the five largest meatpacking companies—Armour, Swift, Morris, Wilson, and Cudahy—controlled about 55 percent of the market.

The early twentieth century had trusts, but it also had trust busters, progressive government officials who believed that cor-

porations with too much power were a threat to American freedom and democracy. Starting with President Woodrow Wilson
in 1920, the U.S. government took a series of actions to break
up companies that had grown too large, protect small companies from unfair business tactics, and insure that the prices were
set by the free market, not by corporate executives meeting in
secret. The beef trust was finally broken up, and for decades
ranchers enjoyed a relatively free and fair market for their cattle.

In 1970 the four largest meatpacking companies controlled only 21 percent of the market. Then the fast-food chains
started to grow, encouraging their meat suppliers to get bigger.
And the U.S. government stopped preventing large companies
from taking over smaller ones. Today the top four meatpacking
companies—Tyson, Swift & Company, Excel, and National
Beef—control about 84 percent of the market. These four companies now slaughter a larger share of America's cattle than the
beef trust ever did.

As the meatpacking companies have grown bigger and
more powerful, independent ranchers have found it harder to
earn a good income. When you buy beef at a supermarket,
some of the money goes to the store, some of it goes to the
meatpacking company that sold the meat to the store, and
some eventually goes to the rancher. Twenty-five years ago,
ranchers got to keep sixty-two cents out of every dollar spent on

beef. Today they get only forty-seven cents. Most of the money goes to the supermarket and the meatpacking company.

Until recently, ranchers usually sold their cattle at auctions. There might be dozens of bidders, and the cattle were sold to whoever offered the highest price. The whole idea of a free market is that a fair price will be set by a lot of potential buyers competing for the same product. The cattle market doesn't work that way anymore. With only four big meatpacking companies left, there isn't much bidding at cattle auctions these days. Independent ranchers now have a hard time figuring out what their cattle are really worth, let alone finding anyone to buy them at a fair price. Every year thousands of ranchers are quitting and selling their land. The great symbols of American freedom are being driven out of business by a market that no longer seems free. The ranchers most likely to be in financial trouble today are the ones who live the life and embody the values supposedly at the heart of the American West. They are self-sufficient, believe in hard work—and as a result are now paying the price.

rotten eggs and burning poop

Greeley, Colorado, is about 150 miles north of the Hanna Ranch. But it might as well be on another planet. You can smell

Greeley long before you can see it. The smell is hard to forget but not easy to describe, a combination of live animals, manure, and dead animals being turned into dog food. Think of rotten eggs mixed with burning hair and stinky toilet, and you get the idea. The smell is worst during the summer months, blanketing Greeley day and night like an invisible fog. Many people who live there no longer notice the smell. It fades into the background, present but not present, like the sound of police sirens and honking horns when you're in New York City. Other people who live in Greeley can't stop thinking about the smell, even after years. It seeps into everything, gives them headaches, makes them nauseous, interferes with their sleep. Greeley is a modern-day factory town where cattle are the main units of production, where workers and machines turn big animals into small vacuum-sealed packages of meat.

The billions of fast-food hamburgers that Americans eat every year come from places like Greeley. The industrialization of cattle-raising and meatpacking over the past few decades has completely altered the way beef is produced—and the towns that produce it. Responding to the demands of the fast-food and supermarket chains, the meatpacking firms have cut their costs by cutting the wages of workers. They have turned one of the nation's best-paying factory jobs into one of the lowest-paying. They have recruited a workforce of poor immigrants who have little power and suffer terrible injuries on the job. The harms of this new meatpacking system are being felt not only by the workers employed by it but also by the animals processed by it—and by consumers who eat its meat. WELCOME TO GREELEY, a sign along the highway says: AN ALL-AMERICAN CITY.

Swift & Co. runs one of the nation's biggest meatpacking plants just a few miles north of downtown Greeley. Weld County, which includes Greeley, earns more money every year from livestock than any other county in the United States. Swift & Co. is the largest private employer in Weld County, running a beef slaughterhouse and a sheep slaughterhouse as well as processing facilities. Outside town, a pair of enormous feedlots supply the beef slaughterhouse with cattle. Each feedlot can hold up to 100,000 cattle. At times the animals are crowded so closely together it looks like a sea of cattle, a mooing, moving mass of brown-and-white fur that goes on for acres. These cattle don't wander the prairie, eating fresh grass. During the three months before slaughter, they eat special grain dumped into long concrete troughs that look like highway dividers. The grain is designed to fatten the cattle quickly, aided by growth hormones that have been implanted beneath their skin.

Male cattle that will be processed for their meat are called steers. A typical steer will eat almost 3,000 pounds of grain during its stay at a feedlot, just to gain 400 pounds in weight. The

A Greeley feedlot

process involves a good deal of waste. Each steer deposits about 50 pounds of urine and manure every day. Unlike human waste, this stuff isn't sent to a treatment plant. It's dumped into pits—gigantic pools of pee and poop that the industry calls lagoons. Slaughterhouse lagoons can be as big as 20 acres and as much as 15 feet deep, filled with millions of gallons of really disgusting stuff. As you might expect, the lagoons smell incredibly bad, and sometimes they leak, sending raw sewage into nearby rivers and streams. In 1991 one billion fish were killed in North Carolina by a disease linked to the runoff from slaughterhouse lagoons. People had to use bulldozers to bury the dead fish. The amount of waste created by the cattle that pass through Weld County is staggering. The two big feed-lots outside Greeley produce more pee and poop than the cities of Denver, Boston, Atlanta, and St. Louis—combined.

The smell from slaughterhouse lagoons isn't just unpleasant. It can also be harmful. The pools of waste emit various dangerous gases, including hydrogen sulfide and ammonia. Hydrogen sulfide—also known as "sewer gas" or "stink damp"—can be harmless in very small doses. Our own digestive system produces it: bad breath gets some of its bad smell from tiny amounts of hydrogen sulfide. Large concentrations of hydrogen sulfide can kill you (although nobody's breath has ever been that bad), and even small amounts, inhaled over a long period of time, can cause all kinds of health problems. Slaughterhouse lagoons release tons of hydrogen sulfide into the air. People who live nearby often complain about headaches, nausea, asthma, shortness of breath, and dizziness. Some studies suggest that breathing air polluted with hydrogen sulfide can cause permanent damage to the nervous system and the brain.

Farmers and ranchers have always used some of the manure from their animals as fertilizer. Putting manure on a field can be a good way to help crops grow. But no society in human history has ever had feedlots and slaughterhouses as big as the ones near Greeley. There have never been so many animals and so much manure in one place before. Strange things can happen when you don't watch out. In the fall of 2004, a pile of manure at a large feedlot in Milford, Nebraska, caught on fire. As manure decomposes, it gets hot and releases gases that burn easily, such as methane. If there's enough manure, it can catch on fire without anyone's lighting a match. Big manure fires are no longer unusual. At the Milford feedlot, once

4 million pounds of burning poop

the 4-million-pound, 30-foot-high pile of manure started to burn, it was hard to put out. The local fire department tried twice, without success. When the owner flattened the pile with heavy equipment, the smoldering fire spread. Spraying a lot of water on it threatened to pollute nearby streams. The massive pile of poop burned for nearly four months, with smoke drifting from it for miles.

mr. mcdonald's breasts

Many cattle ranchers now fear that the beef industry is deliberately being changed to operate like the chicken industry. And ranchers don't want to wind up like chicken growers—who in recent years have become largely powerless, trapped by debt and by strict contracts written by the meatpacking companies. Four chicken companies now control more than half the American market. These companies have shifted almost all of their chicken production to the rural South, where the weather tends to be mild, labor unions are weak, and farmers are desperate to find some way to stay on their land. Although many factors are responsible for changing the chicken industry, one invention played an especially important role. The Chicken McNugget turned a bird that once had to be carved at a table into something that could easily be eaten behind the wheel of a car. It turned an agricultural commodity into a manufactured product. And it encouraged a system of production that turns many chicken farmers into economic serfs who must always obey company orders.

"I have an idea," Fred Turner, the chairman of McDonald's, told one of his suppliers in 1979. "I want a chicken finger food without bones, about the size of your thumb. Can you do it?" The supplier, an executive at Keystone Foods, ordered a group of researchers to get to work in the lab, where they were soon joined by food scientists from McDonald's. At the time, doctors were praising the health benefits of eating chicken instead of beef. People in the United States were starting to eat a lot more chicken—a trend with worrisome implications for a fast-food chain that only sold hamburgers.

The nation's chicken meat had traditionally been provided by hens who had grown too old to lay eggs. In the early twentieth century, most chicken farms were small. The birds lived as long as six years, roaming outdoors and eating grass. After World War II, chicken farms emerged in Delaware and Virginia on a much larger scale. Raising chickens to be eaten and raising hens to lay eggs became two separate businesses. They had one thing in common: both started to operate much more like factories than like old-fashioned farms.

Fred Turner wanted McDonald's to sell a chicken dish that

Southern California chicken farm, 1913

would fit neatly with the chain's other menu items. After six months of intensive research, the Keystone Foods lab developed new technology for the manufacture of McNuggets—small pieces of ground-up chicken meat that were stuck together with edible paste, breaded, fried, frozen, and then reheated. The initial test-marketing of McNuggets was so successful that McDonald's soon asked another company, Tyson Foods, to start manufacturing them, too. Based in Arkansas, Tyson was one of the nation's leading meatpacking companies, and it

A modern chicken farm

soon developed a whole new breed of chicken for the production of McNuggets. Named Mr. McDonald, the new breed of chickens had unusually large breasts.

Chicken McNuggets were introduced in 1983. Within a month, the McDonald's Corporation had become the second largest purchaser of chicken in the United States, surpassed only by KFC. McNuggets tasted good, they were easy to chew, and they seemed to be healthier than other items on the menu at McDonald's. After all, they were made out of chicken. But their health benefits were an illusion. When a researcher at Harvard Medical School performed a chemical analysis of

McNuggets, he discovered that they contained many of the same unhealthy fats as beef. How could that be? The McNuggets were being cooked in beef fat, just like McDonald's fries. The chain soon switched to vegetable oil, adding beef flavoring to the McNuggets to maintain their familiar taste. Chicken McNuggets, which became wildly popular among small children, no longer get their flavor from beef additives—but they still contain more fat per ounce than a hamburger.

The McNugget helped transform not only the American diet but also its system for raising poultry. "The impact of McNuggets was so huge that it changed the industry," the president of ConAgra Poultry, the nation's second largest chicken company, later said. Twenty-five years ago, most chicken was sold whole in the United States. Today about 90 percent of the chicken sold has already been cut into pieces, cutlets, or nuggets. Gaining the McNugget contract helped turn Tyson Foods into the world's largest chicken processor. Tyson now manufactures about half the nation's McNuggets and supplies chicken to ninety of the one hundred largest restaurant chains. It now breeds, slaughters, and processes chicken. It does not, however, raise the birds. It leaves most of the expense and the risk of that task to thousands of farmers.

A Tyson chicken farmer never owns the birds in his or her own poultry houses. Like most of the other leading processors,

Tyson supplies its farmers with one-day-old chicks. Between the day they are born and the day they are killed, the birds spend their entire lives on the farmer's property. But they belong to Tyson. The company supplies the chicken feed, veterinary services, and technical support. It decides the feeding schedules, demands the purchase of certain equipment, and employs "flock supervisors" to make sure that these corporate orders are being followed. It hires the trucks that drop off the baby chicks and return six weeks later to pick up full-grown chickens ready for slaughter. At the processing plant, Tyson employees count and weigh the birds. A farmer's earnings are determined by Tyson's count of the birds, Tyson's measure of their weight, and the amount of Tyson feed that has been used.

The chicken farmer provides the land, the fuel, the chicken houses, and the hard work. Most farmers must borrow money to build the houses, which cost about $150,000 each. A typical chicken farmer has been raising the birds for fifteen years, owns three chicken houses, still remains deeply in debt, and after expenses earns about $12,000 a year. About half the nation's chicken growers leave the business after just three years, either selling out or losing everything. The back roads of the rural South are now littered with abandoned chicken houses.

mccannibals

Norah Smith raises chickens in West Virginia. Like the farmers who supply Tyson, she never owns the birds in her chicken houses. Another company drops off day-old chicks at her farm and comes back with a truck a little more than a month later to take the chickens to the slaughterhouse. While the birds are at her place, the company tells her when to feed them and how to take care of them, sending over supervisors to make sure she's doing everything the way they want it done. After the company picks up the chickens, it decides how much to pay her. She has no control over the price given for her birds. Norah originally went into the business because she wanted to be "an independent farmer." She thought raising chickens might enable her and her husband to have a comfortable life. But now she has three different jobs and works sixty hours a week just to make ends meet. A few years ago her husband had a heart attack, and Norah works hard to pay for his health insurance.

On a recent morning at the farm, Norah pulled open the door to one of her chicken houses. The building was as long as a football field, and inside you could see 30,000 chickens, packed closely together. The squawking of so many birds made a tremendous noise. The air was full of dust, white feathers, and a really bad smell. The birds were nineteen days old. They had only eighteen more days to live. Aside from their first day and their last day of life, they would never set foot outdoors. They were being fed a grayish mixture of old pretzels and cookies covered with a layer of fat. Chicken feed is often made out of whatever can be bought inexpensively. Sometimes the leftover waste from cattle slaughterhouses is added to chicken feed. Sometimes the leftover meat, fat, blood, and bones from *chicken* slaughterhouses is added to chicken feed, turning the birds into cannibals. The aim is to provide feed that will fatten chickens as quickly and as cheaply as possible. In the wild, chickens don't eat other chickens. They prefer grass. "These chickens will never see grass in their entire lives," Norah said.

The industrialization of meatpacking has not only changed the way chickens are raised, it has also changed the birds themselves. In 1994, Japanese scientists discovered that every chicken in the world could trace its origins back eight thousand years to a wild bird in Thailand called the red jungle fowl. Deep in the forests of Thailand, Pakistan, and India, red jungle fowls still live in their original

Red jungle fowls

habitat. The birds are colorful; the feathers of the male are green, red, and gold. Unlike today's chickens, red jungle fowls can fly. They can't soar high like a hawk, but they can fly short distances. Thousands of years ago people began to keep red jungle fowls in cages, using them first in religious ceremonies, later as food. Farmers mated large birds with one another, eventually producing a bird with a thick chest that looked a lot like the modern chicken. It had more meat but could no longer fly. Unable to escape from predators, chickens became a tasty meal for foxes, skunks, dogs, cats, and hawks as well as people.

Like Mr. McDonald, the chickens raised for the fast-food industry have been bred to develop large breasts and reach maturity in a short time. In 1965 chickens gained roughly three and a half pounds during about two months on the farm. Today they gain about five and a half pounds in little more than half that time. If a child gained weight that fast, he or she would weigh 286 pounds by the age of six. Some chickens grow such big breasts that they have a hard time walking (when they have any room to walk). Their legs become crooked from all the weight and fill with fluid. They live in constant pain. Today's chickens also develop heart problems. They're big and fat and don't have any chance to exercise. Norah has been surprised lately by how many of her birds are having heart attacks. It seems to happen every day now. A chicken having a heart attack will suddenly stand up, get a startled look in its eyes, then flip over and die. If you cut the dead bird open, you find a thick layer of fat around the heart. Chickens that die from heart attacks have been struck by "flip-over disease." It's most likely caused by gaining too much weight too fast. Norah collects the dead birds in a bag and uses them as compost.

shocking

In 2006, about 9 billion chickens will be raised in the United States, slaughtered, and then eaten. That works out to almost thirty chickens for every man, woman, and child in the country. Killing a chicken has never been pleasant. The old-fashioned method, used by farmers for centuries, is to chop off their heads with an ax. You've probably heard that a chicken can run around for a few moments without its head. That's true, although it's not something farmers like to see. The billions of chickens slaughtered every year to make McNuggets and KFC Crispy Strips don't get a chance to run around without their heads. They are killed at enormous slaughterhouses, hanging upside down, their legs shackled to a fast-moving chain that carries thousands of birds. Unlike the assembly lines at an automobile factory, where cars are put together, the production lines at a modern slaughterhouse are geared for disassembly, as one animal after another is killed and then rapidly taken apart.

Fifteen miles from Norah's farm there's a slaughterhouse run by a company with an all-American name: Pilgrim's Pride. The name suggests a product that's wholesome and pure. Many of the farmers in Norah's neighborhood raise birds for Pilgrim's Pride, which sells chicken meat to KFC and other fast-food chains. The slaughterhouse is a white building with a chain-link fence around it. Little smokestacks rise from different parts of the roof, sending puffs of steam into the air. It doesn't look like a scary place full of death and dying. It looks like a factory that could be making chocolate bars, lawn chairs, or tennis shoes. You can tell it's a slaughterhouse when big trucks start pulling up, full of rustling and squawking chickens in cages, their white feathers visible behind metal bars.

When chickens arrive at the Pilgrim's Pride slaughterhouse, their cages are rolled onto conveyor belts and tipped over. The birds tumble down a ramp that resembles a playground slide. When they land at the bottom, workers grab their legs and attach them to a moving overhead chain. Sometimes chickens break their legs trying to wriggle free. The chain carries them upside down to a huge tank of water that's charged with electricity. When the birds are dunked into the water, the electricity is supposed to knock them unconscious. Chickens that have been properly shocked don't feel what happens next.

But some birds manage to avoid the water by twisting their bodies and flapping their wings or come out of the water still wide awake. Several years ago McDonald's admitted that one or two out of every one hundred chickens processed by the company's suppliers aren't knocked out by the "stun bath."

What happens next is painless for birds that are unconscious but cruel to those still awake. The moving chain carries the chickens to a sharp rotating blade that slits their throats. The blade reliably kills almost all the chickens. Every so often, however, a bird that's still awake moves its head out of the way and dodges the blade. Moments later that bird suffers a painful death. The chain dunks the chickens into a tank of boiling water. Called the scald tank, it helps remove their feathers. It looks like a witch's brew of bubbling, bloody liquid. No chicken has ever been known to survive the scald tank. The birds that somehow live to this point are boiled to death.

The company motto at Pilgrim's Pride is "Fresh from the Farm . . . Every Day," and the company Web site features cartoons of happy, smiling chickens. Yet a 2004 videotape shot inside the slaughterhouse near Norah's farm reveals little to smile about. The video was made by an animal rights activist upset by how the chickens were being treated at the plant. On some days so many chickens would arrive there at once that workers didn't have enough time to shackle every bird's legs.

Pilgrim's Pride slaughterhouse, Moorefield, West Virginia

Instead of attaching them to the overhead chain, workers would throw leftover birds against the wall. Some of the chickens that hit the wall were knocked out, but others continued to squawk and flap around. The video shows frustrated workers jumping up and down on the birds or picking them up and throwing them against the wall again. According to the animal rights activist, one worker put three live chickens on the floor and jumped on each of them. "I like to hear the popping sound they make," said the worker.

The cruelty at the Pilgrim's Pride slaughterhouse was caused by a production line that moved too quickly and by workers who were poorly supervised. But even a well-run American slaughterhouse inflicts unnecessary suffering on birds. At many European slaughterhouses, chickens aren't dumped from cages, grabbed, shackled to a chain, and then dropped into an electrified stun bath. They are kept in crates, placed in a sealed chamber, and then forced to breathe a gas that painlessly knocks them unconscious. At slaughterhouses that use this "controlled atmosphere stunning" system, workers never have to handle live birds. And chickens never get boiled alive. A study of controlled atmosphere stunning released by McDonald's in July 2005 concluded that it was more efficient than using a stun bath, better for the welfare of the birds, and better for the workers in the plant, without affecting the quality of the meat. But it was also more expensive, and McDonald's currently has no plans to ask chicken suppliers to get rid of their shackles and stun baths.

the jungle

As bad as things can be at a chicken slaughterhouse, they can be even worse at a cattle slaughterhouse. Today's chickens are nearly identical in size, allowing most of the slaughterhouse work to be done by machines. But cattle still come in all sizes and shapes, varying in weight by hundreds of pounds. As a result, much of the work in a cattle slaughterhouse must be done by hand. Human error can cause unnecessary pain for the animals, injure workers, and contaminate the meat. Working at one of these plants is a dangerous and unpleasant job. It seems hard to believe, but at the dawn of the twenty-first century, in an era of high-speed computers and tiny cell phones, the most important tool in a cattle slaughterhouse is a sharp knife.

The dangers of working at a slaughterhouse are nothing new. A hundred years ago the novelist Upton Sinclair traveled to Chicago, which at the time was the heart of the meatpacking industry. He investigated the mistreatment of poor immigrants from eastern Europe who worked in the Chicago slaughter-houses. Angered by what he saw, Sinclair wrote a novel, *The Jungle,* based on his research. The book described a long list of slaughterhouse horrors that workers faced: severe back and shoulder injuries, deep cuts, amputated limbs, exposure to dangerous chemicals, and, memorably, a workplace accident in which a man fell into a vat and got turned into lard. The plant kept running, and the lard was sold to the public. Human beings at the slaughterhouse, Sinclair argued, had been made into "cogs in the great packing machine," easily replaced and entirely disposable.

The Jungle also described filthy working conditions that

threatened the health of everyone who ate meat. "This is no fairy story and no joke," Upton Sinclair wrote. "The meat would be shoveled into carts, and the man who did the shoveling would not trouble to lift out a rat even when he saw one— there were things that went into the sausage in comparison with which a poisoned rat was a tidbit." Diseased animals were routinely slaughtered and processed. The book was full of other disgusting details. Chemicals such as borax and glycerine were used to disguise the rancid smell of spoiled meat. Canned meat was deliberately mislabeled. And workers who needed to go to the bathroom weren't allowed to take a break. They were forced to pee right on the slaughterhouse floor, near meat that people would soon be eating.

When *The Jungle* was published in 1906, it became a huge bestseller. The meatpacking companies that ran the beef trust immediately attacked the book and called Upton Sinclair a liar. After reading *The Jungle,* President Theodore Roosevelt ordered an independent investigation of its claims. When government investigators later told President Roosevelt that the book was accurate, he was outraged. Despite strong opposition from the meatpacking industry, he fought hard to gain congressional approval of the Meat Inspection Act of 1906 and the Pure Food and Drug Act of 1906. Roosevelt won the battle, and both of these laws were passed by Congress. For the first time the U.S. government had the power to regulate the meatpacking industry and make sure that the meat being sold was safe to eat. Upton Sinclair was glad that these new food-safety laws had been passed as a result of his book, but terribly disappointed that nothing had been done to help poor meatpacking workers. He had written *The Jungle* in order to create sympathy for the workers—and instead had created an uproar about the filthiness of the meat. "I aimed for the public's heart," Sinclair wrote many years later, "and by accident I hit it in the stomach."

It took decades for the working conditions in America's slaughterhouses to improve. Labor unions battled the meatpacking companies to gain higher wages, health benefits, and workplace safety rules. By the 1950s the unions had largely won the battle. Working at a slaughterhouse was still a dirty job—but it had finally become a good job. In fact, meatpacking workers were soon among the highest-paid factory workers in the United States. When they got hurt, they received good medical care. When the production line moved too fast, they could speak up and ask that it be slowed down. The wages were high enough to provide a decent middle-class life for workers and their families. It was considered a desirable way to make a living. There were waiting lists for work at meatpacking plants.

During the 1970s, the lives of American meatpacking workers took a turn for the worse. As meatpacking companies grew bigger to serve the needs of the fast-food industry, they began to cut wages. They moved slaughterhouses away from cities like Chicago, where unions were strong, and opened them in rural areas, where unions were weak. They recruited poor workers from Mexico, many of them illegal immigrants. And they sped up the production line. One company, IBP, led the way in changing how meatpacking workers were treated, breaking unions, reducing health benefits, and lowering wages by as much as 50 percent. Companies that wanted to compete with IBP had to imitate its low-cost tactics—or risk going out of business. As fast-food chains spread across the country, the workers producing the meat for all those Whoppers and Big Macs saw their incomes plummet and their jobs become much harder.

Today meatpacking workers are among the lowest-paid factory workers in the United States. And they have one of the most dangerous jobs. There aren't long waiting lists at American slaughterhouses anymore. In fact, the typical meatpacking worker now quits or is fired after just one year on the job.

don't complain

When a worker is badly injured, a government agency called the Occupational Safety and Health Administration (OSHA) often writes a report on the cause of the accident. The titles of some OSHA reports on meatpacking injuries give a sense of the potential dangers that workers confront every day: *Employee Severely Burned After Fuel from His Saw Is Ignited. Employee Hospitalized for Neck Laceration from Flying Blade. Employee's Finger Amputated in Sausage Extruder. Employee's Finger Amputated in Chitlin Machine. Employee's Fingers Amputated by Guillotine Blade. Employee's Fingers Amputated in Meat Blender. Employee's Eye Injured When Struck by Hanging Hook. Employee's Arm Amputated in Meat Auger. Employee's Arm Amputated When Caught in Meat Tenderizer. Employee Burned in Tallow Fire. Employee Burned by Hot Solution in Tank. One Employee Killed, Eight Injured by Ammonia Spill. Employee Killed When Arm Caught in Meat Grinder. Employee Killed in Unguarded Meat Grinder. Employee Killed When Head Crushed by Conveyor. Employee Killed When Head Crushed in Hide Fleshing Machine. Employee Killed by Stun Gun. Caught and Killed by Gut-Cooker Machine.*

Serious accidents don't happen every day. But the risk of one happening is always present. During a visit to a cattle slaughterhouse, the dangers of the job were easy to see. Hundreds of workers—about half of them women, almost all of them young and Latino—sliced meat with long slender knives. They stood at a table about chest-high, grabbed meat off a conveyor belt, trimmed away fat, threw meat back on the belt, tossed the scraps onto a conveyor belt above them, and then grabbed more meat, all in a matter of seconds. Even though the room was cooled to about forty degrees, many of the workers were sweating. Hundreds of them were pressed closely together, constantly moving and slicing. You saw their hardhats, white coats, flashes of steel. Nobody was smiling or chatting—they were too busy, anxiously trying not to fall behind.

In another part of the plant, cattle that had been sliced in half were suspended from an overhead trolley and swinging toward a group of men. Each worker had a large knife in one hand and a steel hook in the other. They grabbed the meat with their hooks and attacked it fiercely with their knives. As they hacked away, using all their strength, grunting, the place suddenly felt different. It didn't seem like a modern factory anymore. The machinery seemed beside the point. What was happening there had been going on, one way or another, for thousands of years: the meat, the hook, the knife, men straining to cut more off the bone.

Knocker, Sticker, Shackler, Rumper, Knuckle Dropper, Navel Boner, Splitter Top/Bottom Butt, Feed Kill Chain—even the names of job assignments at a cattle slaughterhouse give a sense of the brutality involved in the work. Twelve-hundred-pound animals are sliced apart, largely by hand. Cuts are the most common injuries suffered by meatpacking workers, who often stab themselves or accidentally stab someone nearby. Many workers make the same knife cut every two or three seconds, which adds up to about 10,000 cuts in an eight-hour shift. Doing anything that many times, again and again, is bound to hurt you. Meatpacking workers frequently develop back problems, shoulder problems, wrist pain, and "trigger finger" (an injury in which a finger becomes locked in a curled position). If a worker's knife becomes dull, additional pressure is placed on his or her muscles, joints, and nerves. It can cause pain to extend from the cutting hand all the way down the spine. Workers often take their knives home after work, spending at least forty minutes a day keeping the edges smooth and sharp.

Perhaps the leading cause of injuries at slaughterhouses today is the speed of the disassembly line. The old meatpacking plants slaughtered about 50 cattle an hour. Thirty years ago, new plants in the countryside slaughtered about 175 cattle an hour. Today some plants slaughter up to 400 cattle an hour— about half a dozen big animals every minute, sent down a single production line, carved by workers desperate not to fall behind. As the pace increases, so does the risk of injuries.

The reason the line moves so fast is easy to explain. Once a slaughterhouse is up and running, fully staffed with workers, the profits it will earn are directly related to the speed of the line.

A faster pace means higher profits for the meatpacking company. The Occupational Safety and Health Administration is supposed to insure that American workplaces are safe. But the meatpacking industry, through its friends in Congress, has made sure that OSHA inspections are rare and that OSHA fines are kept low. The maximum fine that OSHA can impose on a company for the death of a worker is $70,000. That may sound like a lot—but keep in mind that Tyson, now the world's largest meatpacking company, takes in almost 400,000 times that amount of money every year (roughly $27 billion). OSHA has the authority to demand criminal charges against meatpacking executives who carelessly or recklessly endanger workers. But it rarely uses that power. A meatpacking executive who deliberately violates OSHA safety rules has a better chance of winning a state lottery than of facing criminal charges for causing the injury of a worker.

In the days when labor unions were strong, meatpacking workers could complain about line speeds and injuries without fear of getting fired. Today many workers don't belong to a union, and even those who do are reluctant to complain. Most of the workers are recent immigrants from Mexico who can't speak English. Many are illegal immigrants who lack the proper documents to be in the United States. And meatpacking workers are often employed "at will," which means they can be fired without warning, for just about any reason. Such an arrangement doesn't encourage people to complain about what's wrong. Workers who have traveled a great distance for these jobs—who have families to support, who are earning far more in an American meatpacking plant than they could earn back home in Mexico—are understandably afraid to speak out and risk losing everything. They are under tremendous pressure not to report injuries to the government. If a worker agrees not to report an injury, a supervisor will usually shift him or her to an easier job for a while, providing some time to heal. If the injury seems more serious, a Mexican worker is often given the chance to return home for a while and get better there. Workers who obey these unwritten rules get to keep their jobs. Those who disobey are likely to be punished or let go.

From a purely business point of view, injured workers aren't good for profits. They are less productive. Getting rid of them and refusing to pay their medical bills makes sense, especially when new workers are readily available and inexpensive to train. Injured workers are often given some of the most unpleasant tasks in the slaughterhouse. Their hourly wages are often cut. And through a variety of methods they are encouraged to quit. Injured, unemployed, no longer able to do manual labor, these workers often become trapped in poverty.

cook it well

In January 1993, doctors at a hospital in Seattle, Washington, noticed that an unusual number of children were being admitted with bloody diarrhea. Some were suffering from a rare disorder that causes kidney damage. Health officials soon realized that the sick children had recently eaten undercooked hamburgers served at local Jack in the Box restaurants. Tests of the hamburger patties revealed the presence of *E. coli* O157:H7, a bacterium that can cause severe food poisoning. Jack in the Box issued an immediate recall of the contaminated ground beef. Nevertheless, more than seven hundred people in at least four states were sickened by Jack in the Box hamburgers, nearly two hundred people were hospitalized, and four died. Most of the victims were children. One of the first kids to become ill, Lauren Beth Rudolph, ate a hamburger at Jack in the Box a week before Christmas. She was admitted to the hospital on Christmas Eve, suffered terrible pain, had three heart attacks, and died in her mother's arms on December 28, 1992. She was six years old.

The Jack in the Box outbreak received a great deal of attention on television and in the newspapers, alerting the public to the dangers of *E. coli* O157:H7. The Jack in the Box chain almost went out of business amid all the bad publicity. But this wasn't the first outbreak of *E. coli* O157:H7 linked to fast-food hamburgers. In 1982 dozens of children were sickened by contaminated hamburgers sold at McDonald's restaurants in Oregon and Michigan. McDonald's had quietly cooperated with government investigators, providing ground beef samples contaminated with *E. coli* O157:H7—samples that for the first time linked the germ to serious illnesses. In public, however, the McDonald's Corporation denied that its hamburgers had made anyone sick. A spokesman for the chain acknowledged only "the possibility of a statistical association between a small number of diarrhea cases in two small towns and our restaurants."

Every day in the United States, roughly 200,000 people are sickened by something they ate, 900 are hospitalized, and 14 die. More than one quarter of the American population suffers a bout of food poisoning each year. Most of these cases are never reported to authorities or properly diagnosed. The widespread outbreaks that are detected and identified represent a small fraction of the number that actually take place. And there is strong evidence that the number of people getting sickened by food has gone

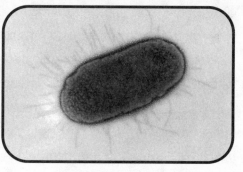

E. coli

up in the past few decades. Much of this increase can be blamed on recent changes in the way American food is produced.

A generation ago, the typical outbreak of food poisoning involved a small gathering: a church supper, a family picnic, a wedding reception. Contaminated food made a group of people in one local area get sick. Such traditional outbreaks still take place. But the nation's current system of food processing has created a whole new sort of outbreak, one that can potentially sicken millions of people.

The construction of huge feedlots, slaughterhouses, and hamburger grinders has made it easier for E. coli O157:H7 and other nasty germs to spread through the nation's food supply. In the 1970s there were thousands of small slaughterhouses in the United States. Today thirteen large slaughterhouses supply most of the beef eaten by almost 300 million Americans. The meatpacking system that arose to supply the nation's fast-food chains—an entire industry molded to serve their needs, to provide gigantic amounts of uniform ground beef so that all McDonald's hamburgers would taste the same—has proven an extremely efficient system for spreading disease.

While medical researchers have pointed out the links between modern food processing and the rise in food poisoning, the nation's leading meatpacking companies have strongly opposed government efforts to pass tough food-safety laws. For years the meatpacking industry has managed to avoid the kind of rules that apply to the manufacturers of most consumer products. If a defective toy somehow poses a risk to small children—for example, if a piece could easily break off and be swallowed—the U.S. government can demand that every one of those toys be removed from stores. But the U.S. government cannot order a meatpacking company to remove contaminated, potentially lethal ground beef from fast-food kitchens and supermarkets—even if that meat can kill children. The government can't even fine companies that knowingly sell bad meat. "We can fine circuses for mistreating elephants," the head of the USDA once admitted, "but we can't fine companies that violate food-safety standards."

The ability of the meatpacking companies to avoid strict food-safety rules has been made possible by their close ties to members of Congress. Every year the industry gives millions of dollars to politicians who support its point of view. Meatpacking companies don't want people to get sick. But they also don't want to be held legally responsible when bad meat does make people sick. Being held legally responsible would require these companies to pay the medical bills of everyone sickened by their meat. The industry's attitude today is much the same as it was a hundred years ago, when a member of the beef trust told Congress why his company opposed the Meat Inspection Act of

1906. "There is no limit to the expense that might be put on us," he said. "In all reasonableness and fairness *we are paying all we care to pay.*"

The risk of contamination begins in the feedlot. Far from their natural habitat on the prairie, cattle in feedlots become prone to all sorts of illnesses. They get little exercise and live amid pools of manure. "You shouldn't eat dirty food and dirty water," a government health official says. "But we still think we can give animals dirty food and dirty water." Modern feedlots have become places where germs are easily spread from one animal to another. *E. coli* O157:H7 can live in cattle troughs and survive in cattle manure for up to ninety days.

The germs from infected cattle are spread not only in feedlots but also at slaughterhouses and hamburger grinders. The slaughterhouse tasks most likely to contaminate meat are the removal of an animal's furry hide and of its digestive system. If the hide hasn't been cleaned well, chunks of dirt and poop may fall from it onto the meat. The digestive system is still pulled out of cattle by hand. If the job is not performed carefully, the contents of the stomach and intestines may spill everywhere. The speed of today's production lines makes the task much more difficult. A single worker at a "gut table" may have to pull the guts out of sixty cattle every hour. Doing the job properly takes a fair amount of skill. Doing it wrong spills the stomach contents, full of germs, all over the meat. Knives are supposed to be cleaned and disinfected every few minutes, something that workers in a hurry tend to forget. A contaminated knife spreads germs to everything it touches. The faster the line, the more likely that people will make mistakes.

The risk of widespread contamination grows when the meat is turned into ground beef. A generation ago, local butchers made hamburger meat out of leftover scraps. Ground beef was sold locally, and it was often made from cattle slaughtered locally. Today enormous slaughterhouses and grinders dominate the production of ground beef. A modern plant can produce almost a million pounds of hamburger meat a day, shipping it throughout the United States and even overseas. A single animal infected with *E. coli* O157:H7 can contaminate 32,000 pounds of that ground beef.

To make matters worse, the animals used to make about one quarter of the nation's ground beef—old dairy cattle—are those most likely to be sick and diseased. Dairy cows can live as long as forty years, but they are often slaughtered at the age of four, when their milk production starts to fall. McDonald's relies heavily on dairy cattle for its hamburger supplies, since the animals are relatively cheap and yield leaner meat. The days when hamburger meat was ground in the back of a little butcher shop, out of leftover scraps of beef, are long gone. The mixing together of meat from a large number of animals at ground beef plants has played a crucial role in spreading *E. coli* O157:H7. A single fast-food hamburger now contains meat from hundreds or even thousands of different cattle.

Children who eat ground beef must make sure that it has been completely cooked. It should be well done. There shouldn't be a single particle of meat that still looks pink. Cooking the meat thoroughly kills germs like *E. coli* O157:H7. But it doesn't change a rather unappetizing fact. There are all sorts of complicated scientific explanations for how germs are spread in feedlots, how germs are spread in slaughterhouses, how germs are spread in hamburger plants. Behind them lies a simple explanation for why eating a hamburger can now make you seriously ill: there is poop in the meat.

run

Chickens are pretty dumb. Cattle are smarter, and pigs are rather intelligent. In fact, pigs are even smarter than dogs. Pigs are also sensitive, highly social animals. Contrary to what many people think, they like being clean and roll in the mud only on hot days to cool themselves off. For thousands of years pigs have been raised by farmers, allowed to roam outdoors until it's time to be turned into bacon, pork, or ham. During the past twenty years, however, pigs have been raised indoors at giant hog factories that look more like prisons than farms. The mother pigs are often confined for months in crates that are so small they can't walk or turn around. Piglets are taken away from their mothers at the age of three weeks—about three months earlier than they would separate from each other in the wild. The piglets are crammed into pens with steel floors. The pens are so crowded that the piglets, which are friendly by nature, start biting each other's tails. To prevent injuries and infections, workers now cut the tails off.

Scientists have little idea what pigs, cows, and chickens might be thinking as they head to their deaths at a slaughterhouse. It's unlikely that they know what's about to happen. Many farm animals have been bred to be calm. Most of the time they appear to lack emotions. But you can tell when cattle are frightened: they tend to bellow. The latest slaughterhouses are designed to keep cattle quiet and relaxed as they march up the ramp to their doom. The ramps curve and have walls on either side to prevent the cattle from seeing what's ahead. While most livestock never realize that they're about to become pieces of meat, every so often an animal seems to know exactly what's going on.

On January 8, 1998, at the V & G Newman slaughterhouse in Malmesbury, England, two pigs were just minutes

Sundance and Butch

away from being killed when they wriggled through a hole in the fence, swam across a nearby river, and ran off. Newspapers soon called the pigs Butch and Sundance, nicknames referring to the Wild West outlaws in the movie *Butch Cassidy and the Sundance Kid.* Despite an intensive search by television crews, local police officers, and animal rights activists, Butch and Sundance roamed free for more than a week. Sundance was finally cornered and shot with a tranquilizer dart that made him feel sleepy. Butch was discovered in somebody's backyard garden, looking for a snack. Butch, it turned out, was actually female. She was thought to be Sundance's girlfriend. A British newspaper, the *Daily Mail,* bought the two pigs and donated them to a farm in Kent. Butch and Sundance still live there today, happily playing and sunbathing outdoors.

A few years earlier, an American dairy cow named Emily attempted a similarly daring escape. Although she was only two years old, her owner thought that she wasn't producing enough milk and sent her to a slaughterhouse in Hopkinton, Massachusetts. On November 14, 1995, Emily stood in a line with other cattle inside the slaughterhouse gates. Moments before it was her turn to enter the building, Emily suddenly decided to run off. Workers said she leaped over a five-foot-high fence, kept on running, and disappeared into the woods. For more than a month she lived in the woods amid herds of deer, foraging for food. A couple of vegetarians found Emily, adopted her, and took her home to their farm. Children from a nearby school helped take care of her. A group of Hindu priests from India visited her and blessed her as a sacred cow. When Emily died of natural causes in 2003, dozens of people attended her funeral, and a statue was later placed at her grave.

Emily's statue

BIG

Sam and Charlie Fabrikant, 2003

On a hot July morning in 2004, Sam Fabrikant sat on the edge of a bed at the Mirage, a hotel in Las Vegas. He was facing the toughest decision of his life. His mother and his twin brother, Charlie, sat beside him. It was the last day of their family vacation, and before returning home to Buffalo Grove, Illinois, Sam needed to make up his mind. His family wanted him to have gastric bypass surgery. Sam had just turned sixteen years old—and weighed almost 300 pounds. The operation would reduce his stomach from about the size of a football to the size of a golf ball. It would limit the amount of food absorbed by his small intestine. It would make Sam want to eat less and help him to lose weight. But the operation also posed some risks. If something went wrong, it could kill him.

Sam had tried not to think about the operation while on vacation. This trip was supposed to be fun. The Mirage is one of the most famous hotels in Las Vegas. It has swimming pools, game rooms, a casino, Siegfried & Roy's white tiger habitat, dolphins swimming in enormous tanks, and a manmade volcano that erupts every fifteen minutes in the evening, shooting fire a hundred feet into the air. Sam had enjoyed wandering around the Mirage, checking out the stores and eating at the restaurants. For years he'd dreamed of becoming a hotel manager and had even written letters to Steve Wynn, the founder of the Mirage. Although he felt great admiration for Wynn, Sam no longer wanted to run a hotel. Now he wanted to become a high school history teacher. Despite all the excitement at the Mirage, this trip to Vegas was ending on a bittersweet note. Sam realized that he'd gained a lot of weight over the past year, and it made him sad.

As a young boy, Sam had always been thin. His family used to call him "string bean." At about the age of ten, he started to get too big. He loved eating large meals at home—and really loved going out for fast food. After reaching his teens, Sam began to eat at fast-food restaurants three or four times a week. His parents both worked long hours and often took him to McDonald's after school. Sam liked to order two hamburgers and French fries. He also drank a lot of soda—about two quarts a day.

Sam's eating habits were by no means unusual at his high school. Every morning at Buffalo Grove High School, a buzzer sounded at 11:10 to release students from fourth-period classes. Some people called the buzzer the school bell, but it didn't sound anything like a bell. It sounded like the noise a McDonald's French fry machine makes when the fries are done—which seemed fitting, since the fry machines were buzzing throughout the day at the McDonald's right across the street. And as soon as fourth period ended, kids would leave campus for their Big Macs, McNuggets, and McFlurries. Sometimes the Buffalo Grove McDonald's sold hamburgers for just a quarter and cheeseburgers for thirty-five cents. Kids would buy as many as five or six burgers at a time. They would rush across Dundee Road for fast-food lunches, often ignoring the traffic light. Students were struck by cars every year. After being hit by a car on Dundee Road, one kid asked some friends, as medics loaded him into an ambulance, to bring his burger to the hospital.

Buffalo Grove High School opened in 1973, on land that used to be a cornfield. The McDonald's on Dundee Road was the first building to open near the school. And by the time Sam became a freshman at Buffalo Grove, there was an ice cream parlor right next to the McDonald's, as well as a Popeyes, a Pizza Hut, a Dunkin' Donuts, a Brown's Chicken & Pasta, and a Burger King. Students who didn't care for those options could drive a few minutes down the road to Taco Bell, KFC, Subway, Dairy Queen, Super China, Jimmy John's, another Burger King, Portillo's, Walker Brothers, Chuck E. Cheese's, White Castle, Wendy's, another Pizza Hut, Denny's, Einstein Bros Bagels, Fuddruckers, or Culver's (home of the ButterBurger). The cafeteria at Buffalo Grove High School wasn't large enough for all the students, and so when the buzzer sounded at 11:10, out they went, by foot or by car, to the fast-food joints of Dundee Road.

Sam's twin brother, Charlie, attended the same school. Charlie also loved to eat fast food. At Burger King he'd usually order two Whoppers with fries. In 2003, at the age of fifteen, Charlie had gastric bypass surgery. He weighed 350 pounds at the time. The operation was a success. Within a year, Charlie had lost 100 pounds. The doctors had made his stomach so small that he couldn't eat more than half a cup of food at a meal. If he tried to eat more, he might stretch his new little stomach and gain weight. So he ate six small meals a day. And he never chewed gum, because the doctors said if he swallowed it, they might have to perform another operation to remove it.

Charlie had learned a great deal about gastric bypass surgery from his mother. She'd had the operation in 1998 and had lost 75 pounds since then. Despite the risk and the inconvenience and the limits on what they could eat, she and Charlie felt glad they'd had the surgery. They hoped Sam would do it, too.

At times during the Las Vegas vacation, Sam resented his twin brother. Although the two had always been very close, Sam now felt a twinge of jealousy. When they went to clothing stores, Charlie could find shirts and pants that fit. Sam couldn't. He felt insecure and self-conscious about his body. The recent weight gain had made his asthma worse. He needed to use his inhaler more often and had trouble walking around Las Vegas. He thought about all the ways in which being so big had made his life more difficult. Sam loved to play sports but now had to sit down after playing basketball for just a few minutes. He wanted to attend the prom but felt too embarrassed. He was a baseball fan and loved to watch the Cubs play at Wrigley Field, but he no longer fit comfortably into the seats at the stadium. Although he knew that surgery had helped his brother and his mother, Sam was afraid of the operation. For months he'd come close to making the decision—and had always backed away at the last minute. Sitting on the bed at the Mirage, Sam decided to take the risk. He just couldn't live this way anymore.

monster thickburgers

The huge popularity of gastric bypass surgery has a simple explanation. Over the past few decades, as the fast-food industry has grown, so have the waistlines of most Americans. Today almost two thirds of the adults in the United States and about one sixth of the children are overweight or obese. Almost 50 million Americans are now obese. An additional 6 or 7 million are "morbidly obese": they weigh about 100 pounds more than they should. Since the early 1970s, the rate of obesity among American adults has increased by 50 percent. Among preschoolers it has doubled. And among children aged six to eleven it has tripled. According to James O. Hill, a nutritionist at the University of Colorado, "We've got the fattest, least fit generation of kids, ever."

Scientists are just beginning to understand why so many people have gotten so fat recently in the United States. Obesity clearly has a number of complex, interconnected causes. What you eat, how much of it you eat, and how much you exercise help to determine your weight. The genes that you inherit from your parents can also play a role. Some families—and even some racial groups—may be more likely than others to gain weight easily. But the basic family and racial traits of the American people haven't changed in the past thirty years. What's changed are their eating and living habits. When people eat more and move less, they get fat.

For thousands of years human beings had to struggle for food. Getting enough food to survive usually required hard work—hunting, farming, fishing. And when food supplies ran low, people had to survive for days or weeks without eating much. For most of human history, getting too fat wasn't the problem. Getting food was the problem. Scientists think that our bodies developed fat cells in order to store energy for those periods when food was hard to find. Today few of us have to hunt, farm, or fish for our daily meals. All we have to do is open the refrigerator, go to the supermarket, or stop at a drive-through. Our bodies, however, still function as though the food may run out at any moment. As a result, it's much easier to gain weight (and store energy as fat) than it is to lose it.

A typical person has 25 to 35 billion fat cells. The body needs those fat cells to stay healthy. They communicate with the brain, signaling how much energy has been stored and when it's time to eat. They also play an important role in the immune system, helping the body protect itself from cancer and diseases. Fat cells are good for you. But in this case, you don't want too much of a good thing. An obese person can develop as many as 275 billion fat cells. That's almost eight times the normal amount. All these fat cells don't just sit there. They require new blood vessels and place new demands on vital organs. They create chemical imbalances. Instead of helping the immune system, these billions of new fat cells make the body much more vulnerable to illnesses.

Once you've got so many fat cells, it's hard to get rid of them. Going on a diet only shrinks them. That may be one of the reasons why many people go on a diet, lose weight—and then gain back all the weight a few months later. Their fat cells rarely vanish. They just shrivel for a while, like empty little balloons, and then fill up with fat again. Becoming obese early in life may fundamentally change a person's body chemistry, making it difficult to become thin. If you are obese by the age of thirteen, there's a 90 percent chance you will be overweight in your midthirties.

The rise of suburbia, changes in the American workplace, and the triumph of the automobile have made it easier to grow obese. A hundred years ago, few people worked behind a desk. They worked outdoors on a farm or indoors at a factory. They worked hard and burned a great deal of energy throughout the day. Today many people work in offices, talking on the phone, typing at a computer, sitting on their butts for most of the day. They drive to work instead of walking. They drive to the mall. They sit on the couch and play video games instead of exercising. And they eat a lot of fast food. The inactivity of American kids has played a large role in the spread of obesity. Less than 30 percent of high school students in the United States attend daily physical education classes, and only 12 percent of students walk to school.

Most fast-food meals are low in fiber, low in nutrients, high in salt, high in starch, high in sugar, high in fat, and high in calories. They are the perfect meals for making you unhealthy. The fast-food industry says that if people get fat from eating burgers and fries, it's their own fault. The industry argues that it's a question of "personal responsibility." But fast foods have been carefully designed to make you want to eat them again and again. In fact, the industry earns most of its money from a small group of customers who eat at fast-food restaurants at least three or four times a week. According to one former McDonald's executive, the company has a reliable business formula: the "80-20 rule." About 80 percent of the money that McDonald's earns comes, he said, from just 20 percent of its customers. These fast-food fanatics, who go to McDonald's all the time, have an unfortunate nickname in the industry. They're called "heavy users."

The fast-food chains encourage people not only to eat things full of fat, salt, and sugar but also to eat larger portions at every meal. If you went to a fast-food restaurant during the 1950s and bought a Coca-Cola, you'd probably get about eight ounces of soda. That was the adult portion: eight ounces. Today the smallest Coke that McDonald's sells (a child's Coke) is twelve ounces. That's a 50 percent increase in size. Many customers purchase a large Coke, which is thirty-two ounces—four times bigger than the Cokes that fast-food restaurants used to sell. One of these large Cokes has 310 calories and contains the equivalent of almost thirty teaspoons of sugar.

The hamburgers have gotten bigger, too. In 1957 the typical fast-food burger patty weighed one ounce. Today the typical burger patty weighs six ounces. Indeed, fast-food chains are now proud of how big their hamburgers have become. At Hardee's, the Monster Thickburger contains two thirds of a pound of beef, four strips of bacon, and three slices of cheese, with mayonnaise on top. That one hamburger has 1,410 calories. To put those numbers in perspective, the average person aged nine to thirteen should eat about 1,800 calories in a single day. At Wendy's, a Classic Triple hamburger with cheese, Great Biggie French fries, and a Biggie cola have about 1,760 calories. If you eat that meal at Wendy's, you probably shouldn't eat anything else that entire day. Even the children's meals at fast-food restaurants have gotten bigger. In 1999, Burger King started selling the Big Kids Meal, and two years later McDonald's introduced the Mighty Kids Meal. Eating too many of those two could turn you into a mighty big kid. A Burger King Big Kids Double Cheeseburger Meal has 900 calories.

Although the major fast-food chains have led the way in encouraging Americans to eat larger portions of food, nothing that they sell comes near the burgers you can buy at Denny's Beer Barrel Pub in Clearfield, Pennsylvania. The family-owned restaurant started offering super-duper-sized hamburgers in 1991, gradually increasing the size of the ground beef patties from two pounds to six pounds. The six-pound burger patty came with five pounds of toppings. In January 2004, a college student named Kate Stelnick ordered one of these eleven-pound hamburgers and ate the whole thing. She weighed about a hundred pounds before eating it—and increased her weight by more than 10 percent at this one meal. In April 2005, Denny's Beer Barrel Pub started offering what may be the largest hamburger on any menu in the world. The Beer Barrel Belly Buster weighs fifteen pounds. It features ten pounds of ground beef, twenty-five slices of cheese, three tomatoes, two onions, a head of lettuce, mayonnaise, ketchup, mustard, relish, and peppers on a seventeen-inch bun.

the american disease

Children who eat too much food and become obese often feel bad about themselves. In a society that celebrates being thin, they are made to feel unattractive. They're frequently teased at school. They're far more likely than other kids to feel sad and depressed. One study of obese children in California found that their poor self-image and bleak view of the future was similar to that of children undergoing treatment for cancer. Obesity, however, can harm more than a child's feelings. It can permanently damage his or her body.

Obesity has been linked to health problems such as heart disease, colon cancer, breast cancer, asthma, high blood pressure, and strokes. Obese people are two to three times more likely to die young than people of normal weight. Obesity kills more than twice as many Americans every year as car accidents. According to one recent estimate, obesity is responsible for about 110,000 deaths every year in the United States. And that estimate may be low. Some Americans have gotten so big that their coffins have to be supersized.

Type II diabetes is one of the most serious illnesses that can be caused by obesity. Diabetes can harm the circulation in a person's feet and legs. Sometimes the damage is so severe that a limb needs to be amputated. Diabetes can cause kidney failure, blindness, and heart disease. It is now the sixth leading cause of death in the United States. Thirty years ago doctors rarely saw a child with Type II diabetes. The disease was nicknamed "adult-onset diabetes" because it seemed that children never developed it. Today Type II diabetes has become commonplace among kids, thanks to the rise in childhood obesity. Children who don't exercise, who drink too much soda and eat too much high-fat, high-calorie food, have a much higher risk of developing diabetes. A study conducted by the federal government predicts that if American kids continue to become obese at the current rate, one out of every three children born in the year 2000 will develop diabetes. Among African-American and Latino children, perhaps one out of every two will develop diabetes. The life of a ten-year-old child who has Type II diabetes will be, on average, between seventeen and twenty-six years shorter than that of a healthy child.

As people in other countries have started to eat a lot of American fast food, they've begun to look more like Americans, at least in one way. They've gotten a lot bigger. Between 1984 and 1993, the number of fast-food restaurants in Great Britain roughly doubled—and so did the obesity rate. During the 1980s, the sale of fast food in Japan more than doubled—and so did the obesity rate among Japanese children. Overweight people used to be rare in Japan. The first McDonald's opened there in 1971, introducing the Japanese to American fast food. Today McDonald's is by far the largest restaurant chain in Japan. And today about one third of Japanese men in their thirties—members of the first generation raised on Happy Meals and Big Macs—are overweight.

The traditional diet in Okinawa, an island off the coast of Japan, is thought to be one of the healthiest in the world. For generations, Okinawans followed a diet that included a lot of soy, fish, fruits, and vegetables, with small amounts of meat. People in Okinawa lived longer than just about anyone anywhere else in the world. Many Okinawans could expect to live past the age of a hundred. The first McDonald's opened on the island in 1976, and the presence of large U.S. military bases there also encouraged the Okinawans to adopt an American diet. Today Okinawa has the most hamburger restaurants, per person, in Japan. Okinawa also has the highest obesity rate in Japan. The life expectancy is falling. Many elderly Okinawans, who never learned to like fast food and still eat the island's traditional foods, may outlive their children.

windows of the soul

What we eat changes not only how we look on the outside but also how we look on the inside. In order to demonstrate this

Dr. Mehmet Oz

point, Dr. Mehmet Oz stands before a long metal table in the gloomy basement of a New York City hospital. Dr. Oz is one of New York's leading heart surgeons. He thinks that many heart operations could be avoided if people exercised more and ate less fast food. He thinks that hearing about, or reading about, what a poor diet can do to your body isn't always enough. Seeing is believing. That's why some real body parts, removed from people who've recently died at the hospital, are spread across the table.

On the right side of the table, a human brain sits in a glass jar. Nearby there are pieces from two different aortas (the artery that carries blood from the heart to the rest of the body), kidneys, livers, and spines. An unopened white bucket on the left side of the table has a tag on it that says, "Hearts for Dr. Oz."

"When you're young, you don't have power over many things," Dr. Oz says. "Your body is one thing over which you do have some power. You can function better physically and mentally if you make some good choices."

Dr. Oz begins his tour of the human body by opening the glass jar and removing the brain. It's wet and glistening in his hands. He says that eating unhealthy foods can damage the brain. Foods that contain too much sugar and the wrong kinds of fats can cause your blood vessels to thicken and narrow. That can limit the amount of blood reaching your brain, reducing its ability to work properly. Over a long period of time, the damage to blood vessels can lead to infarcts, or strokes, killing brain tissue. Although many people recover from such brain damage, sometimes it can kill you, paralyze you, or make it difficult for you to think clearly or speak.

Dr. Oz puts the brain back into the jar and picks up the aortas. The first one is a healthy aorta. It's tan and smooth. It

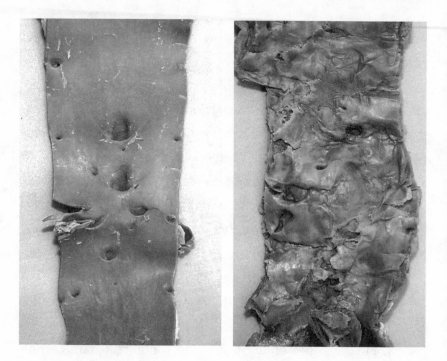

A healthy aorta, left, and an atherosclerotic aorta

has a slight bounce and feels a lot like a thick rubber band. The second one looks twisted and gnarled. It's covered in thick yellowish spots. It feels like a hard piece of plastic. The second aorta was removed from a person with advanced atherosclerosis, a heart disease that causes blood vessels to stiffen. As an artery gets hard, pieces of fat (called plaque) stick to it. If a big piece of plaque suddenly breaks off, it can block the flow of blood and cause a heart attack.

"With this aorta, you can literally peel the plaque off," explains Dr. Oz. "It's like an old can of paint that has paint chips coming off. I call these pieces of plaque 'aorta chips.'"

Atherosclerosis and other heart diseases can be caused by eating certain foods with too much fat in them. "Trans fat" is probably the worst kind of fat. It's an artificial, manmade fat that's found in many processed and fast foods. Trans fats are cheap, and they extend the length of time that a product can sit on the shelf without spoiling. But what's good for the companies that make this food isn't so good for the people who eat it. Trans fats increase the amount of fatty plaque in your blood and may also stiffen your arteries. Researchers at Harvard University believe that trans fats alone are now responsible for the deaths of at least 30,000 Americans every year. Many popular fast foods (French fries, fried chicken, chicken nuggets) and junk foods (doughnuts, cookies, packaged cakes) contain a lot of trans fat. All of these products can be made with healthier fats, but it's a little more expensive to do so.

When investigators at the National Academy of Sciences tried to determine how much trans fat a person should eat, they came up with a surprising conclusion: none. As of January 2006, a new federal rule insists that all fast-food and processed-food companies must reveal how much trans fat is in their products. For years these companies have refused to provide this information. Look at the label before you buy cookies, crackers, doughnuts, or fast food. And if you see any trans fat there, maybe you should buy something else.

The two pieces of backbone on the metal table look very different from each other, just like the two aortas. The first backbone feels thick and solid. It came from a person with a healthy diet. The other backbone is full of holes; Dr. Oz describes it as "crunchy." It came from a person with osteoporosis, a disease that weakens bones.

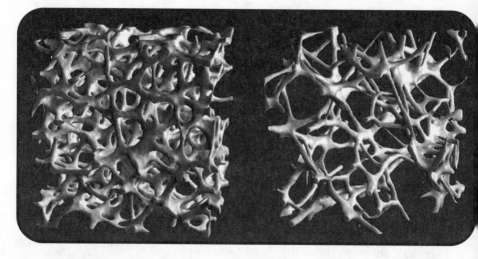

Computer drawing of a healthy backbone, left, and a backbone with osteoporosis

"One of the big contributors to osteoporosis is soft drinks," Dr. Oz says. You need a lot of calcium to develop strong bones, and children traditionally got much of their calcium by drinking milk. Today American teenagers drink much more soda than milk. As a result, they're not getting enough calcium and their bones break more easily. A study of high school kids in Massachusetts found that ninth- and tenth-grade girls who drank soda were far more likely to suffer broken bones than girls who didn't drink any.

The two livers on the table are especially gross. They seem like something from one of those Halloween fairs at school, where you close your eyes, put your hand in a bucket, and feel something cold and wet and slimy. Your liver is the biggest organ in your body, and one of the most important. It produces bile to help you digest fats, stores vitamins, maintains the right amount of sugar in your blood, and cleans toxins out of your blood. The healthy liver on the table is smooth and reddish brown. It could be a piece of meat at a butcher shop. The unhealthy liver has a green tinge, and it's covered with thick yellow globs that are stiff to the touch.

"The liver processes all the junk you eat when you go to a fast-food restaurant," Dr. Oz says. "When it gets full of fat, it doesn't behave normally." When the film director Morgan Spurlock ate nothing but fatty, sugary McDonald's food for an entire month—as depicted in the movie *Super Size Me*—his liver began to malfunction. Although liver damage usually takes much longer to occur, Spurlock began to feel (and look) pretty ill after just a few weeks on a fast-food diet.

To complete the guided tour of what can happen inside your body, Dr. Oz reaches into the white plastic bucket and pulls out two hearts. The healthy heart is round and pinkish brown. It feels springy when you touch it. The unhealthy heart is much bigger and darker, its color closer to black than pink. More oblong than round, it looks like a little deflated football.

"People talk about their hearts all the time," Dr. Oz says, holding one in each hand. "There's a reason. It's a window into our soul. I try to hammer that home whenever I talk to kids about what they eat and how much they exercise and how it can affect the health of their hearts. Heart disease isn't something that just might happen to your dad. It could be what's happening right now inside your own body."

It would be nice to think that heart problems occur only when you're old and gray. Unfortunately, that's not the case. In 2000, Thomas Robertson had severe chest pain and was rushed to a hospital in New Orleans. He was five foot four and weighed 215 pounds. He often ate fast-food hamburgers and fries. Doctors at the hospital were surprised to find that Thomas was having a heart attack. He was only eighteen years old. Although heart attacks among teenagers are unusual, there is evidence that they may become more common. A study published in the spring of 2004 found that some ten-year-old obese children already had heart damage similar to that of forty-five-year-old men who'd been smoking cigarettes for ten years.

weighing in

Sam arrives at the WISH Center, August 3, 2004

After returning home from Las Vegas, Sam Fabrikant made an appointment to see Dr. Chris Salvino, a surgeon who specializes in gastric bypass operations. Dr. Salvino knew the Fabrikant family well, having already operated on Sam's brother. During the previous ten years, a type of surgery once considered unusual had become almost routine. In 1993 surgeons performed about 16,000 gastric bypass operations. As the number of obese Americans skyrocketed, so did the number of gastric bypasses. By 2004 surgeons performed about 150,000 of them. Many doctors viewed the surgery as an important tool to prevent the health problems associated with obesity. But some doctors also viewed the surgery as a good way to make money. The cost for one of these operations could be anywhere from $20,000 to $50,000.

Dr. Salvino had an unusual background for a bariatric surgeon (the kind of doctor who operates on the stomach and intestines). For years he'd trained to become an astronaut. He'd earned six college degrees—in biology, aerospace medicine, flight aeronautics, mechanical engineering, space studies, and "technology in flight"—and worked as a surgeon in the air force. His hopes of blasting into space were dashed by poor eyesight: NASA requires its astronauts to have at least 20-200 vision, and Salvino was just a bit too nearsighted. After working as a surgeon in Africa, he returned to the United

States and performed his first gastric bypass surgery in 1998.

Dr. Salvino soon realized that this was an operation with a great future. In 2000 he put together a business plan for opening clinics devoted solely to weight-loss surgery. His first Weight Intervention and Surgical Healthcare (WISH) Center was in Downer's Grove, Illinois, a suburb of Chicago. By 2004 others had been launched in Texas, Arizona, Florida, Washington, and Ohio. Before choosing their locations, Dr. Salvino carefully studied the obesity rates in nearby communities and the number of rival bariatric surgeons.

On August 3, 2004, Sam visited the WISH Center headquarters in Downer's Grove. A nurse asked him to get on a scale. Sam was five foot nine and weighed 290 pounds. Dr. Salvino warned that before having the operation, Sam would have to see an independent psychiatrist to make sure that he could mentally handle the procedure and its aftermath. Having gastric bypass surgery is very stressful, and some people don't have the emotional strength to deal with it. For the next four months, Sam would have to meet with doctors at the WISH Center to make sure he was a good candidate for the operation. He would have to complete on-line training seminars to prepare him. And he would have to start eating six small meals a day, so that his mind and body could get used to the habit. Sam felt better prepared for the surgery than most people, having already watched his mother and his brother go through it. But he was scared.

Despite the large number of gastric bypass surgeries that are performed every year, it remains a risky operation. Patients may suffer from internal bleeding, intestinal leaks, blood clots, or infections. Perhaps one out of every hundred patients dies within thirty days of having the operation. When gastric bypass surgery is done by an unskilled surgeon, the death rate can be even higher. At least ten hospitals in six states no longer allow the operation because so many of their patients had died.

Even when the patient survives, gastric bypass surgery can have serious complications. Some patients suffer nerve damage that can cause lifelong pain. Others need to undergo a second operation after the first one somehow goes wrong. Even a successful operation can lead to serious complications or even death months later. Gastric bypass patients must take large doses of vitamins for the rest of their lives, because their new digestive systems are too small to absorb the necessary amounts from food. If a patient stops taking those vitamins, he or she can develop life-threatening deficiencies of calcium, iron, vitamin B, and vitamin D.

In April 2004, Warren Allen died ten months after having gastric bypass surgery at Cincinnati Children's Hospital. He had stopped taking his vitamins, which led to kidney problems, gangrene, wounds that wouldn't heal, and blood clots in the brain. At the time of his operation, Allen was eighteen years old and weighed more than 500 pounds. Although for years he'd eaten too much food, at the time of his death Allen was suffering from malnutrition—from not getting the crucial vitamins his body needed. Some gastric bypass patients have even developed beriberi, a disease common among starving and malnourished children in Africa. Kids with beriberi develop large, unnaturally round bellies.

Many doctors refuse to perform gastric bypass surgery on teenagers, worried not only about the risk of life-threatening complications but also about the possibility of stunting their growth. A teenager who has a gastric bypass operation may never reach his or her full height. Dr. Salvino is one of the few bariatric surgeons willing to perform the operation on teens. He believes that for some young patients, the health risk of *not* having surgery is too great—that is, the lifelong risk of developing cancer, heart disease, or diabetes from remaining obese. Dr. Salvino is an experienced surgeon, having performed more than 1,500 gastric bypass operations. The death rate among patients at his WISH Centers is lower than the national average. About one out of every 1,700 patients dies within a month of surgery there.

As Sam left his first appointment at the WISH Center, he was glad to be getting ready for surgery. The WISH Center seemed like the right place to have the operation. The company was trying to do for gastric bypass surgery what McDonald's had done for fast food: create a reliable, predictable national brand. The WISH Center had even started to run ads on television, suggesting to obese people that surgery might be the answer to their problems. At the WISH Store, you could buy bottles of WISH Protein Plus Vanilla meal replacement powder, WISH Protein Plus Chocolate convenience packs, WISH angel pins, WISH 25-ounce Protein Shaker cups with twist-off tops, and DVDs like *Fitness with Bliss: Sitting Aerobics*. On the wall in one of the offices at the WISH Center, there was a large map of the United States. Colored pins marked the six locations where WISH Centers had already opened. And the company was planning to open more.

On the drive home from the WISH Center, Sam and his mother passed within a couple of miles of McDonald's corporate headquarters in Oak Brook, Illinois. It seemed fitting that the headquarters of these two companies should be so close to each other. One sold the inexpensive fast food that could make you obese, while the other sold a painful and expensive remedy. A glass display case at McDonald's headquarters holds an old photograph of Ray Kroc in his office during the 1950s, when McDonald's was just getting started. A map of the United States was mounted on his wall, and the locations of new

McDonald's restaurants were proudly marked by little round lights.

complicated

On December 19, 2004, the day before his operation, Sam wasn't allowed to eat anything. His stomach needed to be completely empty when the doctors made it smaller. He drank apple juice and water all day, trying not to feel too hungry. He was scared. Before going to bed that night, Sam asked his parents, "Are you sure I'm doing the right thing?" They told him that the surgery would go just fine and that it was perfectly normal to feel nervous. He didn't sleep well that night.

At quarter past four the next morning, Sam and his family headed to Provena Mercy Medical Center. It was still dark when they arrived at the admissions desk. After checking in, Sam changed into a hospital gown, got a shot of Valium in the arm to help him relax, and was wheeled into the operating room. The nurses asked him to lie down on a cold metal table, and an anesthesiologist explained that a powerful drug would soon put him to sleep. Before Sam realized what was happening, he lost consciousness, and then Dr. Salvino cut into his abdomen to begin the operation.

When Dr. Salvino peered inside Sam's belly, things didn't

look right. Sam had a rare disorder. His intestines were oddly twisted and in an unusual place. Dr. Salvino needed help from other surgeons to make sure that Sam's internal organs wouldn't be damaged by the operation. The doctors had to move around the intestines a great deal and knew that as a result, Sam would feel a lot of pain later. They stapled part of his stomach to create a small pouch, attached a section of his small intestine to it, and then sewed his belly shut. The operation lasted about three hours, much longer than usual, and Sam was wheeled out of the operating room around noon.

A few hours later, Sam's mother sat beside his bed in the recovery room. He was still unconscious, connected by wires and tubes to all sorts of machines. She noticed that his breathing seemed a little odd. And his blood pressure was also unusually high. Hours passed without Sam's waking up or responding when people spoke to him. The doctors became concerned and conducted a series of tests. They found that a blood clot had formed in Sam's leg and traveled to his lung. If the clot blocked an artery, it could damage his lung—or kill him.

Sam spent the next five days in the intensive care unit of the hospital, where the sickest and most vulnerable patients are kept. In order to get rid of the blood clot, the doctors gave Sam blood-thinning medicine. It made the clot smaller but also made his wounds bleed. A metal screen was inserted into a large vein near his groin to insure that no other blood clot could travel to his lungs or his brain. Sam was awake but groggy, not really sure where he was or what was happening. There was a chance that he might die. A doctor from the WISH Center spent the night in Sam's room two days after the operation, worried that he might not make it. Sam's mother was at the hospital day and night.

Sam finally left the hospital on New Year's Eve, eleven days after the operation. He felt weak, but his life was no longer in danger. After getting out of the car and stepping into the snow on the driveway, he paused and took a deep breath. It felt good to be home. He couldn't eat any solid food for a week. His mother gave him three shots a day of a drug to dissolve any blood clots. And his brother, Charlie, had to give him baths, like a little baby might get. Sam was too exhausted to be embarrassed.

Two weeks after the operation, Sam and Charlie and their mother appeared on NBC's *Today Show* to talk about gastric bypass surgery. Sam still wasn't feeling well. The most he could eat at one sitting was a few spoonfuls of pudding. He wanted to feel excited about appearing on TV but just couldn't. The family had to get up really early and leave the house at four in the morning to make it to the WISH Center on time. Before going on the air, Sam's face was patted with makeup, and his hair styled with gel. He'd never used gel before (let alone make-up), and the whole thing felt weird. When Matt Lauer, one of the show's hosts, asked how the surgery had gone, Sam tried to sound upbeat. "Unfortunately, I was one of the few who did have complications," he said. "But you know, the doctors here were able to catch it, and knock on wood, I'm doing great now."

A year after his operation, in December 2005, Sam weighed less than half of what he did before the operation. He'd lost 147 pounds. Whenever he looked in the mirror, Sam saw a different person. Classmates would stop him in the hallway at school and say, "Wow, you're looking terrific." He felt grateful to Dr. Salvino and to everyone at the WISH Center. The company, however, wasn't doing as well as Sam. In the spring, it had gone bankrupt. Health insurance firms were increasingly reluctant to pay for gastric bypass surgery, and the WISH Center in Florida had to shut down. The company went through a rough time, though it eventually emerged from bankruptcy.

Sam's new life became much happier, but it wasn't easy. He thought the WISH Center protein drinks tasted lousy, and he didn't always follow the doctors' instructions. One morning he realized that some of his hair was falling out—a sign of malnutrition. He'd been forgetting to take his vitamins. Eating used to be one of his great pleasures; after the operation, it became a chore. He couldn't eat more than a few bites of anything at one sitting. If he ate more than that, he felt like vomiting.

Every now and then Sam craved a fudge sundae or a Coca-Cola, foods that he could never have again. The sugar in the sundae would give him an intense headache, and the bubbles in the soda would cause terrible stomach pain. He could still eat hamburgers, however. It just took a while. If Sam wanted to eat a Big Mac, he'd have to cut it into six small pieces and then eat one piece every three hours. The same burger that most people can finish in a few minutes would take Sam about fifteen hours to eat.

YOUR WAY

Welcome to Burger King, Baghdad

On April 9, 2003, a U.S. Marine armored vehicle pulled down the gigantic statue of Saddam Hussein in central Baghdad, showing the world that the United States had finally driven him from power. Nine weeks later the first Burger King opened in Iraq. American soldiers waited as long as two hours to buy Whoppers and Chicken Royales at the new restaurant, located in Baghdad International Airport. Pizza Huts, Burger Kings, and Subways soon opened at U.S. military bases throughout Iraq. Running a Burger King in the middle of a war zone presented all sorts of unusual challenges. Hamburger buns, ground beef, chicken, and French fries had to be airlifted into the country and then carried by trucks along dangerous roads. Joe Petrusich—a Canadian businessman employed by a Kuwaiti company to operate many of the restaurants for the U.S. Department of Defense—had to fly from one restaurant to another in Black Hawk helicopters to make sure everything was done properly. "It is very, very challenging," Petrusich told a reporter. "You are dealing with problems every day. I get phone calls saying bridges have been blown up and we can't get our trucks through." Not long after the restaurant at the Baghdad airport opened, it became one of the most successful Burger Kings in the world, selling more than five thousand sandwiches a day.

The opening of Pizza Huts and Burger Kings in war-torn Iraq shows how badly the fast-food chains want to expand overseas. As competition has become fiercer in the United States, fast-food companies have looked to foreign markets as the source of future growth. In 1991, McDonald's had fewer than 4,000 restaurants outside the United States. Today it has about 18,000 restaurants in 120 foreign countries. Classes at McDonald's Hamburger University in Oak Brook, Illinois, are now taught in twenty different languages. McDonald's now earns the majority of its profits outside the United States, as does KFC. The values, tastes, and marketing practices of the American fast-food industry are being exported to every corner of the globe. In the same way that American cities are beginning to look similar—filled with identical chain restaurants and stores—many foreign cities are being to look a lot like each other. They are becoming Americanized. This international spread of uniformity and conformity, according to political scientist Benjamin R. Barber, is creating a "McWorld."

People in poor and developing nations often view McDonald's and the other fast-food chains as symbols of American freedom, progress, and technology. They can't wait for fast-food joints to open nearby. In 1990, when McDonald's opened its first Moscow restaurant, five hundred Russians patiently stood in line to eat there. In 1994, when a McDonald's opened in Kuwait, the line of cars waiting for the drive-through window extended for seven miles. Around the same time, a KFC restaurant in Saudi Arabia's holy city of Mecca set a new sales record for the chain, earning $200,000 in a single week.

Few places on earth now seem too distant or too remote for Colonel Sanders or the Golden Arches.

Much like the cigarette companies, which started to target people in poor and developing countries when Americans cut back on smoking, soda companies are now trying to expand their sales overseas. They are not only opening bottling plants in poor countries, they are also supplying stores with refrigerators and providing electricity to run these fridges. Driven by the belief that "a bottle cold is a bottle sold," soda companies have given away hundreds of thousands of refrigerators to stores in Africa. The soda industry is trying to increase its "throat share" overseas, making sure that whenever people are thirsty, they drink soda. In 1998, Coca-Cola's partner in Latin America launched a marketing scheme called the 100 Meters Program. "The objective of this program is simple," Panamco, Coke's business partner, said. "In any urban center, no one should have to walk more than 100 meters [about 300 feet] to buy our products." It aimed to put Coke products everywhere, at all times of the day. In addition to supplying supermarkets and fast-food restaurants, Panamco planned to sell soda at schools, factories, office buildings, newsstands, beauty salons, and drugstores. It hired street vendors to sell Cokes at traffic lights in Venezuela and even put coolers in Colombian taxicabs.

storming kfc

America's fast-food companies have become so big and so powerful worldwide that it may seem like nothing can stop them. But their rapid expansion overseas, which looks so impressive on a map, may actually be a sign of their growing weakness in the American market. One of the reasons McDonald's started to open so many restaurants overseas is that it was running out of places to open them in the United States. All the good locations seem to be taken, and new customers will have to be found elsewhere. As the fast-food industry grows more dependent on foreign sales, it faces new and unexpected risks. When people overseas love the United States, they're eager to buy American products and shop at American stores. But when anti-American feelings rise, the anger is often directed at U.S. companies that sell hamburgers, sodas, and fries.

"Resist America beginning with Cola," said a banner at Beijing University in May 1999. "Attack McDonald's, Storm KFC." The U.S. Air Force had just accidentally bombed the Chinese embassy in Belgrade, Yugoslavia, and anti-American demonstrations were erupting throughout China. At least a dozen McDonald's and four KFC restaurants were damaged by Chinese protesters. For some reason, no Pizza Huts were harmed. "Maybe they think it's Italian," said a Pizza Hut spokesman in Shanghai.

A generation ago American embassies and oil companies were the most likely targets of overseas demonstrations against the United States. Today fast-food restaurants have assumed that role, with McDonald's a particular favorite. In 1995 a crowd of four hundred Danish protesters looted a McDonald's in downtown Copenhagen, made a bonfire of its furniture in the street, and burned the restaurant to the ground. In 1998 bombs destroyed a McDonald's in St. Petersburg, Russia; two

Ronald McDonald after an apple attack in France

McDonald's near Athens, Greece; a McDonald's in the heart of Rio de Janeiro, Brazil; and a Planet Hollywood in Cape Town, South Africa. In 1999, Belgian vegetarians set fire to a McDonald's in Antwerp, and a year later protesters tore the sign off a McDonald's in London's Trafalgar Square, destroyed the restaurant, and handed out free hamburgers to the crowd. A few months later, a French farmer named José Bové demolished a McDonald's under construction in his hometown of Millau. Angry about the devastating impact of cheap, industrialized American food, Bové later wrote a best-selling book entitled *The World Is Not for Sale—And Nor Am I!*

The war in Afghanistan and the invasion of Iraq prompted a series of new fast-food attacks. In 2002 three people were killed by a bomb blast at a McDonald's in Indonesia; McDonald's restaurants were destroyed in Russia, Ecuador, Saudi Arabia, and Lebanon; and Burger King restaurants were attacked in Egypt, Qatar, Oman, Bahrain, and Lebanon. Over the next few years a McDonald's in Turkey was bombed, a protester blew himself up outside a McDonald's in northern Italy, and two firebombs were discovered outside a McDonald's in Rome. KFC restaurants in Saudi Arabia and Bahrain were attacked. And one KFC restaurant in Karachi, Pakistan, was destroyed twice. After being rebuilt after the first attack, it was burned to the ground in May 2005, killing six KFC workers inside. So many fast-food restaurants have now been bombed overseas that the major chains are installing shatterproof windows, special ceiling tiles that can absorb bomb shrapnel, and large outdoor containers, made of cement and planted with flowers, to protect against car bombs.

The violence directed at McDonald's and KFCs is the most dramatic sign of the fast-food industry's problems overseas. Even more serious, however, is the way in which popular attitudes toward food are beginning to change, especially in the European Union and Japan—two of the industry's largest markets. European and Japanese consumers want to know where their food comes from and how it's made. The spread of a deadly, mysterious disease played a large role in opening their eyes.

During the 1980s, cattle in Great Britain started to act strangely, became ill, and then died. A new disease, bovine spongiform encephalopathy, nicknamed "BSE" or "mad cow disease," was literally destroying their brains. British scientists linked mad cow disease to an unlikely ingredient that some agribusiness companies were quietly putting into cattle feed: dead cows. The leftover meat and blood from slaughter-houses were being fed to cattle as a cheap form of protein. The news disgusted British consumers. They were outraged that cattle were being turned into cannibals and afraid that mad cow disease might spread to human beings. For years the British government assured the public that the disease couldn't harm people who ate beef. And then, in March 1996, the British health secretary announced that eating meat from cattle with mad cow disease did indeed pose a risk to people. It could cause an incurable illness, a human form of mad cow disease that destroyed a person's brain.

Throughout Europe and Japan, governments had promised for years that beef was perfectly safe to eat. That proved to be a lie. Soon millions of cattle potentially infected with mad cow disease had to be removed from farms, slaughtered, and then burned. So many needed to be killed that in Denmark a company built a power plant to generate electricity by burning cattle. The sale of beef plummeted, and consumers in Europe and Japan began to demand tough food-safety rules. And the sale of organic foods—produced naturally, without growth hormones, antibiotics, or pesticides—skyrocketed. Amazed that companies would feed dead cattle to other cattle just to save money, consumers demanded a return to traditional forms of agriculture. The German government took the lead, declaring that one fifth of the country's farmland would be organic by the year 2010. Germany also became the first country in the European Union to add language guaranteeing animal rights to its constitution. And its minister for agriculture declared that cattle would no longer be given feed that could harm them. "Our cows," she said, "should get only water, grain, and grass."

the new ronald

Facing criticism overseas and in the United States, McDonald's has worked hard in recent years to improve its public image. In 2001 the company responded to American fears about mad cow disease by imposing strict rules on its beef suppliers. The Food and Drug Administration (FDA), the U.S. government agency responsible for the safety of animal feed, had already banned the practice of feeding dead cattle to cattle. But the FDA hadn't done much to insure that feed companies were obeying the rules. As panic about mad cow disease spread throughout Europe and hamburger sales there plummeted, McDonald's told the leading U.S. meatpacking companies that they would have to keep dead cattle out of their cattle feed and make sure that the FDA's rules were being followed—or McDonald's wouldn't buy any more of their beef. Meatpacking companies that routinely fought tooth and nail against any new government regulations quickly agreed to do exactly what McDonald's wanted. The fast-food chain was their largest customer. "Because we have the world's biggest shopping cart," a McDonald's spokesman explained, "we can use that leadership to provide more focus and more order throughout the beef system."

In 2001, McDonald's also instructed its meat suppliers to do a better job of treating animals humanely. People for the

Ethical Treatment of Animals (PETA) was threatening nationwide protests against the chain, and McDonald's decided to use its power over the meatpacking industry to eliminate some of the most obvious abuses at factory farms. McDonald's told its egg suppliers that hens should have enough room to stand in their cages. Previously the hens were crammed so tightly together that they often couldn't stand on their own feet. The egg suppliers agreed to McDonald's request; after all, McDonald's was the nation's largest purchaser of eggs. The hens got a little more space: about 72 square inches for each bird, roughly the size of a piece of computer paper. That was better, but still not enough room for the hens to walk around. McDonald's also told its chicken, pork, and beef suppliers to minimize the amount of suffering that animals endured at their slaughterhouses. Other fast-food chains soon followed McDonald's animal welfare policies. None of them, however, has insisted on strict new rules to protect the human beings in meatpacking plants—the workers being injured on the job every day.

Over the past few years McDonald's and other fast-food chains have added healthier items to their menus. The new marketing campaigns about healthy eating may reflect a sincere concern for the well-being of their customers. Or they may simply be a public relations effort to avoid blame for America's obesity epidemic. In 2005, McDonald's became the largest purchaser of apples in the United States, and it now sells more salads than any other company. Healthier options, unfortunately, don't always lead to healthier eating. The *Washington Post* estimated that almost 98 percent of McDonald's customers don't order a salad. "The most popular item on our menu," a McDonald's spokesman admitted to the newspaper, "continues to be the double cheeseburger, hands down." The most successful new item on the Burger King menu isn't the Veggie Burger. It's the Enormous Omelet breakfast sandwich, which contains more calories (740) and more grams of fat (46) than a Whopper.

The fast-food industry would like people to believe the problem isn't the food, it's the customers' behavior. "There are no good foods or bad foods," the industry argues, implying that if you're overweight, it's your own fault. The emphasis is on changing what the customers do, not what the fast-food companies do. With that goal in mind, Ronald McDonald has undergone a makeover. Instead of being a silly clown who plays only with small children, Ronald has become a snowboarding, skateboarding hipster who wants to influence preteens. McDonald's hopes he will serve as a "global ambassador of fun, fitness, and children's well-being." The actors who visit restaurants dressed as Ronald McDonald have been told to exercise and get into shape—or they'll be fired. Despite all the talk about healthy eating, McDonald's has not yet offered to pay hip-hop artists millions of dollars to sing about eating fresh fruits and vegetables. A recent marketing campaign for the Big Mac, aimed at young teens, ignores the whole idea of healthy eating and focuses instead on a subject that really has nothing to do with hamburgers: sex. Ray Kroc, who tried to keep flirting teenagers out of his restaurants, might not have appreciated the sexual overtones of the latest slogans advertising Big Macs. "Bite me like it's your first time" is one. "My buns demand both hands" is another.

kids with knives

As a child in the 1950s, Alice Waters was a picky eater. She didn't like foods with thick sauces. She didn't like stews, creamy spinach, or overcooked meat. She liked simple things, like the fruits and vegetables her father grew in the backyard garden of their little house in Chatham, New Jersey. Her family didn't have a lot of money, so they didn't go to restaurants frequently. They ate meals at the dining room table. Alice didn't like the food at school, and in those days kids were allowed to eat in the cafeteria or go home for lunch. Most days Alice went home. She was picky but still enjoyed eating certain junk foods every now and then: potato chips, orange soda, jelly doughnuts, chili cheeseburgers.

Alice moved to Berkeley, California, for college. The University of California at Berkeley was known for its radical thinking, for students who liked to make waves and challenge conventional wisdom. During the 1960s, Berkeley students campaigned for racial equality, for women's rights, for an end to the war in Vietnam. Alice fit in well at Berkeley; there was nothing ordinary about her. At the age of nineteen she took a year off and lived in France. The experience changed her forever. She fell in love with the food there. She felt like she'd never eaten before. The people she met in France cared intensely about food, about how it was bought and sold and prepared and served at the table. Meals were more than a way to fill your belly. They were a way to enjoy conversation, family, and friendship. They weren't something rushed and soon forgotten. They were meant to bring people together.

Alice returned home determined to learn how to cook. She wanted to introduce the United States to a whole new outlook on food. She studied French cookbooks and started making meals for friends. And then, in 1971, she opened a restaurant in Berkeley and gave it a French name: Chez Panisse. At the restaurant she offered food that was simple and fresh, food that mainly got its taste not from fancy sauces and seasonings but from the quality of the basic ingredients. Alice always sought out the best-tasting tomatoes, the best peaches, the best plums. When she couldn't buy them at the market, she found people to grow them for her. She formed close ties with local farmers and ranchers, refusing to buy food that was out of season or that had been transported thousands of miles. The food she bought had to be organic, locally produced, and delicious.

Chez Panisse was soon considered one of the finest restaurants in the United States, and Alice Waters was hailed as one of the nation's greatest chefs. She was a true radical—not the kind who wants to destroy things or tear them down, but the kind who looks past the surface to the fundamental nature of things. During the same years that fast-food chains were turning restaurant kitchens into little factories and live-stock into industrial commodities, Alice championed an old-fashioned view of food. It stood for a different set of American values: honesty, integrity, wholesomeness, and, most of all, community.

Every day, while driving to Chez Panisse in the morning and driving home late at night, Alice passed Martin Luther King Jr. Middle School. It seemed like a sad place, with graffiti on the windows and burned-out grass on the lawn. Although students still attended classes there, the school looked neglected. Alice wondered how the people of Berkeley, who considered them-selves so high-minded and aware, could allow a public school to fall apart this way. She made this point during a newspaper interview, and not long afterward got a call from Neil Smith, the school's principal. He invited her to Martin Luther King Jr. Middle School and asked her to help beautify the place.

During a visit to the school, Alice became less concerned about how the place looked—and much more concerned about what the kids were being fed there. Martin Luther King Jr. Middle School had been built in the 1920s to educate five hundred children. Now it had about twice that many students. The cafeteria was too small to feed so many kids. It had been shut down for years and was being used to store old tables and chairs. There was still nasty old leftover food in the ovens. Lunch was served at a snack bar on the edge of the playground. Alice watched kids standing around eating reheated frozen hamburgers, chicken nuggets, and fries. She was appalled. The sight of the abandoned cafeteria and the cheap fast food made her realize that something had to be done right away to change the way these kids thought about food. And she decided to do it.

Twelve years after Alice's first visit to Martin Luther King Jr. Middle School, it has the most innovative and remarkable food program in the United States. Called the Edible Schoolyard, it doesn't just provide healthy, nutritious meals. It gives kids a firsthand education in the role that food plays in society. It teaches skills they can use for the rest of their lives. After raising money through her Chez Panisse Foundation, Alice supervised the planting of an enormous garden at Martin Luther King Jr. Middle School. An acre of asphalt was torn up, topsoil was hauled in, and all sorts of plants, flowers, fruit trees, and vines were planted. Today this school garden produces strawberries, potatoes, tomatoes, lettuce, herbs, beans, corn, pumpkins, asparagus, broccoli, beets, carrots, garlic, cucumbers, peppers, cabbage, and Brussels sprouts, among other things. There's a chicken coop where hens can wander freely and lay eggs. There's a wood-burning outdoor oven for cooking pizza and baking bread. The place looks like a small farm in the heart of a lovely town.

The sixth-, seventh-, and eighth-graders at Martin Luther King Jr. come from a wide variety of backgrounds. About twenty different languages are spoken at students' homes. Roughly one third of the kids are African-American, one third are white, and the rest are mainly Asian or Latino. All of them have to work in the garden, planting, tending, and harvesting food. And all of them have to work in the school's new kitchen, learning how to prepare food, how to serve it, and how to clean up after everybody's eaten it. Esther Cook, the chef-teacher at the Edible Schoolyard, has thought up many ingenious ways to combine cooking and gardening with learning. In the classroom, food-related subjects are used to help teach science, history, and ecology. A science project might involve earthworms in the garden; a history project might unfold in the kitchen, with samples of what European serfs ate during the Middle Ages. Teachers work with their students in the garden and the kitchen. At Martin Luther King Jr. Middle School, food isn't something you scarf down quickly and then forget about. It's an integral part of daily life.

On a recent day in the kitchen, thirty-two sixth-graders got ready to make a simple fruit salad. They were new to the school. They washed their hands, put on green aprons, and grabbed sharp knives. Esther Cook told them to keep the knives at their sides, pointed downward. She didn't want anyone to get stabbed. The kids sat at three big tables. A few seemed afraid of the knives. "You guys can handle it," Esther said. "They're not toys, but you can handle it." The kids started peeling, slicing, and dicing the fruit. Large steel tubs were soon filled with pieces of kiwi, orange, and *pepino dulce* (a pear-shaped fruit with greenish flesh that tastes like honeydew melon or cantaloupe). Napkins and plaid tablecloths were brought out, the tables were set, the food was served, and everyone started to eat. For some students, long accustomed to eating microwave dinners in front of the TV, those school meals were the first ones they'd ever made from scratch.

Alice Waters at Martin Luther King Jr. Middle School

The Edible Schoolyard has proven to be a tremendous success. Other schools throughout the United States have sent teachers to study it and then planted their own gardens. In 2004, the Chez Panisse Foundation agreed to help the Berkeley Unified School District change the food that is served in every one of its schools. Alice is now supervising the creation of new gardens and new kitchens, finding new suppliers of organic food, figuring out how to prepare healthy meals for nine thousand students every day, and privately raising the money to do all of those things. It is a mammoth undertaking. While other famous chefs are opening chain restaurants and putting their names on frozen meals, Alice is trying to protect the environment, support independent farmers, and change the way American children think about food. Her work demonstrates the importance of learning from the past. Sometimes new ideas aren't really that new. More than a century ago, a California educator argued that every school in the United States should have a garden. These gardens, he said, will teach children that "actions have consequences, that private citizens should take care of public property, that labor has dignity, that nature is beautiful."

changing the world

The U.S. Congress should ban advertising that exploits children. It should prevent soda companies and fast-food companies from marketing unhealthy foods in schools. It should pass tough food-safety laws. It should raise the minimum wage. It should pass tough worker-safety laws. It should punish companies that mistreat animals. It should insure that independent farmers and ranchers have a free and fair market for their products. It should fight against dangerous concentrations of corporate power. It should promote the kind of agriculture and the kind of eating habits that are sustainable. Congress should do all those things—but it isn't likely to do any of them soon. The political power of the fast-food companies and their big suppliers makes a discussion of what Congress should do largely meaningless.

The fast-food industry spends millions of dollars every year trying to influence politicians and billions more trying to influence people through advertising. The wealth and power of the major chains make them seem invincible. And yet these corporations must obey the demands of a·group that's even more powerful, a group whom they desperately want to attract and please: consumers.

Nobody is forced to buy fast food. The first step toward real change is by far the easiest. Stop buying it. If you don't like the way fast-food companies behave, don't give them any of your money. Every dollar that you spend on food is like a vote. When you buy something from a company, you are in effect voting for its policies and its behavior. Burger King, KFC, and McDonald's choose to do business one way—selling highly processed food, keeping wages low, seeking to make everything everywhere the same. Other companies have chosen a different path and still earn large profits.

In 1948, the same year that the McDonald brothers introduced the Speedee Service System, Harry and Esther Snyder opened their first In-N-Out Burger restaurant on the road between Los Angeles and Palm Springs. It was America's first drive-through hamburger stand. Today there are almost two hundred In-N-Outs in California and Nevada. Harry Snyder died in 1976, but at the age of eighty-five, Esther still serves as president of the family-owned company. The Snyders have declined countless offers to sell the chain, refuse to franchise it, and have succeeded by rejecting just about everything the rest of the fast-food industry does.

In-N-Out isn't your typical fast-food chain. There are verses from the Bible on the bottom of its soda cups. More importantly, the chain pays the highest wages in the fast-food industry. Full-time workers get a benefits package that includes medical, dental, vision, and life insurance. The typical In-N-Out restaurant manager has a salary about three times higher than that of managers at other fast-food chains. The In-N-Out managers have, on average, been with the company for more than a decade. The high wages at In-N-Out haven't led to higher prices or lower-quality food. The most expensive item on the menu costs $2.50. There are no microwaves, heat lamps, or fancy machinery in the kitchens at In-N-Out restaurants. The ground beef is fresh, the potatoes are peeled every day to make French fries, and the milk shakes are made from real ice cream. Treating workers well and using fresh food instead of frozen makes a big difference. For the past seven years in a row, a survey by *Restaurants & Institutions* magazine has found that among fast-food hamburger chains, In-N-Out ranks first in food quality, value, service, atmosphere, and cleanliness. As a result, the company earns some of the highest profits, per restaurant, in the industry.

Burgerville is another chain that proves that a fast-food company can behave responsibly. Founded in 1961 by George Propstra, the chain now operates thirty-nine restaurants in Oregon and Washington State. It's also a family-owned company, distinguished by a long-standing commitment to selling fresh, locally produced food. Most of Burgerville's ingredients are purchased from farmers and ranchers in the Pacific Northwest. Instead of transporting frozen food thousands of miles, the chain allows items to come and go from the menu, depending on the time of year.

When local strawberries and huckleberries are in season, Burgerville uses them to make milk shakes. When the onions are ripe in Walla Walla, Washington, it uses them to make onion rings. The cheese for its cheeseburgers comes from Tillamook, Oregon. The beef comes from Oregon Country Beef, a group of ranching families that refuse to give their cattle growth hormones, antibiotics, genetically engineered grain, or feed that contains dead animals. In August 2005, Burgerville began to purchase renewable wind power for all the electricity at its restaurants. And instead of toys inspired by the latest Hollywood cartoons, the kids' meals at Burgerville often include packets of seeds and a gardening tool with which to plant them.

In-N-Out and Burgerville aren't perfect. But they show that fast-food companies can do well by doing good. Thousands of independent restaurants across the United States are guided by the same spirit. The executives who run the giant fast-food chains aren't bad people. They are people who need to broaden their views and accept responsibility for their actions. They will pay higher wages if you demand it. They will treat workers and animals and the land differently if you insist on it. They want your money, your vote. A hundred books could be written about the problems of the fast-food industry. But the solution starts with you.

Pull open the glass door, feel the rush of cool air, walk inside, get in line, and look around you. Look at the kids working in the kitchen, at the customers in their seats, at the ads for the latest toys. Study the backlit color photographs above the counter. Think about where the food came from, about how and where it was made, about what is set in motion by every single fast-food purchase, the ripple effect near and far—think about it. Then place your order. Or turn and walk out the door. It's not too late. Even in this fast-food nation, you can still have it your way.

PHOTO CREDITS

pp. v and 259 McDonald's door, author photo

p. 13 Hamburger Charlie, courtesy of Bill Collar, Home of the Hamburger, Inc.

p. 16 Headline from April 25, 1904, *New York Times*

p. 17 Preference for hamburger © Joyce White

p. 21 Carhops at the Chicken Villa © Covello and Covello Photography

p. 28 Harland Sanders © AP Photo

p. 31 Ray Kroc © Art Shay/Time & Life Pictures/Getty Images

p. 37 Sonic French fry mascot © Chris Rusche

p. 43 Walt Disney © Hulton Archive/Getty Images

p. 46 Willard Scott as the original Ronald © Jay Pingree

p. 54 NeuroMarketing © Angela Stanton/Center for Neuroeconomics Studies and Loma Linda University Medical Center

p. 60 Ronald McDonald Beanie Baby, author photo

p. 63 Martinsburg a century ago © Berkeley County Historical Association

p. 66 The Martinsburg "strip," author photo

pp. 68 and 69 Aerial photos of Martinsburg © Air Photographics, Inc.

p. 71 Danielle Brent, courtesy of Danielle Brent

p. 73 1913 Ford assembly line © AP Photo/Ford Motor Company

p. 82 Sadi Lambert, author photo

p. 89 Pascal McDuff and Maxime Cromp, photo composite © Films en Vue and Magnus Isaacson, Monique Simard, and Marcel Simard

p. 92 J. R. Simplot © Louis Psihoyos/Science Faction Images

p. 107 Human taste bud © Indigo Instruments, www.indigo.com

p. 109 Baby formula pictures, reproduced with permission from *Pediatrics*, Vol. 113, p. 843 © 2004 by the American Academy of Pediatrics

p. 118 Taste testing © International Flavors & Fragrances

p. 122 Dactylopius coccus costa © Jay Pingree

p. 125 Jain nuns © AFP/Raveendran/Getty Images

p. 128 Kasigluk, Alaska, author photo

p. 135 School menu, Gibson City-Melvin-Sibley Unit #5 School District, Gibson City, Illinois

p. 136 Hungry kids, 1909, Lewis Hine, courtesy of Library of Congress, Prints & Photographs Division. National Child Labor Committee Collection, LC-DIG-nclc-00032.

NOTES

Although we did a great deal of firsthand reporting and research for this book, we also benefited from the hard work of others. In these notes we've tried to give credit to the many people whose writing and research helped ours. The notes may also be useful to readers who'd like to know where we found a particular fact or who'd like to read more about a particular subject. By providing these sources, we hope to make our work transparent and reveal how *Chew On This* was put together. Perhaps someday the fast-food chains will be more open about how they assemble their food.

INTRODUCTION

McDonald's played a leading role in the creation of the fast-food industry, and several books about the company discuss its impact on the world. Ray Kroc's memoir with Robert Anderson, *Grinding It Out: The Making of McDonald's* (New York: St. Martin's, 1987), gives a strong sense of the man who turned the chain into a household name. John F. Love's *McDonald's: Behind the Arches* (New York: Bantam, 1995) is a history of McDonald's that was approved by the company. Nevertheless, it is fascinating, thoughtful, sometimes critical, and extremely well researched. *Big Mac: The Unauthorized Story of McDonald's* (New York: Dutton, 1976), by Max Boas and Steve Chain, looks behind the cheerful image of McDonald's and finds behavior that is often unpleasant. John Vidal's *McLibel: Burger Culture on Trial* (New York: New Press, 1997) uses the story of a British court case to look at the international consequences of McDonald's. We found a great deal of little-known information in restaurant industry publications like *Restaurant Business, Restaurant & Institutions, Nation's Restaurant News,* and *ID: The Voice of Foodservice.* For years some of the best reporting on the fast-food industry has appeared in the *Wall Street Journal.*

7   *Every day about one out of fourteen Americans:* The U.S. Census Bureau estimates that the U.S. population was approximately 295,734,134 in July 2005. During the previous year, the McDonald's Corporation said that its restaurants in the United States served more than 21,800,000 customers every day. Using those statistics, our calculations found that every day about one out of every 13.57 Americans eats at a McDonald's.

7   *Every month about nine out of ten American children visit one:* Cited in Rod Taylor, "The Beanie Factor," *Brandweek,* June 16, 1997.

7   *In 1968 there were about 1,000 McDonald's restaurants. . . . Now there are more than 31,000:* In 1968 the one thousandth McDonald's restaurant opened in Des Plaines, Ill. See "McDonald's Timeline," McDonald's Corporation, 2005. The latest figure comes from "FAQ's," McDonald's Canada, October 2005.

7   *McDonald's buys more processed beef, chicken, pork, apples, and potatoes:* See Love, *Behind the Arches,* pp. 4–5. Amount of beef purchasing cited by the president of the National Cattlemen's Beef Association in "NCBA, McDonald's Form Hamburger Task Force: Improving Value of U.S. Beef Products by Exporting Trimmings," *Food & Drink Weekly,* Apr. 29, 2002. For potato purchasing, see "Quality McFacts," McDonald's Corporation, 2005. For apple purchasing, see Gary Younge, "McDonald's Grabs a Piece of the Apple Pie," *Guardian* (UK), April 7, 2005.

8   *It spends more money on advertising and marketing:* According to *Advertising Age,* in 2004 McDonald's spent $1.4 billion on advertising in the United States. McDonald's was the third most widely advertised brand, surpassed only by Verizon Wireless and Cingular Wireless. See "Superbrands: A Special Report," *Brandweek,* June 20, 2005, p. 52, "Info McNuggets," *Advertising Age,* July 25, 2005.

8   *America's most famous food brand:* See "Best Global Brands 2005," *Business Week,* July 2005.

8   *The Golden Arches:* A survey by a marketing firm called Sponsorship Research International—conducted among 7,000 people in the United States, the United Kingdom, Germany, Australia, India, and Japan—found that 88 percent could identify the Golden Arches and 54 percent could identify the Christian cross. See "Golden Arches More Familiar than the Cross," *Cleveland Plain Dealer,* Aug. 26, 1995.

8	*Most fast-food visits are impulsive:* See Joyce A. Young, "Food Service Franchisors and Their Co-branding Methods," *Journal of Product and Brand Management*, 2001.
10	*Chicken McNuggets since 1983:* See "McDonald's Expands Chicken McNuggets Line," *PR Newswire*, Aug. 9, 1983.
10	*In 1970, Americans spent about $6 billion . . . In 2005, they spent about $134 billion:* These figures were provided by the National Restaurant Association.
10	*Americans now spend more money on fast food than on college education:* According to the National Restaurant Association, in 2003 Americans spent $121 billion on fast food. That same year they spent $110 billion on higher education, $98 billion on new cars, and $46.5 billion on computer equipment and software. See National Income and Product Accounts Table, Table 2.5.5., "Personal Consumption Expenditures by Type of Expenditure," U.S. Chamber of Commerce, 2003.
10	*They spend more on fast food than on movies:* In 2003 Americans spent $9.9 billion on movie tickets, $39 billion on books and maps, $11.9 billion on recorded music, and $35.9 billion on magazines, newspapers, and sheet music. That adds up to $96.7 billion, which is much less than the $121 billion Americans spent on fast food. See "Personal Consumption Expenditures by Type of Expenditure" and "2003 Year-end Statistics," Recording Industry Association of America.

THE PIONEERS

A number of good books explore the southern California culture that produced the fast-food industry. Among them are *Southern California Country* (New York: Duell, Sloan & Pearce, 1946), by Carey McWilliams; *The Dream Endures: California Enters the 1940s* (New York: Oxford University Press, 1997), by Kevin Starr; *Crabgrass Frontier* (New York: Oxford University Press, 1985), by Kenneth T. Jackson; and *The American Drive-In: History and Folklore of the Drive-In Restaurant in American Car Culture* (Osceloa, Wis.: Motorbooks International, 1994), by Michael Karl Witzel. Many of the founders of the fast-food industry have written books describing its early days. Taken together, these accounts are a fine collection of American success stories. Ray Kroc's *Grinding It Out* reveals the challenges and struggles of building the McDonald's Corporation. For the history of Burger King, read *The Burger King: Jim McLamore and the Building of an Empire* (New York: McGraw-Hill, 1998), by James W. McLamore. For the origins of Domino's, there's *Pizza Tiger* (New York: Random House, 1986), by Tom

Monaghan with Robert Anderson. For the origins of KFC and some entertaining tales of the South, pick up a copy of *Life As I Have Known It Has Been "Finger Lickin' Good"* (Carol Stream, Ill.: Creation House, 1974), by Colonel Harland Sanders. *Never Stop Dreaming: 50 Years of Making It Happen* (San Marcos, Calif.: Robert Erdmann, 1991), by Carl Karcher with B. Carolyn Knight, tells the story of Carl's Jr., while *Dave's Way: A New Approach to Old-Fashioned Success* (New York: Putnam's, 1991), by R. David Thomas, tells the story of Wendy's.

Richard J. McDonald, one of the founding brothers of McDonald's, wrote the foreword to Ronald J. McDonald's fascinating book, *The Complete Hamburger: The History of America's Favorite Sandwich* (New York: Birch Lane, 1997). We learned a great deal of hamburger history from *Hamburger Heaven: The Illustrated History of the Hamburger* (New York: Hyperion, 1993), by Jeffrey Tennyson. David Gerard Hogan's history of the White Castle chain, *Selling 'em by the Sack* (New York: New York University Press, 1997), has an excellent section on the terrible public image the hamburger had for many years.

13   *Charlie was going:* For the disputed history of America's first hamburger, see Hogan, *Selling 'em by the Sack,* pp. 21–23, and McDonald, *The Complete Hamburger,* pp. 3–10. We learned much about Hamburger Charlie from Bill Collar, a resident of Outagamie County who plays him during the hamburger festival every year. The description of Seymour, Wisconsin, in the late nineteenth century and details of its county fair were found in a newspaper article, "Seymour's First Annual Fair an Unprecedented Triumph," *Appleton Post,* Appleton, Wis., Oct. 15, 1885.

15   *"a food for the poor"* and *"The hamburger habit is just about as safe":* Quoted in Hogan, *Selling 'em by the Sack,* pp. 22, 32.

15   *In 1910, Alexander J. Moody:* See "Poison in Steak Killed Rich Baker: Chicago Chemist Finds Arsenic in Remnants of Meal and in Organs of Alexander J. Moody," *New York Times,* Mar. 29, 1910. See also "Pie Maker Was Poisoned," *New York Times,* Apr. 23, 1910. For public concern about arsenic poisoning and the general safety of hamburgers, see a letter to the editor by John E. Wooland, *New York Times,* May 9, 1935, as well as "The Restaurant Enjoys a Revival," *New York Times,* July 29, 1934.

16   *Death by hamburger, April 1904:* This is a headline from a *New York Times* article published on Apr. 25, 1904.

16   *frustration among butchers:* See "Steaks Head Sales List: Meat Council Shows How Cheaper Cuts Can Be Made Popular," *New York Times,* July 27, 1923.

17   *hamburger ranked nineteenth:* See "Beef and Cabbage Our Favorite Dish: Poll of New York Restaurants for 3 Weeks Gives Victory to Humble Fare," *New York Times,* June 15, 1925.

19   *Between 1920 and 1940:* According to the U.S. Census Bureau, the population of southern California in 1920 was 1,347,050—and in 1940 it was 3,572,263. That means the number of people in southern California was 2.7 times larger in 1940 than it was in 1920. See Carey McWilliams, *California: The Great Exception* (1949; reprint, Berkeley: University of California Press, 1999), p. 14.

19   *By 1940 there were about a million cars:* Cited in McWilliams, *California,* p. 236.

20   *"People with cars are so lazy":* Quoted in Witzel, *American Drive-In,* p. 24.

24   *"Imagine—No Car Hops":* The ad is reprinted in Tennyson, *Hamburger Heaven,* p. 62.

25   *"Working-class families could finally afford":* Love, *Behind the Arches,* p. 41.

25   *"Our food was exactly the same":* George Clark, one of the founders of Burger Queen, made this admission. Quoted in Stan Luxenberg, *Roadside Empires: How the Chains Franchised America* (New York: Viking, 1985), p. 76.

25   *Carl Karcher:* Author interview with Carl Karcher. See also B. Carolyn Knight, *Making It Happen: The Story of Carl Karcher Enterprises* (Anaheim, Calif.: Carl Karcher Enterprises, 1981), and Karcher with Knight, *Never Stop Dreaming.*

26   *Glen W. Bell, Jr.:* For the story of Taco Bell, see Love, *Behind the Arches,* pp. 26–27, and John A. Jakle and Keith A. Sculle, *Fast Food: Roadside Restaurants in the Automobile Age* (Baltimore: Johns Hopkins University Press, 1999), pp. 257–58.

26   *William Rosenberg:* For the story of Dunkin' Donuts, see Luxenberg, *Roadside Empires,* pp. 18–20.

26   *Thomas S. Monaghan:* For the story of Domino's, see Tom Monaghan, *Pizza Tiger* (New York: Random House, 1986).

27   *Frederick DeLuca:* For the history of Subway, see Fred DeLuca and John P. Hayes, *Start Small, Finish Big* (New York: Warner Business Books, 1991).

30   *"That was where I learned":* Kroc, *Grinding It Out,* p. 17.

30   *"If you believe in it":* Transcribed from voice recording at Ray A. Kroc Museum, Oak Brook, Ill.

33   *"We have found out":* Quoted in Love, *Behind the Arches,* p. 117.

33   *"This is rat eat rat":* Quoted in Boas and Chain, *Big Mac,* pp. 15–16.

34   *"grinding it out":* Kroc, *Grinding It Out,* p. 123.

34   *In 1961, Kroc borrowed money:* See Love, *Behind the Arches,* pp. 187–201.

34   *more than $180 million a year:* In 1961 the McDonald brothers gave up their 1 percent share of the McDonald's Corporation's annual sales. In 1998, the year that Richard McDonald died, that company had sales of about $18.1 billion. A 1 percent share of McDonald's sales that year would have brought Richard McDonald an income of $181 million.

34   *"Eventually I opened a McDonald's":* Kroc, *Grinding It Out,* p. 123.

35   *increased from 200 to almost 3,000:* The McDonald's Corporation opened its two

hundredth restaurant on April 15, 1960. The three thousandth McDonald's opened in Woolwich, England, in 1974. See "McDonald's Timeline," McDonald's Corporation, 2005.

36   *Altogether, Americans now eat:* This figure is a 2003 estimate by NPD FoodWorld CREST Research.

36   *If you put all those burgers in a straight line:* This is our own estimate. The average fast-food hamburger is about 4 inches wide, so if you could somehow put 13 billion hamburgers next to one another, they would stretch for approximately 52 billion inches. That's about 820,707 miles. The circumference of the earth at the equator is 24,901.55 miles. And if you divide 820,707 by 24,901.55, you wind up with 32.96.

THE YOUNGSTER BUSINESS

Steven Watts's *The Magic Kingdom: Walt Disney and the American Way of Life* (Boston: Houghton Mifflin, 1997) is perhaps the best biography of Walt Disney, drawing on material from the Disney archive and interviews with Disney associates. Although some of Watts's conclusions are debatable, his research is impressive. *The Disney Version: The Life, Times, Art, and Commerce of Walt Disney* (New York: Avon Books, 1968), by Richard Schickel, offers a more complex and much less flattering view of the man. Amid the growing literature on marketing to children, three books are particularly revealing: *What Kids Buy and Why: The Psychology of Marketing to Kids* (New York: Free Press, 1997), by Dan S. Acuff with Robert H. Reiher; *Creating Ever-Cool: A Marketer's Guide to a Kid's Heart* (Gretna, La.: Pelican, 1998), by Gene Del Vecchio; and *Kids as Customers: A Handbook of Marketing to Children* (New York: Lexington Books, 1992), by James U. McNeal. Susan Linn's *Consuming Kids: The Hostile Takeover of Childhood* (New York: New Press, 2004) and Juliet B. Schor's *Born to Buy: The Commercialized Child and the New Consumer Culture* (New York: Scribner, 2004) take a more critical view of marketing to kids.

A number of useful reports examine the issue. "Captive Kids: A Report on the Commercial Pressures on Kids at School" was issued by the Consumers Union in 1998. That same year, "Sponsored Schools and Commercialized Classrooms: Schoolhouse Commercializing Trends in the 1990s," by Alex Molnar, was released by the Center for the Analysis of Commercialism in Education, at the University of Wisconsin-Milwaukee. Some studies look at the subject from a global perspective. "Broadcasting Bad Health: Why Food Marketing to Children Needs to Be Controlled" was prepared by the International Association of Consumer Food Organizations and published by the World Health Organization in July 2003. Corinna Hawkes has written eye-opening papers for the World Health Organization, including "Marketing Activities of Global Soft Drink and Fast Food Companies in Emerging Markets: A Review," in *Globalization, Diets, and Noncommunicable Diseases* (Geneva, Switzerland: World Health Organization, 2002).

37 *"Give me a Y!":* One of us attended the conference in Singapore.

39 *Today companies selling all kinds of products:* Cited in speech by Paul Kurnit, "Youth Minded: Decoding the Youth Psyche and Implications for Your Brands," Youth Marketing Forum 2004, Singapore.

39 *in the United States children are responsible:* Paul Kurnit of KidShop and Kurnit Communications has estimated that the youth market is actually worth more than $1 trillion: $200 billion in personal spending by children; $300 billion in spending by parents and other adults directly influenced by children; and $500 billion in spending by adults indirectly influenced by children (on such items as family vacations, the family car, and the family home). The $500 billion estimate for the U.S. market comes from "Packaged Facts," *The Kid's Market* (New York: Marketresearch.com), Mar. 2000.

41 *"Hundreds of young people were being trained and fitted":* Quoted in Watts, *The Magic Kingdom,* p. 170.

44 *the number of children in the United States had increased:* See "Baby Boom Brought Biggest Increases Among People 45-to-54 Years Old," *U.S. Department of Commerce News,* October 3, 2001.

44 *"Dear Walt":* Quoted in Leslie Doolittle, "McDonald's Plan Cooked Up Decades Ago," *Orlando Sentinel,* Jan. 8, 1988.

45 *"A child who loves our TV commercials":* Kroc, *Grinding It Out,* p. 114.

46 *"world's newest, silliest, and hamburger-eatingest clown!":* The first Ronald McDonald television ad can be found on "The Multimedia Mixer: An Interactive Look at Ray Kroc and the Founding of McDonald's Corporation: Millennium Edition," a CD-ROM issued by the McDonald's Corporation in 1999. Other early commercials featuring Willard Scott as Ronald McDonald can be viewed at McDonald's Hamburger University in Oak Brook, Ill.

47 *Willard Scott was fired:* For the story of Willard Scott and Ronald McDonald, see Love, *Behind the Arches,* pp. 218–22, 244–45. Additional information about the flying hamburger ads can be found in Philip H. Dougherty, "Advertising: A Network Drive for Drive-Ins," *New York Times,* Apr. 5, 1967.

47 *more than nine out of ten American kids:* Cited in "Welcome to McDonald's," McDonald's Corporation, 1996.

49 *"brand loyalty" may begin:* Cited in "Brand Aware," *Children's Business,* June 2000.

49   *recognize a company logo:* See "Brand Consciousness," *IFF on Kids: Kid Focus,* No. 3, and James McNeal and Chyon-Hwa Yeh, "Born to Shop," *American Demographics,* June 1993, pp. 34–39.

49   *"It's not just getting kids to whine":* Quoted in "Market Research: The Old Nagging Game Can Pay Off for Marketers," *Selling to Kids,* Apr. 15, 1998.

50   *"but kids tend to stick":* For a list of the different kinds of nags, see James U. McNeal, *Kids as Customers: A Handbook of Marketing to Children* (New York: Lexington Books, 1992), pp. 72–75.

51   *The idea of creating:* See Schor, *Born to Buy,* p. 117.

52   *"Marketing messages sent through a club":* McNeal, *Kids as Customers,* p. 175.

52   *increased sales of Burger King Kids Meals:* Cited in Karen Benezra, "Keeping Burger King on a Roll," *Brandweek,* Jan. 15, 1996.

52   *"Children are important":* Quoted in Kim Foltz, "'Kids Club' Helps to Lift Burger King," *New York Times,* July 27, 1990.

52   *A government investigation:* Cited in "Children's Online Privacy Proposed Rule Issued by FTC," press release, Federal Trade Commission, Apr. 20, 1999.

56   *twenty-five hours a week watching television:* Cited in D. A. Gentile and D. A. Walsh, "A Normative Study of Family Media Habits," *Applied Developmental Psychology* 23 (Jan. 28, 2002): 157–178.

57   *more time watching television:* Cited in "Policy Statement: Children, Adolescents and Television," *American Academy of Pediatrics,* Oct. 1995.

57   *more than 40,000 TV commercials:* Cited in "Report of the APA Task Force on Advertising and Children," American Psychological Association, 2004.

57   *About 20,000 of those ads:* Food advertisements represent more than half of all ads on children's programming. Cited in Mary Story and Simone French, "Food Advertising and Marketing Directed at Children and Adolescents in the U.S.," *International Journal of Behavioral Nutrition and Physical Activity,* Feb. 10, 2004.

57   *fast-food chains now spend more than $3 billion:* Interview with Lynn Fava, Competitive Media Reporting.

57   *McDonald's has opened more than eight thousand:* Cited in "Fast Food and Playgrounds: A Natural Combination," promotional material, Playlandservices, Inc.

57   *"Playlands bring in children":* Ibid.

58   *"The key to attracting kids":* Sam Bradley and Betsey Spethmann, "Subway's Kid Pack: The Ties That Sell," *Brandweek,* Oct. 10, 1994.

59   *"McDonald's is in some ways":* Interview with a retired senior fast-food executive, who prefers not to be named.

59   *more than 1.5 billion toys:* Cited in Julian E. Barnes, "Fast-Food Giveaway Toys Face Rising Recalls," *New York Times,* Aug. 16, 2001.

59   *Almost one out of every three new toys:* Ibid.

59   *In 2000 a reporter for the* South China Morning Post: For details of the working

conditions at factories that make toys for McDonald's, see Martin Wong, "Childhood Lost to Hard Labour: Lax Age Checks Open Door to Underage Workers At Shenzhen Factory Producing Toys for Fast-Food Chain," *South China Morning Post,* Aug. 27, 2000; Mike Carlson, "U.S. Customs Joins McDonald's Probe," *South China Morning Post,* Aug. 31, 2000; and "McDonald's Toys: Do They Manufacture Fun or Mere Exploitation?" (Hong Kong: Hong Kong Christian Industrial Committee), 2000. We are grateful to Monina Wong, a researcher for the Hong Kong Christian Industrial Committee, for speaking to us in the summer of 2005 about what is currently happening to workers at Chinese toy factories.

59   *less than twenty cents an hour:* In late August 2000, one American dollar was worth roughly 8.28 Chinese yuan renminbi. Children at the City Toys factory were reportedly being paid about 24 yuan for a sixteen-hour workday. That means they were earning less than $3 per day—and only 18 cents per hour. The U.S. minimum wage is $5.15 per hour.

60   *paid less than ten cents an hour:* Cited in Martin Wong and Antoine So, "McDonald's Investigates Claims of Labour Abuse," *South China Morning Post,* Dec. 10, 2000. Workers at the Chit Tat Industrial Co. Ltd. were being paid as little as 11 yuan (or $1.33) for seventeen-hour days. That is a wage of about 8 cents per hour.

60   *about 10 million Happy Meals:* The story of McDonald's Teenie Beanie Baby promotion can be found in Rod Taylor, "The Beanie Factor," *Brandweek,* June 16, 1997.

61   *"We believe that the McDonald's brand":* Quoted in Marc Graser, "Did Somebody Sing McDonald's?: 'Adversongs' Urge Fast Food into Hip-Hop Lyrics," *Crain's Chicago Business,* Apr. 4, 2005.

MCJOBS

Two fine books tell the story of how the automobile transformed the American countryside: *The Geography of Nowhere: The Rise and Decline of America's Man-Made Landscape* (New York: Touchstone, 1994), by James Howard Kunstler; and *Once There Were Greenfields: How Urban Sprawl Is Undermining America's Environment, Economy, and Social Fabric* (Washington, D.C.: National Resources Defense Council, 1999), by F. Caid Benfield, Matthew D. Raimi, and Donald D. T. Chen. For the details of Martinsburg's early history, we consulted William T. Doherty's *Berkeley County, U.S.A.: A Bi-Centennial History of a Virginia and West Virginia County, 1772–1972* (Parsons, W. Va.: McClain, 1972), and *The Architectural and Pictorial History of Berkeley County* (Martinsburg, W. Va.: Berkeley County Historical Society, 1992). Miriam J. Williams Wilson and members of the

Berkeley County Clerk and Assessor's Office helped us find information about the strip along Interstate 81. Mona Kissel, at Air Photographics, Inc., tracked down the aerial photographs that show how the land surrounding I-81 has changed over the years. We are grateful to Betsy Morgan, a guidance counselor at Martinsburg High, who introduced us to students there—and to the many young fast-food workers who took the time to share their stories. Robin Leidner and Ester Reiter are sociologists who worked at chain restaurants in order to write about fast-food jobs. Reiter's *Making Fast Food: From the Frying Pan into the Fryer* (Montreal: McGill-Queen's University Press, 1991) focuses on Burger King, while Leidner's *Fast Food, Fast Talk: Service Work and the Routinization of Everyday Life* (Berkeley: University of California Press, 1993) looks at McDonald's. The benefits and harms of teenage employment are addressed at length in a study conducted by the Institute of Medicine, *Protecting Youth at Work: Health, Safety and Development of Working Children and Adolescents in the United States* (Washington, D.C.: National Academy Press, 1998).

64 *At J. C. McCrory Co.:* We found infomation about these old stores in Martinsburg's 1913–1914 *Polk City Directory* and *The Architectural and Pictorial History of Berkeley County.*

65 *The number of people living in the area:* According to the U.S. Census Bureau, the population of Berkeley County, West Virginia, in 1970 was 36,356. In 2000, it was 75,905.

65 *Martinsburg now sits:* See "Population Estimates for the 100 Fastest Growing U.S. Counties with 10,000 or More Population in 2004: April 1, 2000, to July 1, 2004," U.S. Census Bureau, 2005.

65 *In 1942 there were about 3 million:* For the number of fruit trees in 1942, see Martinsburg's *Polk City Directory,* 1942, p. 12. For the current number, see "2004 West Virginia Orchard & Vineyard Survey," West Virginia University, Kearneysville Tree Fruit Research and Education Center, 2005.

66 *During the 1980s the land was sold:* The information about Martinsburg land sales came from records in the Berkeley County Clerk and Assessor's Office. A farm owned by Sarah Miller was originally bought for $149,000; it later sold for $25,097,379. A farm owned by Norma Grant was originally bought for $200,000. It was later subdivided, and the parcels sold at prices ranging between $450,000 and $1.2 million. The land is now occupied by fast-food restaurants, a mall, and strip malls.

67 *"They paved paradise":* The line comes from a wonderful Joni Mitchell song, "Big Yellow Taxi."

67 *In 1970, Martinsburg had six:* The 1970 *Polk City Directory* listed six fast-food restaurants in Martinsburg, while the 2004 edition listed forty-five.

67 *"When you're up a thousand feet":* Quoted in "The Multimedia Mixer," McDonald's Corporation, 1999.

70 *one of the world's largest purchasers:* Author interview with Elliott Olson, chairman of Dakota Worldwide Corporation, which distributes software that many businesses use to select new locations.

70 *Danielle Brent is a seventeen-year-old:* Interview with Danielle Brent.

74 *"Everything's 'add water'":* Interview with a Taco Bell worker.

75 *In 1958, Turner wrote a training manual:* Cited in Love, *Behind the Arches,* p. 140.

75 *"Smile with a greeting":* Quoted in Ester Reiter, *Making Fast Food: From the Frying Pan into the Fryer* (Montreal: McGill-Queen's University Press, 1991), p. 85.

76 *the largest group of low-income workers:* Interview with Alan B. Krueger, author with David Card of *Myth and Measurement: The New Economics of the Minimum Wage* (Princeton, N.J.: Princeton University Press, 1995).

76 *the rate at which fast-food workers quit:* The annual turnover rate, or the rate at which an employee quits or is fired in any given year, varies by restaurant but can often be 250 percent or higher in the fast-food business. (See Carolyn Walkup, "Safe and Sound: Security of Food Supply, Keeping Workers Motivated Top Confab's Agenda; Special Report: Coex Wrap-Up," *Nation's Restaurant News,* Mar. 17, 2003.) By comparison, the annual average turnover rate for all occupations is about 20 percent. (See U.S. Department of Labor, Bureau of Labor Statistics, "Employee Turnover Rates, Annual U.S. Voluntary Turnover by Industry," Nov. 9, 2004.) Denise Fugo, treasurer of the National Restaurant Association, suggested that the annual turnover rate in the fast-food business may be as high as 400 percent. (See Lornet Turnbull, "Restaurants Feeding Off Fit Economy," *Columbus Dispatch* [Ohio], Feb. 23, 1999.) The National Restaurant Association publicly claims that the annual turnover rate is much lower—perhaps 80 percent. (See Todd Henneman, "Jack in the Box Going Upmarket in Benefits as Well as Its Eateries," *Workforce Management,* Mar. 1, 2005.)

77 *Between 1968 and 1990:* See Aaron Bernstein, "A Perfect Time to Raise the Minimum Wage," *Business Week,* May 17, 1999.

77 *nine out of every ten fast-food workers:* Of the roughly fifty to sixty employees at a typical McDonald's, only four or five are full-time, salaried managers. See Leidner, *Fast Food, Fast Talk.*

78 *They tend to earn about $25,000:* In November 2003, the Bureau of Labor Statistics estimated that the average annual income of "First-line supervisors/managers of food preparation and serving workers" was $24,990. That same year the typical full-time worker earned $36,520 a year. See *Occupational Outlook Handbook.*

79 *a McJob is a job:* Merriam-Webster defines *McJob* as a "low-paying job that requires little skill and provides little opportunity for advancement." The *Oxford English Dictionary* defines it as "an unstimulating, low-paid job with few prospects, esp. one created by the expansion of the service sector." The *American Heritage Dictionary* defines it as "a job, usually in the retail or service sector, that is low paying, often temporary, and offers minimal or no benefits or opportunity for promotion." These three major dictionaries seem to agree that a McJob is a lousy job.

80 *Other kids are eager:* Interview with fast-food workers at Martinsburg High School, May 2004.

82 *Sadi Lambert, a friend:* Interview with Sadi Lambert.

83 *Pascal McDuff sent job applications:* We are grateful to Pascal McDuff for the time he spent describing the battle with McDonald's in Montreal. A good documentary film about the union struggle, *Maxime, McDuff & McDo,* directed by Magnus Isacsson, is available from Films en Vue in Montreal, Canada. The picture of Pascal and Maxime used in *Chew on This* is a publicity shot created for the documentary. See also Konrad Yakabuski, "Arch Enemy," *Report on Business Magazine,* November 2001.

86 *In 1960 about one out of every three American workers:* For the 2004 proportion, see "Union Members Survey," Bureau of Labor Statistics, Jan. 27, 2005; 12.5 percent of U.S. wage and salary workers were union members in 2004. For the 1960 proportion, see "Figure 2, U.S. Union Density, 1930–2001," in Ian Graham, "It Pays to Be Union, U.S. Figures Show," *Labour Education,* International Labour Organization, 2002/2003, no. 128.

90 *The odds against a McDonald's restaurant in Canada:* Roughly three McDonald's closed per year in Canada during the early 1990s, while about eighty new ones annually opened. See Mike King, "McDonald's to Go," *Montreal Gazette,* Feb. 15, 1998.

90 *"Did somebody say McUnion?":* Bill Tieleman, "Did Somebody Say McUnion?" *National Post,* Mar. 29, 1999.

THE SECRET OF THE FRIES

Food: A Culinary History (New York: Columbia University Press, 1999), edited by Jean-Louis Flandrin and Missimo Montanari, traces the changes in how food is prepared from prehistoric campfires all the way to the kitchens at McDonald's. A good account of the history of American food processing can be found in John M. Connor and William A. Schiek, *Food Processing: An Industrial Powerhouse in Transition* (New York: Wiley, 1997). The reference books on flavor technology are a pleasure to read. They are like medieval texts on black magic, full of strange, unfamiliar words. Some of the most interesting ones are Giovanni Fenaroli and George A. Burdock, *Fenaroli's Handbook of Flavor Ingredients,* vol. 2 (Ann Arbor, Mich.: CRC Press, 1995); Henry B. Heath, *Source Book of Flavors* (Westport, Conn.: Avi, 1981); Carl W. Hall, A. W. Farrall, and A. L. Rippen, *Encyclopedia of Food Engineering* (Westport, Conn.: Avi, 1986); and *Flavor Science: Sensible Principles and Techniques,* edited by Terry E. Acree and Roy Teranishi (Washington, D.C.: American Chemical Society, 1993).

Julie Mennella, a biopsychologist at the Monell Chemical Senses Center in Philadelphia, spoke to us about how children develop their sense of taste. Terry E. Acree, a professor of food science technology at Cornell University, was a wonderful resource on the subjects of smell, taste, flavor, and the flavor industry. Bob Bauer, executive director of the National Association of Fruits, Flavors, and Syrups, outlined when and where the flavor industry settled in New Jersey. We are grateful to Carol Brys, Brian Grainger, Diane Mora, and Marianne Swaney-Stueve at International Flavors & Fragrances. They not only answered our questions patiently but allowed us a glimpse of how flavors are manufactured and tested. A number of flavorists whom we interviewed asked that their names and the names of their companies not appear in this book. While respecting their privacy, we'd like to thank them for their help.

92   *"The French fry [was]":* Kroc, *Grinding It Out,* p. 10.

93   *J. R. Simplot:* Interview with J. R. Simplot.

93   *Although Thomas Jefferson had brought:* See "The French Fries," a chapter in Elizabeth Rozin's *The Primal Cheeseburger* (New York: Penguin, 1994), pp. 133–52.

95   *At the time McDonald's bought fresh potatoes:* Cited in Love, *Behind the Arches,* p. 329.

95   *McDonald's had about 725 restaurants:* See "McDonald's Timeline," McDonald's Corporation, 2005. By the end of 1964, McDonald's had 657 restaurants. Its thousandth store opened in 1968, and its three thousandth store opened in 1974.

96   *In 1960 the typical American:* See Bling-Hwan Lin, Gary Lucier, Jane Allshouse, and Linda Scott Kantor, "Fast Food Growth Boosts Frozen Potato Consumption," *Food Review,* Jan.–Apr. 2001, and Economic Research Service/USDA, "French Fries Driving Globalization of Frozen Potato Industry," *Agricultural Outlook,* Oct. 2002.

96   *Close to 90 percent:* Cited in "Fast Food Growth Boosts Frozen Potato Consumption," p. 42.

96   *A study recently found:* "Feeding Infants & Toddlers Study by Gerber Products Co.," Mathematica Policy Research Inc. Cited in "Junk Food Starts Early," *Time,* Nov. 10, 2003.

96   *"I've been a land hog":* Simplot interview.

97   *Altogether, J. R. Simplot controls:* Delaware has about 1.6 million acres of land.

97   *three companies control about 80 percent:* Cited in Timothy J. Richard, Paul M. Patterson, and Ram N. Acharya, "Price Behavior in a Dynamic Oligopsony: Washington Processing Potatoes," *American Journal of Agricultural Economics,* May 1, 2001.

97   *Out of every dollar-fifty:* A large order of fries weighs about one quarter of a pound. It takes about a half pound of fresh potatoes to make a quarter pound of fries. A typical farm price for fresh processing potatoes is four to five dollars per hundredweight—or four to five cents a pound.

98   *Idaho has lost about half:* Interview with Bert Moulton of the Potato Growers of Idaho.

103   *more saturated beef fat:* A small McDonald's hamburger weighed 102 grams and had 3.6 grams of saturated fat; a small order of fries weighed 68 grams and had 5.05 grams of saturated fat. See "Where's the Fat," *USA Today,* Apr. 5, 1990; Marian Burros, "The Slimming of Fat Fast Food," *New York Times,* July 25, 1990.

104   *Americans now spend more than $1 trillion:* "Personal Consumption Expenditures by Major Type of Product and Expenditure," Bureau of Economic Analysis, Mar. 19, 2004.

106   *The aroma of a food can be responsible:* Cited in Ruth Sambrook, "Do You Smell What I Smell? The Science of Smell and Taste," *Institute of Food Research,* Mar. 1999.

108   *Babies like sweet tastes:* See Julie A. Mennella and Gary K. Beauchamp, "Early Flavor Experiences: Where Do They Start?" *Nutrition Today,* Sept. 1994.

108   *"It's during childhood":* Interview with Julie Mennella.

108   *an experiment on how tastes are formed:* See Julie A. Mennella, Coren P. Jagnow, and Gary K. Beauchamp, "Prenatal and Postnatal Flavor Learning by Human Infants," *Pediatrics* 107, no. 6 (June 2001).

109   *In another experiment, Mennella proved:* See Julie A. Mennella, Cara E. Griffin, and Gary K. Beauchamp, "Flavor Programming During Infancy," *Pediatrics* 113, no. 4 (Apr. 2004): 840–45.

113   *The flavor in a twelve-ounce can of Coke:* An industry source told us the cost of the flavor in a six-pack of Coke, and we did the math.

114   *And what does that artificial strawberry flavor contain?:* This tasty recipe comes from Fenaroli and Burdock, *Fenaroli's Handbook of Flavor Ingredients,* vol. 2, p. 831.

117   *Universal TA.XT2 Texture Analyzer:* For a description of such contraptions, see Ray Marsili, "Texture and Mouthfeel: Making Rheology Real," *Food Product Design,* Aug. 1993.

120   *"Children's expectation of a strawberry":* Interview with Brian Grainger, the director of flavor creation for North America at IFF.

120 *"We could do it very easily":* Ibid.

122 *Boys are more likely than girls:* Interview with Marianne Swaney-Stueve, a senior sensory and consumer researcher, and Brian Grainger at IFF.

123 *Small children have tried to drink:* See Anastasia Ustinova, "Labels on Toxic Items Often Entice Children," *Augusta Chronicle,* Mar. 19, 2004.

123 *Carmine can cause allergic reactions:* See James L. Baldwin, Alice H. Chou, and William R. Solomon, "Popsicle-Induced Anaphylaxis Due to Carmine Dye Allergy," *Annals of Allergy, Asthma & Immunology* 79 (Nov. 1997): 415–19.

123 *Tartrazine, a yellow food coloring:* See "Effect of Artificial Food Colors on Childhood Behavior," *Archives of Disease in Childhood* 65 (1990): 74–77; "Tartrazine Sensitivity," *American Family Physician* 42 (1990): 1347–50.

124 *A study conducted in 2004:* Cited in "Something Fishy: Could This Spell the End of E Numbers?" *Independent* (London), July 6, 2004.

124 *"We assume that because these things do not make us drop dead":* Interview with Dr. Vyvyan Howard.

126 *"Eating a cow for a Hindu":* Quoted in Laurie Goodstein, "For Hindus and Vegetarians, Surprise in McDonald's Fries," *New York Times,* May 20, 2001.

126 *"If you visit McDonald's anywhere":* Quoted in "Healthy Eating," McDonald's Corporation, Australian Web site, www.McDonalds.com.au, 2001.

STOP THE POP

The harmful impact of fast food in rural Alaska is a good example of how this industry is changing traditional cultures and remote societies throughout the world. The mayor of Bethel opened the town's first Subway restaurant in 2000, and Yupik Eskimo teens now work there behind the counter. Several books examine the history and culture of the Yupik people. *Minuk: Ashes in the Pathway* (Middleton, Wis.: Pleasant Company, 2002), a novel by Kirkpatrick Hill, tells the story of a Yupik girl's first contact with outsiders a century ago. Mary Lenz and James H. Barker have written a thorough history of the area, *Bethel: The First Hundred Years* (Bethel: A City of Bethel Centennial History Project, 1985). Ann Fienup-Riordan's book, *The Living Tradition of Yupik Masks* (Seattle: University of Washington Press, 1996), includes photographs of the masks and explains their meaning. *Always Getting Ready, Upterrlainarluta: Yupik Eskimo Subsistence in Southwest Alaska* (Seattle: University of Washington Press, 1993), by James H. Barker, combines beautiful photographs with a graceful text. Barker's respect for the Yupik is evident on every page.

We are grateful to Mary Kapsner for all her help. She is an honest, idealistic, hard-working state legislator, and we look forward to her becoming the governor of Alaska someday. Jonathan Kapsner was a gracious host, willing to drive around

Bethel at a moment's notice. Meera Ramesh, the juvenile diabetes coordinator at the Yukon Kuskokwim Health Corporation, was generous with her time, as were Paulette Pasco, Dr. Stan Shulman, and Dr. Edwin Allgair, who have seen the rise in tooth decay among children in the region. Among the many people who helped with research in Alaska, we'd like to thank Teresa Altenburg, Carol Ballew, Carol Cozzen, Felecia Griffith-Kleven, Dana Hall, Chris Ho, Michael Johnson, Allen M. Joseph, Don Kashevaroff, Jodie Malus, David Matthews, and Julian Naylor. Michael Jacobson's report "Liquid Candy: How Soft Drinks Are Harming Americans' Health" (Center for Science in the Public Interest, Oct. 1998) examines the increase in soda consumption in the United States over the past thirty years and its effect on the health of young people.

130 *A child caught speaking Yupik:* See Rhonda Barton, "Nets & Paddles: Fish and Canoes Carry Meaningful Lessons," *Northwest Education Magazine,* Spring 2004.

130 *"upterrlainarluta":* See Barker, *Always Getting Ready.*

131 *About half of the village's adults are unemployed:* According to 2000 U.S. Census data, 53.55 percent of the adults in Kasigluk were not employed. Cited in Alaska Community Information Summaries.

133 *"We don't know if there will or won't":* Quoted in Rona Cherry, "McDonald's Goes to School in Arkansas," *New York Times,* Sept. 30, 1976.

133 *Thirty years later, about 19,000:* This is our own estimate, based on the following data. In 2000 the Centers for Disease Control and Prevention estimated that 20.2 percent of American public schools offer brand-name fast food to students. According to the Department of Education, there are about 94,000 public schools. See "School Health Policies and Programs Study," Centers for Disease Control and Prevention, 2000, and "Overview of Public Elementary and Secondary Schools and Districts: School Year 2001–2002," U.S. Department of Education, National Center for Education Statistics, 2003.

133 *"We want to be more like":* Quoted in Janet Bigham, "Corporate Curriculum: And Now a Word, Lesson, Lunch, from a Sponsor," *Denver Post,* Feb. 22, 1998.

134 *"I don't think it's healthy":* Quoted in "Battle of the Bulge: Fast Food Is King at Arroyo High," *San Francisco Chronicle,* June 29, 2003.

134 *a group of students protested with signs:* See Elizabeth Weil, "Heavy Questions," *New York Times,* Jan. 2, 2005.

134 *Half of the boys and one third of the girls:* Ibid.

137 *"an absolute waste":* Quoted in Gordon W. Gunderson, *The National School Lunch Program: Background and Development* (Washington, D.C.: U.S. Government Printing Office, 1971).

137 *"whereby the pupils may obtain":* Ibid.

137 *By 1946 the national school lunch program:* Ibid.

138   *The National Soft Drink Association:* For a history of the case, see the report of the Democratic Staff of the Senate Committee on Agriculture, Nutrition and Forestry, "Food Choices at School: Risks to Child Nutrition and Health Call for Action," May 18, 2004. The case was *National Soft Drink Ass'n v. Block,* 721 F.2d 1348 (1983).

138   *43 percent of elementary schools:* Cited in U.S. General Accounting Office, "School Lunch Program: Efforts Needed to Improve Nutrition and Encourage Healthy Eating" (Washington, D.C.: U.S. General Accounting Office, May 2003), p. 17.

138   *Jade Alexander is a thirteen-year-old:* Interview with Jade Alexander.

139   *More than 40 percent of the children:* See Loma E. Thorpe et al., "Childhood Obesity in New York City Elementary School Students," *American Journal of Public Health* 94, no. 9 (Sept. 2004).

140   *"Go ahead and enjoy them!":* Cited in a report by the Consumers Union, "Captive Kids: A Report on Commercial Pressures on Kids at School," 1998.

141   *The Pizza Hut "Book It!" program:* See press release, "Pizza Hut BOOK IT! Beginners program for preschoolers features Little Critter: Enrollment for 2005 BOOK IT! Beginners Program Starts November," Pizza Hut, Inc., Oct. 20, 2004.

141   *"Influencing elementary school students":* Quoted in Kent Steinriede, "Sponsorship Scorecard 1999," *Beverage Industry,* Jan. 1, 1999.

142   *"We at McDonald's are thankful":* Quoted in Ernest Holsendorph, "Keeping McDonald's Out in Front: 'Gas' Is No Problem; Chicken May Be Served," *New York Times,* Dec. 30, 1973.

142   *The fast-food chains buy Coca-Cola syrup:* According to *Business Week,* Burger King pays Coke $170 million for 40 million gallons of syrup. That works out to a cost of about $4.25 a gallon—or 3.3 cents an ounce. It is safe to assume that McDonald's, an even larger customer, buys its syrup at a price that is equivalent, if not lower. See Dean Foust, "Man on the Spot: Nowadays Things Go Tougher at Coke," *Business Week,* May 3, 1999.

143   *In 1975 the typical American drank:* This figure comes from the Beverage Marketing Corporation. Cited in Marc Kaufman, "Pop Culture: Health Advocates Sound Alarm as Schools Strike Deals with Coke and Pepsi," *Washington Post,* Mar. 23, 1999.

143   *Today the typical American drinks:* This figure comes from the Beverage Marketing Corporation. Cited in John Rodwan, Jr., "Seeking Growth: Convenience Store Volume Increases to 12 Percent: Convenience Consumer, Carbonated Soft Drinks," *National Petroleum News,* May 1, 2005.

143   *In 1978 the typical teenage boy:* This figure comes from the U.S. Department of Agriculture Nationwide Food Consumption Survey, 1977–78, and is cited in Michael F. Jacobson, "Liquid Candy: How Soft Drinks Are Harming Americans' Health," Center for Science in the Public Interest, Oct. 1998.

143   *today the typical teenage boy drinks:* Ibid.

143   *The amount of soda that teenage girls drink:* Ibid.

143   *Thirty years ago, teenage boys:* For figures from 1977–1978 that show milk consumption double that of soda, see National Food Consumption Survey cited in Jacobson, "Liquid Candy." According to the Beverage Marketing Corporation, in 2002, teen per capita consumption was 53.8 gallons of soda and 23.5 gallons of milk.

143   *About 20 percent of American children:* Cited in Jacobson, "Liquid Candy."

144   *"Location, location, location":* For the story of District 11's shortfall, see Cara DeGette, "The Real Thing: Corporate Welfare Comes to the Classroom," *Colorado Springs Independent,* Nov. 25 to Dec. 1, 1998.

145   *Kristina Clark of Glennallen:* Interview with Kristina Clark. The authors appreciate the assistance of Kristina's mother, Carol Cozzen.

145   *"but no sign of tooth decay":* See Vilhjalmur Stefansson, "Adventures in Diet," *Harper's Monthly,* Jan. 1936.

147   *"Young people in the small villages":* Quoted in press release, "Books & Hoops in Alaska," Coca-Cola Corporation, June 7, 2002.

148   *Edwin Allgair, a dentist:* Interview with Edwin Allgair.

148   *"baby bottle syndrome":* Interview with Stan Shulman, D.D.S., who first alerted us to the frequency of baby bottle syndrome in western Alaska.

151   *In 2003, Mary Kapsner:* Interview with Mary Kapsner.

153   *"Many factors contribute to the formation":* Grocery Manufacturers of America letter to the Honorable Tom Anderson, chair, House Committee on Labor and Commerce, Mar. 3, 2003.

153   *"Why are you singling us out?":* Kapsner interview.

MEAT

Upton Sinclair's *The Jungle* (1906; reprint, New York: Bantam, 1981) remains the essential starting point for an understanding of America's meatpacking industry today. A century after its publication, many of the book's descriptive passages still ring true. Jimmy K. Skagg's *Prime Cut: Livestock Raising and Meatpacking in the United States, 1607–1983* (College Station: Texas A&M University Press, 1986) is a good history of the subject. The best book on today's meatpacking industry is *Slaughterhouse Blues: The Meat and Poultry Industry in America* (Belmont, Calif.: Wadsworth, 2003), by Donald D. Stull and Michael J. Broadway. *From Columbus to ConAgra: The Globalization of Agriculture and Food,* edited by Alessandro Bonanno, Lawrence Busch, William F. Friedland, Lourdes Gouveia, and Enzo Mingione (Lawrence: University of Kansas Press, 1994), contains a fine essay, "Global Strategies and Local Linkages: The Case of the U.S. Meatpacking Industry." Carol Andreas's *Meatpackers and Beef Barons:*

Company Town in a Global Economy (Niwot: University Press of Colorado, 1994) looks at the changes through the prism of a local community, Greeley, Colorado. *Broken Heartland: The Rise of America's Rural Ghetto* (Iowa City: University of Iowa Press, 1996), by Osha Gray Davidson, explains the causes of the rising poverty in American meatpacking towns. In January 2005, Human Rights Watch issued a scathing report on the ways in which the industry violates international human rights laws, "Blood, Sweat, and Fears: Workers' Rights in U.S. Meat and Poultry Plants."

Gail A. Eisnitz's *Slaughterhouse: The Shocking Story of Greed, Neglect, and Inhumane Treatment Inside the U.S. Meat Industry* (Amherst, N.Y.: Prometheus, 1997) suggests that many cattle are needlessly brutalized prior to slaughter. Temple Grandin and Catherine Johnson's *Animals in Translation: Using the Mysteries of Autism to Decode Animal Behavior* (New York: Scribner, 2005) describes how cruelty and poor breeding practices became commonplace in the poultry and meat industry. Nicols Fox has written two excellent books about the hidden dangers of what we eat, *Spoiled: The Dangerous Truth About a Food Chain Gone Haywire* (New York: Basic Books, 1997) and *It Was Probably Something You Ate: A Practical Guide to Avoiding and Surviving Foodborne Illness* (New York: Penguin, 1999).

156   *Emily Hanna grew up:* Interviews with Emily, Maggie, and Ann Hanna.
161   *Today McDonald's is America's largest purchaser of beef:* See Love, *Behind the Arches,* pp. 4–5. Also cited by the president of the National Cattlemen's Beef Association in "NCBA, McDonald's Form Hamburger Task Force: Improving Value of U.S. Beef Products by Exporting Trimmings," *Food & Drink Weekly,* Apr. 29, 2002.
161   *In 1968, McDonald's bought fresh ground beef:* For the consolidation of the chain's beef purchasing, see Love, *Behind the Arches,* pp. 130, 333–38.
161   *In 1917, at the height of the beef trust:* Cited in *Competition and the Livestock Market,* Report of a Task Force Commissioned by the Center for Rural Affairs (Walt Hill, Neb., Apr. 1990), p. 31.
162   *In 1970 the four largest meatpacking companies:* Ibid.
162   *Today the top four meatpacking companies:* See Mary Hendrickson and William Heffernan, "Concentration of Agricultural Markets," National Farmers Union, Feb. 2005.
162   *Twenty-five years ago, ranchers:* See figures provided by Chuck Lambert, chief economist for the National Cattlemen's Beef Association, in Wes Ishmael, "Reality Gap," *Beef,* Aug. 1, 2002.
165   *A typical steer will eat:* Interview with Mike Callicrate, Kansas feedlot operator.
166   *Each steer deposits about 50 pounds:* This figure was determined by researchers at Colorado State University. Cited in Mark Obmascik, "As Greeley Ponders Tax, Cows Keep on Doing Their Thing," *Denver Post,* July 29, 1995.

166   *In 1991 one billion fish were killed:* Cited in Susan Zakin, "Nonpoint Pollution: The Quiet Killer," *Field & Stream,* Aug. 1999, p. 86.

167   *The two big feedlots outside Greeley:* According to O. W. Charles, of the Extension Poultry Science Department of the University of Georgia, one head of cattle generates the same amount of waste as 16.4 people. Cited in Eric R. Haapapuro, Neal D. Barnardd, and Michele Simon, "Animal Waste Used as Livestock Feed: Dangers to Human Health," *Preventive Medicine,* Sept./Oct. 1997. Using that ratio, the roughly 200,000 cattle in those two Weld County feedlots produce an amount of waste equal to that of about 3.2 million people. The combined population of Denver (555,000), Boston (600,000), Atlanta (425,000), and St. Louis (350,000) produce much less excrement than Greeley's cattle.

167   *Some studies suggest that breathing air polluted:* See K. H. Kilburn, "Evaluating Health Effects from Exposure to Hydrogen Sulfide: Central Nervous System Dysfunction," *Environmental Epidemiology and Toxicology* (1999), 1: 207–216.

168   *a pile of manure at a large feedlot in Milford:* See "Burning Manure Pile in Nebraska Goes Out," *Associated Press,* Feb. 23, 2005, and Kevin O'Hanlon, "Massive Manure Fire Burns into Third Month," *Associated Press,* Jan. 28, 2005.

169   *Four chicken companies now control:* Tyson Foods, Pilgrim's Pride, Gold Kist, and Perdue now control about 56 percent of the broiler chickens sold in this country. Cited in Hendrickson and Heffernan, "Concentration of Agricultural Markets."

170   *"I have an idea":* Quoted in Monci Jo Williams, "McDonald's Refuses to Plateau," *Fortune,* Nov. 12, 1984.

172   *Named Mr. McDonald, the new breed:* See Love, *Behind the Arches,* p. 342.

172   *Chicken McNuggets were introduced in 1983:* Cited in Williams, "McDonald's Refuses."

172   *When a researcher at Harvard Medical School:* The researcher was Dr. Frank Sacks, assistant professor of medicine at the Harvard University Medical School, and he utilized gas chromatography to analyze McNuggets for *Science Digest.* See "Study Raises Beef over Fast-Food Frying," *Chicago Tribune,* Mar. 11, 1986, and Irvin Molotsky, "Risk Seen in Saturated Fats Used in Fast Foods," *New York Times,* Nov. 15, 1985.

173   *"The impact of McNuggets was so huge":* Quoted in Timothy K. Smith, "Changing Tastes: By End of the Year Poultry Will Surpass Beef in the U.S. Diet," *Wall Street Journal,* Sept. 17, 1987.

173   *Twenty-five years ago, most chicken was sold whole:* See statistics from the U.S. Egg and Poultry Series, 1960–1990, cited in Michael Ollinger, "Poultry Plants Lowering Production Costs and Increasing Variety—Statistical Data Included," *Food Review,* May–August 2000. In 1982, 51.9 percent of chickens were sold whole; in 1997, only 13.1 percent were sold whole.

173   *Tyson now manufactures about half:* Cited in Sheila Edmundson, "Real Home of

the McNugget Is Tyson," *Memphis Business Journal,* July 9, 1999.

173   *A Tyson chicken farmer:* Interview with Larry Holder, executive director of the National Contract Poultry Growers Association.

174   *A typical chicken farmer has been raising:* See "Assessing the Impact of Integrator Practices on Contract Poultry Growers," Farmers' Legal Action Group, Inc., Sept. 2001.

174   *About half the nation's chicken growers:* Cited in Sheri Venena, "Growing Pains," *Arkansas Democrat-Gazette,* Oct. 18, 1998.

175   *Norah Smith raises chickens:* Author interview. At the request of this chicken farmer, we have not used her real name. She is a real person and not a combination of people.

176   *Sometimes the leftover waste:* The information about chickens being in the chicken feed was confirmed by an interview with Tyson spokesman Gary Mickelson. The information about beef in the chicken feed came through conversations with growers; there is no federal rule blocking beef in chicken feed. See also "Mad Cow Cases Met with Shrug Instead of Safeguards," *USA Today,* July 31, 2005.

176   *In 1994, Japanese scientists discovered:* See "Which Came First? This Chicken," *New York Times,* Dec. 20, 1994; Steve Connor, "Chickens' Ancestry Traced to Thailand," *The Independent* (UK), Dec. 20, 1994.

177   *In 1965 chickens gained roughly:* Figures for weight and growing times cited in Chris Hill, "Chicken Industry Adapts for Future," *Poultry Times,* Apr. 13, 2005.

177   *If a child gained weight:* Cited in Michael McCarthy, "Animal Welfare: The Growing Pains of a Selectively Bred Chicken," *Independent* (London), Dec. 10, 2001. A section near the end of the article explains how researchers arrived at this figure. The researchers suggested that if current trends continue, the typical broiler chicken will soon be the equivalent of a 330-pound six-year-old.

178   *In 2006, about 9 billion chickens:* In 2004, 8.74 billion broiler chickens were slaughtered in the United States. The number should exceed 9 billion in 2006. See U.S. Department of Agriculture, National Agricultural Statistics Service, "Poultry—Production and Value, 2004 Summary," Apr. 2005.

179   *When chickens arrive:* The description of the Pilgrim's Pride slaughterhouse was based on a visit to Moorefield, interviews with local chicken growers with knowledge of the plant, reports by People for the Ethical Treatment of Animals (PETA), and an interview with PETA's director of vegan outreach, Bruce Friedrich. A 2004 PETA report, "The Case for Controlled-Atmosphere Killing of Poultry in Transport Containers Prior to Shackling as a Means for More Humane Slaughter Rather than Electrical Stunning," outlines the different steps of the electrical slaughter process—and what can go wrong. See also Dick Hughes, "Pilgrim's Pride Moves

Quickly to Ensure Humane Processing," *Moorefield Examiner*, July 28, 2004; press conference comments by KFC president Gregg Dedrick, July 21, 2004; and statement from O. B. Goolsby, president and chief operating officer, Pilgrim's Pride Corporation, July 20, 2004. When we contacted Ray Atkinson, a spokesman for the Pilgrim's Pride Corporation, he declined to comment on the PETA video and other allegations of abuse.

180 *Several years ago McDonald's admitted:* Dr. Gomez Gonzales, McDonald's first manager of meat products, made this admission in testimony during a libel suit in England, later known as the "McLibel trial." See verdict of Chief Justice Robert Bell, *McDonald's Restaurants v. Morris & Steel*, Section 8: The Rearing and Slaughter of Animals, 19 June 1997.

180 *Yet a 2004 videotape:* You can see the videotape online at *www.peta.org/feat/ moorefield/*. It's hard to watch.

181 *"I like to hear the popping sound":* Cited in "What the Investigator Saw: Eyewitness Testimony from PETA's Investigation into a Pilgrim's Pride Chicken Slaughterhouse," July 2004.

182 *A study of controlled atmosphere stunning:* See "Report of the Corporate Responsibility Committee of the Board of Directors of McDonald's Corporation: Regarding the Feasibility of Implementing Controlled Atmosphere Stunning for Broilers," McDonald's Corporation, June 29, 2005.

183 *"cogs in the great packing machine":* Upton Sinclair, *The Jungle*, p. 78.

184 *"This is no fairy story and no joke":* Ibid, p. 135.

185 *"I aimed for the public's heart":* Quoted in Skaggs, *Prime Cut*, p. 118.

185 *meatpacking workers were soon among the highest-paid:* See Shelton Stromquist and Marvin Bergman, *Unionizing the Jungles: Labor and Community in the Twentieth-Century Meatpacking Industry* (Iowa City: University of Iowa Press, 1997), pp. 25–33.

186 *lowering wages by as much as 50 percent:* While the meatpacking companies Swift and Armour were paying $17 to $18 an hour, IBP was paying just $8. See Winston Williams, "An Upheaval in Meatpacking," *New York Times*, June 20, 1983.

186 *Today meatpacking workers are among the lowest-paid:* In 1970 meatpacking wages were 19 percent higher than the average wages in American manufacturing; by 2002 meatpacking wages were 24 percent lower than the national average. Cited in Human Rights Watch, "Blood, Sweat, and Fears."

186 *And they have one of the most dangerous jobs:* See Bureau of Labor Statistics, "Table SNR01: Highest Incidence Rates of Total Nonfatal Occupational Injury and Illness Cases, Private Industry," 2003.

186 *the typical meatpacking worker now quits:* Cited in General Accounting Office, "Workplace Safety and Health: Safety in the Meat and Poultry Industry, While

Improving, Could Be Further Strengthened," U.S. Government Accountability Office, Jan. 2005, pp. 31 and 56. This GAO report mentions that a turnover rate of 100 percent is not uncommon at meatpacking plants. At one plant visited by GAO investigators the turnover rate was nearly 200 percent, which means that the typical worker left after only six months.

187   Employee Severely Burned After Fuel from His Saw Is Ignited: These are the titles of Accident Investigation Summaries, U.S. Department of Labor, Occupational Safety and Health Administration.

190   *The maximum fine that OSHA can impose:* See David Barstow and Lowell Bergman, "Deaths on the Job, Slaps on the Wrist," *New York Times,* Jan. 10, 2003. The article points out that during the more than thirty years since OSHA was created, the maximum penalty has only increased once, from $10,000 to $70,000 in 1990.

190   *keep in mind that Tyson:* See "Q2 2005 Tyson Foods Earnings Conference Call—Final," *Fair Disclosure Wire,* May 2, 2005. John Tyson is quoted as projecting 2005 revenues to be between $26 and $27 billion, "down slightly from our previous financial outlook."

190   *A meatpacking executive who deliberately violates:* See David Barstow, "U.S. Rarely Seeks Charges for Deaths in Workplace," *New York Times,* Dec. 22, 2003.

192   *more than seven hundred people:* See "Update: Multistate Outbreak of Escherichia coli O157:H7 Infections from Hamburgers—Western United States, 1992–1993," *Morbidity and Mortality Weekly Report,* Centers for Disease Control and Prevention, Apr. 16, 1993, and Fox, *Spoiled,* pp. 246–68.

192   *Lauren Beth Rudolph:* See Anita Manning, "A Simple Meal Can Shatter a Family," *USA Today,* May 13, 1997.

193   *In 1982 dozens of children were sickened:* Nicols Fox offers the best account of this outbreak. See Fox, *Spoiled,* pp. 220–29.

193   *"the possibility of a statistical association":* Quoted in ibid, p. 227.

193   *roughly 200,000 people are sickened:* Estimate based on figures in Paul S. Mead et al., "Food-Related Illness and Death in the United States," *Emerging Infectious Diseases* 5, no. 5 (Sept.–Oct. 1999).

193   *More than one quarter of the American population:* Ibid.

193   *there is strong evidence:* See Robert V. Tauxe, "Emerging Foodborne Diseases: An Evolving Public Health Challenge," *Emerging Infectious Diseases* 3, no. 4 (Oct.–Dec. 1997). Also see World Health Organization, *Fact Sheet: Foodborne Diseases, Emerging,* Jan. 2002.

194   *Today thirteen large slaughterhouses:* Cited in James M. MacDonald and Michael Ollinger, "U.S. Meat Slaughter Consolidating Rapidly," *USDA Food Review,* May 1, 1997.

195 *"We can fine circuses":* Quoted in Carol Smith, "Overhaul in Meat Inspection No Small Potatoes, Official Says," *Seattle Post-Intelligencer,* Jan. 29, 1998.

196 *"There is no limit":* Quoted in Mary Yeager, *Competition and Regulation: The Development of Oligopoly in the Meat Packing Industry* (Greenwich, Conn.: Jai, 1981), p. 205.

196 *"You shouldn't eat dirty food":* Interview with a government health official who prefers not to be named.

197 *A single animal infected with* E. coli: Cited in Gregory L. Armstrong, Jill Holingsworth, and J. Glenn Morris, Jr., "Emerging Foodborne Pathogens: *Escherichia coli* O157:H7 as a Model of Entry of a New Pathogen into the Food Supply of the Developed World," *Epidemiologic Reviews* 18, no. 1 (1996).

198 *A single fast-food hamburger:* Interview with Dr. Robert Tauxe, chief of foodborne and diarrheal diseases at the Centers for Disease Control, "Modern Meat," *Frontline,* 2002.

199 *at the V & G Newman slaughterhouse:* For the story of the Tamworth Two, see "Pig Tales of the Tamworth Two," *Daily Mail* (London), Oct. 29, 1998; Michael Hornsby, "Tamworth Two Fled Unhygienic Abattoir," *Times* (London), Jan. 30, 1998; Gabrielle Fagan, "Tamworth Two Spark Bills to Help Pigs," *Press Association,* Jan. 20, 1998; and Helen Reid, "Why We All Cheer the Great Escape," *Bristol United Press,* Jan. 19, 1998.

201 *an American dairy cow named Emily:* The story of Emily is based on an interview with Lewis Randa of the Peace Abbey and the following articles: "A Cow Who Took Matters into Her Own Hooves," *AWI Quarterly* 45, no. 1 (Winter 1996): 12; Maureen Sullivan, "Peace Abbey Welcomes Bronze Beloved Bovine," *MetroWest Daily News,* Apr. 26, 2005; and "Holy Cow! She's a Holstein Hero," *People,* Dec. 26, 1996. James Agee wrote a wonderful short story called "A Mother's Tale" that imagines the emotional experience of a cow as it heads to slaughter. It can be found in *The Collected Short Prose of James Agee* (Boston: Houghton Mifflin, 1968).

BIG

Greg Critser's *Fat Land: How Americans Became the Fattest People in the World* (Boston: Houghton Mifflin, 2003) offers a provocative look at the nation's expanding waistlines. In 2004 the National Academy of Sciences issued a fine report, *Preventing Childhood Obesity: Health in the Balance* (Washington, D.C.: National Academies Press, 2004). It provides the most recent scientific findings about the causes and effects of childhood obesity. It also suggests potential solutions.

Charlie and Sam Fabrikant were generous with their time and endured two author visits to Chicago, a day of shadowing at school, and lengthy telephone interviews. Wendy Fabrikant was very helpful in obtaining photographs, answering questions, and setting up a visit to Buffalo Grove High School. We are grateful to Patrice Johannes, the school's principal, for her tour of the school. Dr. Chris Salvino took time out of his busy schedule to explain the history of the WISH Center.

The authors wish to thank Alex Sternberg of the SUNY Downstate Medical Center for arranging interviews with young people at the Downstate Weight Loss Clinic in Brooklyn, New York. Dr. Sternberg runs a youth weight-loss program that could serve as a model for others throughout the country. We'd also like to thank Heidi Guy and David Candy of the New Leaf program at St. Richard's Hospital in Chichester, England; Dr. Vyvyan Howard of the University of Liverpool; Jeanette Orrey, formerly of St. Peter's Church of England Primary School in East Bridgford, Nottinghamshire; and Mary Rudolf of the Watch It clinic in Leeds. Unfortunately, the small number of youth health and weight-loss clinics in Great Britain cannot keep up with the demand for such services.

202   *Sam Fabrikant sat on the edge:* Interviews with Sam, Charlie, and Wendy Fabrikant.

207   *Today almost two thirds of the adults:* For information about the number of adults who are obese or overweight, see Katherine M. Flegal et al., "Prevalence and Trends in Obesity Among U.S. Adults, 1999–2000," *Journal of the American Medical Association* 288 (2002): 1723–27. For children, see C. L. Ogden, K. M. Flegal, M. D. Carroll, and C. L. Johnson, "Prevalence and Trends in Overweight Among U.S. Children and Adolescents, 1999–2000," *Journal of the American Medical Association* 288 (2002): 1728–32.

207   *Almost 50 million Americans are now obese:* Cited in A. H. Mokdad et al., "Prevalence of Obesity, Diabetes, and Obesity Related Health Risk Factors, 2001," *Journal of the American Medical Association* 289 (2003): 76–79.

207   *An additional 6 or 7 million are "morbidly obese":* Ibid. The Body Mass Index (BMI) is a measurement that takes into account a person's height and weight. People who are morbidly obese have a BMI of 40 or greater. Those who are super-obese have a BMI of 50 or higher.

207   *Since the early 1970s, the rate of obesity:* In the 1970–1974 National Health Examination Surveys, 12 percent of the men and 16.7 percent of the women were obese. Cited in "Statistics Related to Overweight and Obesity," Cleveland Clinic, 2005. The obesity rate among U.S. adults in 2001 was 20.1 percent.

207   *Among preschoolers it has doubled:* See Ogden et al., "Prevalence and Trends in Overweight Among U.S. Children and Adolescents." This work defines *obese* as those children who rank in the top five percentiles of children of the BMI. Also see National Academy of Sciences, "Preventing Childhood Obesity," p. 63.

207   *"We've got the fattest, least fit generation":* Quoted in Maggie Fox, "U.S.: Obesity Will Be Hard to Treat, Experts Say," *AAP Newsfeed,* May 29, 1998.

208   *For most of human history:* See Robert William Fogel, *The Escape from Hunger and Premature Death, 1700–2100: Europe, America, and the Third World* (New York: Cambridge University Press, 2004).

208   *A typical person has 25 to 35 billion fat cells:* Cited in Dana D. Sterner, "Abdominal Obesity: How It's Different," *RN,* Nov. 1, 2004.

208   *They communicate with the brain:* See Rob Stein, "Decoding the Surprisingly Active Life of Fat Cells," *Washington Post,* July 12, 2004.

209   *An obese person can develop:* Cited in Brad Evenson, "Research Shows Fat Is an Organ: Guides New Research, Explains Ruined Diets," *National Post* (Canada), Sept. 8, 2003.

209   *If you are obese by the age of thirteen:* See S. S. Guo et al., "Predicting Overweight and Obesity in Adulthood From Body Mass Index Values in Childhood and Adolescence," *American Journal of Clinical Nutrition* (2002): 655.

210   *Less than 30 percent of high school students:* See Centers for Disease Control, "Youth Risk Behavior Surveillance—United States, 2003," *Morbidity and Mortality Weekly Report* 53 (No. SS-2): 21–24; 28.4 percent of students were enrolled in daily physical education classes in 2003, up from 25 percent in 1995.

210   *12 percent of students:* See National Academy of Sciences, *Preventing Childhood Obesity,* p. 41.

210   *"personal responsibility":* See John Arlidge, "McDonald's Says Get Some Exercise, Fatso," *Times* (London), Apr. 17, 2005. Jim Skinner, CEO of McDonald's, told the *Times* reporter that "it's time to shift the focus to personal responsibility. . . . It's not just about our products anymore, it's about what our customers do."

210   *the industry earns most of its money:* See Bret Begun, "A Really Big Idea: Burger King's CEO Has Turned Around the Chain with a Radical Notion: Give People What They Want," *Newsweek,* May 23, 2005, and Jennifer Ordonez, "Cash Cows: Burger Joints Call Them 'Heavy Users'—But Not to Their Faces," *Wall Street Journal,* January 12, 2001.

210   *According to one former McDonald's executive:* Interview with a retired senior executive at McDonald's who prefers not to be named.

211   *One of these large Cokes:* See "McDonald's USA Nutrition Facts for Popular Menu Items," McDonald's Corporation, 2005. A large Coca-Cola Classic has 310 calories and 86 grams of carbohydrates. A twelve-ounce serving of Coke has the equivalent of ten teaspoons of sugar, so a thirty-two-ounce Coke would have somewhere on the order of twenty-nine teaspoons of sugar.

211   *In 1957 the typical fast-food burger patty:* Cited in Amanda Spake, "A Fat Nation: America's 'Supersize' Diet Is Fattier and Sweeter—and Deadlier," *U.S. News & World Report,* Aug. 19, 2002.

211   *That one hamburger has 1,410 calories:* See Hardee's Nutritional Information, 2005.

211   *the average person aged nine to thirteen:* See Report of the Dietary Guidelines Advisory Committee on the Dietary Guidelines for Americans, "Part D: Science Base, Section 3: Discretionary Calories," 2005, p. 8.

211   *At Wendy's, a Classic Triple hamburger:* The sandwich has 970 calories and 59 grams of fat; the fries have 590 calories and 29 grams of fat; and the Biggie cola soft drink has 200 calories and 0 grams of fat. See Wendy's "Build-A-Meal" at www.wendys.com.

212   *A Burger King Big Kids Double Cheeseburger Meal:* The Double Cheeseburger has 530 calories, the Coca-Cola has 140 calories, and the fries have 230 calories. See Burger King, "Nutritional Facts," at www.bk.com.

212   *Denny's Beer Barrel Pub:* See Sarah E. Lockyer, "The Burger Strikes Back," *Nation's Restaurant News,* June 6, 2005.

212   *Kate Stelnick ordered one of these eleven-pound hamburgers:* See "Slender Teen Is First to Gobble 11-Pound Meal," *Ventura County Star* (California), Jan. 18, 2005.

213   *They're frequently teased at school:* See Ian Janssen et al., "Associations Between Overweight and Obesity with Bullying Behaviors in School-Aged Children," *Pediatrics* 113, no. 5 (May 2004): 1187–94.

213   *They're far more likely than other kids:* See Richard S. Strauss, M.D., "Childhood Obesity and Self Esteem," *Pediatrics* 105 (2000).

213   *One study of obese children:* See Jeffrey B. Schwimmer, Tasha M. Burwinkle, and James W. Varni, "Health-Related Quality of Life of Severely Obese Children and Adolescents," *Journal of the American Medical Association* 289 (Apr. 2003): 1813–19.

213   *Obesity has been linked to health problems:* See Aviva Must, Jennifer Spadano, Eugenie H. Coakley, Allison E. Field, Graham Colditz, and William H. Dietz, "The Disease Burden Associated with Overweight and Obesity," *Journal of the American Medical Association* 282 (Oct. 27, 1999): 1523–29.

213   *Obese people are two to three times more likely to die young:* Cited in Eugenia E. Calle, et al., "Body-Mass Index and Mortality in a Prospective Cohort of U.S. Adults," *New England Journal of Medicine* 341 (October 7, 1999): 1097–1105.

213   *Obesity kills more than twice as many Americans:* See National Highway Traffic Safety Administration, press release, "2004 Highway Deaths Projected to Reach 42,800; Transportation Secretary Mineta Calls Fatalities a 'National Epidemic,'" Apr. 21, 2005.

213   *According to one recent estimate:* See Katherine M. Flegal et al., "Excess Deaths Associated with Underweight, Overweight, and Obesity," *Journal of the American Medical Association* 293 (Apr. 20, 2005): 1861.

214   *It is now the sixth leading cause of death:* See "10 Leading Causes of Death, United States, 2002, All Races, Both Sexes," National Center for Injury Prevention

and Control, Centers for Disease Control and Prevention.

214   *A study conducted by the federal government:* See K. M. Venkat Narayan et al., "Lifetime Risk for Diabetes Mellitus in the United States," *Journal of the American Medical Association* 290 (2003): 1884–90.

214   *Among African-American and Latino children:* Ibid.

214   *The life of a ten-year-old child:* Ibid.

214   *Between 1984 and 1993, the number of fast-food restaurants:* Cited in Elizabeth Gleick, "Land of the Fat: It's Time to Shape Up: Europeans Are Facing an Obesity Crisis That May Only Get Worse," *Time,* Oct. 25, 1999.

214   *During the 1980s, the sale of fast food in Japan:* The first figure is cited in Mark Hammond and Jacqueline Ruyak, "The Decline of the Japanese Diet: MacArthur to McDonald's," *East West,* Oct. 1990. The change in the obesity rate is cited in "Western Fast Food Is Blamed for Overweight Children," *Food Labeling News,* May 13, 1998.

215   *Many Okinawans could expect:* See Bryan Walsh, "Asia's War with Heart Disease," *Time International,* May 10, 2004.

215   *The first McDonald's opened on the island:* Ibid.

215   *Today Okinawa has the most hamburger restaurants:* Cited in Norimitsu Onishi, "On U.S. Fast Food, More Okinawans Grow Super-sized," *New York Times,* Mar. 30, 2004.

215   *Okinawa also has:* Ibid.

216   *Dr. Mehmet Oz stands:* Interview with Dr. Mehmet Oz. The authors appreciate the help of Amy Grillo, public affairs assistant at New York-Presbyterian Hospital/Columbia.

219   *Researchers at Harvard University believe:* See Walter C. Willett and Alberto Ascherio, "Trans Fatty Acids: Are the Effects Only Marginal?" *American Journal of Public Health* 84 (1994): 722–24.

221   *A study of high school kids:* See Grace Wyshak, "Teenaged Girls, Carbonated Beverage Consumption, and Bone Fractures," *Pediatrics & Adolescent Medicine* 154 (2000): 610–13.

222   *Thomas Robertson had severe chest pain:* This information came from an interview with Paulette Robertson, Thomas's mother, and John Pope, "Teenage Wake-Up Call; Bad Habits, Disease Taking Hold Earlier," *New Orleans Times-Picayune,* Oct. 13, 2002.

222   *some ten-year-old obese children:* The study was conducted at the Chinese University of Hong Kong by Kam S. Woo, M.D. See "Chinese University of Hong Kong: Exercise Is Key to Reversing Obesity-Related Heart Risk in Children," *Cardiovascular Device Liability Week,* May 2, 2004; David Derbyshire and Roger Highfield, "One in Five Teenagers Shows Signs of Heart Disease," *Daily Telegraph* (London), Sept. 7, 2004.

224 *In 1993 surgeons performed about 16,000 gastric bypass operations:* Figures courtesy of the American Society for Bariatric Surgery.

224 *The cost for one of these operations:* Cited in Robert Steinbrook, "Surgery for
Severe Obesity," *New England Journal of Medicine* 350 (Mar. 11, 2004):
1075–79.

224 *Dr. Salvino had an unusual background:* Interview with Dr. Salvino.

226 *In April 2004, Warren Allen died:* See Todd C. Frankel, "Weighing the Risks for
Obese Teens, a Last Resort," *St. Louis Post-Dispatch*, Mar. 7, 2005, and "Local
Teenager Died Less than Year After Weight-Loss Surgery," *St. Louis Post-Dispatch*,
Mar. 6, 2005.

227 *beriberi:* See Sharon Kirkey, "The Fat Files," *National Post* (Canada), Sept. 9,
2003.

227 *About one out of every 1,700 patients:* Salvino interview.

YOUR WAY

We are grateful to Alice Waters for her hospitality during our visits to the Edible
Schoolyard. Her book, *Fanny at Chez Panisse: A Child's Restaurant Adventures
with 46 Recipes* (New York: Morrow, 1997), explores the life of the restaurant
through the eyes of Alice's daughter and offers some simple recipes. Students inter-
ested in starting a garden at their school should consult the Edible Schoolyard's
Web site, www.edibleschoolyard.org. The National Gardening Association maintains a list of schools around the country that already have gardens. To schedule a
visit to one, call the association at (800) 538-7476 or visit its Web site, www.kids
gardening.org. If you are looking for a delicious alternative to fast food, look for a
farmers' market near your home. The USDA Web site has a map showing where
these markets can be found: www.ams.usda.gov/farmersmarkets/map.htm. Buying
food directly from your local farmer is the best way to support sustainable agriculture and enjoy fresh, healthy meals.

For sixty years, the Soil Association has been promoting organic food and sustainable agriculture in the United Kingdom. Its 2004 report, "Food for Life:
Healthy, Local, Organic School Meals," provides an excellent overview of the
problems with school meal programs in the U.K. as well as a blueprint for schools
everywhere that want to feed children properly.

235 *American soldiers waited:* See Kerry Williamson, "Serving Fast Food in a War
Zone a Whopper of a Task: Calgary's Joe Petrusich Dodges Mortar Rounds
to Bring Burger King and Pizza Hut to U.S. and British Military in Iraq,"
Edmonton Journal (Alberta), Nov. 29, 2004; "Threats to Taste of Home," *Air
Force Times*, Mar. 1, 2004; David Finlayson, "Fast Food Hot Off the Grill Is

Hot Stuff to Troops," *Vancouver Sun,* Nov. 3, 2003; "Burger King in Baghdad—US Troops Dig in for Long Haul," *ONASA News Agency,* July 15, 2003.

235 *"It is very, very challenging":* Quoted in Williamson, "Serving Fast Food."

235 *In 1991, McDonald's had fewer than 4,000 restaurants:* Cited in "McDonald's Opens First Restaurant in Greece; Golden Arches Now in 56 Countries," *PR Newswire,* Nov. 11, 1991.

236 *Today it has about 18,000 restaurants:* As of this writing, McDonald's has more than 13,000 restaurants in the United States and 31,000 total worldwide. See "McDonald's Announces Management Changes & Promotions," McDonald's Corporation, July 15, 2004.

236 *"McWorld":* For a fine examination of the cultural conflict now being waged in many societies, see Benjamin Barber, *Jihad vs. McWorld: How Globalism and Tribalism Are Reshaping the World* (New York: Ballantine, 1996).

236 *five hundred Russians:* Cited in Ann Imse, "McDonald's Opens in Moscow," Associated Press, Jan. 31, 1990.

236 *when a McDonald's opened in Kuwait:* See Kevin Pang, "A Bite of Burger History: A Few Moments in the Fast-Food Burger's Last 50 Years," *Chicago Tribune,* May 26, 2005.

236 *holy city of Mecca:* Cited in Bill McDowall, "The Global Market Challenge," *Restaurants & Institutions,* Nov. 1, 1994.

237 *"The objective of this program is simple":* Quoted in Corinna Hawkes, "Marketing Activities of Global Soft Drink and Fast Food Companies in Emerging Markets: A Review," in *Globalization, Diets, and Noncommunicable Diseases,* World Health Organization, 2002, p. 10.

238 *"Resist America beginning with Cola":* Quoted in Philip F. Zeidman, "Globalization: A Hard Pill to Swallow," *Franchising World,* July–Aug. 1999.

239 *"Maybe they think it's Italian":* Quoted in "U.S. Companies in China Keeping Low Profile," *Colorado Springs Gazette,* May 11, 1999.

241 *A new disease:* For a thorough account of the history and spread of mad cow disease, see Maxime Schwartz and Edward Schneider, *How the Cows Turned Mad* (Berkeley: University of California Press, 2003).

242 *"Our cows":* "Policy Statement by Consumer Protection Minister Renate Künast," *Die Bundesregierung,* Feb. 8, 2001.

243 *"Because we have the world's biggest shopping cart":* Quoted in Philip Brasher, "McDonald's Enforcing Beef Rules," Associated Press, Mar. 13, 2001.

244 *The hens got a little more space:* Cited in Neil Steinberg, "McDonald's Gives Hens More Room," *Chicago Sun-Times,* Aug. 24, 2000.

244 *In 2005, McDonald's became:* Cited in Gary Younge, "McDonald's Grabs a Piece of the Apple Pie," *Guardian* (U.K.), Mar. 23, 2005.

245 *The* Washington Post *estimated:* Cited in Margaret Webb Pressler, "Hold the Health, Serve That Burger," *Washington Post,* Aug. 18, 2005.

245 *The most successful new item:* Ibid.

245 *"There are no good foods or bad foods":* McDonald's representatives have been using this phrase since at least the early 1990s. See the quote of Michael Goldblatt, a former assistant vice president at McDonald's, in "McDonald's Highlights Importance of Good Nutrition in 1990 Annual Report to Shareholders," *Business Wire,* Apr. 11, 1991. Representatives of fast-food companies and junk-food companies continue to use similar language today. Richard Martin, spokesman for the Grocery Manufacturers Association, told a congressional committee in July 2005 that "any food can be responsibly consumed by everyone, including kids." Quoted in Melanie Warner, "Food Industry Defends Marketing to Children," *New York Times,* July 15, 2005.

245 *"global ambassador of fun":* See Kate Macarthur, "Health-Minded Ronald Buffs Image; Iconic Mascot Is Redeployed to Tout Fit Lifestyle to Youth, but Is It an 'Overcorrection'?" *Advertising Age,* July 25, 2005.

246 *"Bite me":* These slogans were found at www.mcdonalds.com/usa/fun/bigmac.html in Sept. 2005.

246 *As a child in the 1950s:* The account of the Edible Schoolyard is based on interviews with Alice Waters, Esther Cook, and other staff members as well as visits to Martin Luther King Jr. Middle School. The authors also appreciate the assistance of Sarah Weiner and Sue DuBois at the Chez Panisse Foundation.

253 *"actions have consequences":* Quoted in "A Delicious Revolution," by Alice Waters, Center for Eco-Literacy, 2004.

256 *survey by* Restaurants & Institutions: See "2005 Consumers' Choice in Chains," *Restaurants & Institutions,* August 22, 2005.

ACKNOWLEDGMENTS

Chew On This has our names on the cover, but many other people made invaluable contributions to the book. Eden Edwards, our editor at Houghton Mifflin, displayed enormous patience, offered wonderful suggestions, and gave us tremendous support from beginning to end. She's also very good with a knife. We are grateful to Eden for all she added to the book and for all she put up with. The flaws in *Chew On This* are entirely our own.

Meredith Mundy Wasinger encouraged us to write a book about fast food for younger readers, and we appreciate her early enthusiasm for the project. At Houghton Mifflin, Liz Duvall and Susan Warhover did a fine job of making us appear much more literate than we really are. We are grateful to Joyce White and Sheila Smallwood for the book's design, to Loren Isenberg for its legality, to Karen Walsh and Megan Butler for its promotion, and to Mike Wartella for its memorable cover. Eamon Dolan deserves some sort of prize.

Ellis Levine is not only an expert on libel law, but also a perceptive critic. His careful reading of the manuscript helps us sleep at night.

Tina Bennett is the best. Without her dedication and wise counsel, this book would not exist. We would like her to run the world.

Although the subject matter in *Chew On This* is often unpleasant, during our research we met far too many pleasant people to name here. Among them, we'd especially like to thank Danielle Brent and Sadi Lambert, who spent so much time describing their work experiences; Kristina Clark and Carol Cozzen, who are warm hearts in the nation's chilliest state; Ann, Emily, and Maggie Hanna, who in every way are the real deal; Mary and Jonathan Kapsner, who were such gracious hosts in Alaska; Alice Waters, who is pure inspiration; and Charlie, Sam, Arnie, and Wendy Fabrikant, who trusted us with their story. The chicken farmer we call Norah gave us a firsthand account of what poultry growers face today. Dr. Mehmet Oz is a walking advertisement for what he preaches. His ideas can change people's lives for the better. Heide Schaffner provided friendly help with photo research. We are grateful to the management of International Flavors &

Fragrances for allowing us another peek at the marvels of their business.

Eric would like to thank his family and friends for being so excited about this book. Mica and Conor, in particular, suffered so that others might learn. Lorelei Linklater was one of the first people to read *Chew On This*, and her response was thoughtful and much appreciated. Once again, without Red, none of these words could have been written.

Charles would like to thank some of the many people who helped him. Maria Mezei read early drafts of several chapters, offering many helpful suggestions. She is a ray of light to all those around her, and she has a bright future as an artist. Crawford Wilson built a ramp around his basement pool table for his grandson, and it has made him feel taller ever since. Arthur C. Kirsch set an example many years ago for his humane engagement with literature and his kindness and decency. Becky Winnette is a beloved sister who brightens up the lives of the children in her special education classroom. The memory of Barrie Winnette's warmth and humor lingers every day. Leila Gazale is not only a valued friend and talented actress but also a legal maven who offered incredible help.

Though Charles can't possibly name all who gave him support, he'd also like to send thanks to Richard Bernstein,

Meredith Blum, Ken and Kathy Bohrer, Ali Burns, Alita Byrd, Jill Campbell, Peter Canby, David Cohen, Kimiye Corwin, Paul English, Sophie Fels, Patrick Flynn, Andy and Tara Friedman, Colin Gardner, Dwight Garner, Jake Goldstein, Adam Goodheart, Chad and Krista Hoeppner, Diana Kane, Jose Lantigua, Jay Leahy, Kelly Munly, Al Nazemian, Alexandra Neil, Joanna Parson, Kim and Lori Peckham, Whitney Peeling, Jay Pingree, Cristina Posa, Mary Ramsey, Rebecca Reich, Jacky Reres, Aaron Retica, Allison Rhodes, Melissa Salmons, Sandy Schechter, Pamela Scorza, Karen Shelby, Sarah Harrison Smith, Frances Stead Sellers, Rory Stanton, Heather Won Tesoriero, Mike Wartella, Robert Wilson, and Amanda Winfree.

Charles L. and Miriam J. Wilson offered tremendous support and have made their own roads by walking. They have lived in a way that has demonstrated compassion and quiet courage, and they are deeply loved.

INDEX

A

additives
  color, 121–24
  flavor, 103, 104–5, 110–16, 120,
    173
  fragrance, 106, 114–15
  health effects of, 123–24
advertising. *See* marketing
Alaska, Kasigluk, 128–32, 145–50,
  151–55
animal welfare, 165–66, 175–77,
  179–82, 196, 199, 243–44

B

baby bottle syndrome, 148–49
beef industry, 156–69, 184–86, 194,
  241–42
brain damage, 217, 241–42
brand name recognition, 8, 24, 47, 49
Brent, Danielle, 70–72, 80–81
Burger King
  assembly-line production, 74
  creation, 25–26
  demonstrations against, 240
  fry flavoring, 127
  healthier choices, 245
  in Iraq, 235
  manual, 75
  number of restaurants, 57
  portion sizes and calories, 212
  promotions by, 52, 58, 61
  in schools, 134
Burgerville, 256–57

C

California, 19–20, 246–53. *See also*
  fast-food restaurants, history
candy, 120, 121–24
cannibalism, 176, 183, 241, 242, 243
Carl's Jr., 25, 211
cereal, 140–41
Chez Panisse, 247–48, 250, 252
chicken industry, 169–82, 194
Clark, Kristina, 145–47, 149–50,
  154–55
Coca-Cola, 55, 113, 142, 143,
  145–50, 211
Coca-Cola Company
  at marketing conferences, 38, 56
  marketing strategies, 144, 147–48,
    152–55, 237
  repetitive ads, 53

color additives, 121–24
Colorado, 156–60, 163–68
ConAgra Poultry, 173
Confederation of National Trade
  Unions (CNTU), 87–90
corporations, large, 7–8, 35, 98,
  161–63, 243, 254
Cramer, Keith G., 25–26
Cromp, Maxime, 85–91
culture
  California, 19–20, 247
  cars in our, 19, 23, 67, 81, 94,
    141, 169–70
  cattle ranching, 156–60, 163
  effects of strip malls, 63–67, 205,
    236
  Japan, 214–15
  obesity factors, 209–10
  working parents, 48–49, 58, 81,
    204
  Yupik Eskimos, 128–32, 145–50,
    151–55

D

Denny's, 61, 127, 212
diabetes, Type II, 213–14, 227
Disney, Walt, 39–40, 44. *See also*
  Disneyland; Walt Disney Studios
Disneyland, 40–43, 44, 62
Domino's Pizza, 27, 74
drive-ins and drive-throughs, 20–22,
  255
Dunkin' Donuts, 26

E

E. coli O157:H7, 192–98
economics
  annual advertising costs, 57
  annual food costs, 104
  cattle ranching, 160–61, 162–63
  cost of gastric bypass surgery, 224
  80–20 rule, 210

fast-food profits, 32, 97, 142
  increase in fast-food sales, 10–11,
    52, 58
  junk food sales in schools, 138
  McDonald's worth, 34
  real estate, 66, 160
  restaurant deals, 11, 75, 142
  spending power of children, 39
  wages (*See* salary)
education
  cooking, 250–51
  Edible Schoolyard garden,
    249–53
  on flavor and eating habits, 108
  on nutrition, 57, 245–53
  school materials by fast food
    companies, 140–42
eggs, 244

F

Fabrikant, Sam, 202–7, 223–33
farming issues, 96–98, 255–57
fast food
  cleanliness issues, 18, 80
  cooking oil, 102–3, 125–27, 173
  eating nothing but, 18, 221–22
  form delivered to restaurant, 74
  French fries (*See* French fries)
  hand-eaten, 23, 94, 169–70
  health effects of, 215–23 (*See also*
    obesity)
  healthier choices, 244–46, 255–57
  impacts on Yupik culture, 131–32
  meat (*See* chicken; hamburger;
    meat used in fast food)
  mouthfeel, 116–17
  in other countries, 126–27,
    214–15, 234–42
  poor nutrition in, 210, 211,
    219–20, 227, 245
  profits, 32, 97, 142

sales, 10–11, 52, 58, 210
in schools, 132–35
the source of, 9–10, 241, 255–57
taste (*See* taste)
fast-food restaurants
cash registers, 75
competition among, 33–34
customer relations, 75
demonstrations against, 126,
238–41
drive-ins and drive-throughs,
20–22, 255
effects on the American landscape,
63–70
history, 18, 20–36
location strategies, 10, 35, 67, 70,
133, 238
of multinational corporations, 35
playlands, 57–58
responsibly managed, 255–57
sameness as a goal, 32–33, 36,
236 (*See also under* McDonald's)
fat. *See* obesity; trans fats
feedlots, 163–69, 196
food containers, 23, 58–62, 257
food poisoning, 192–98
franchise system, 32–33, 35–36, 236.
See also taste, sameness
French fries
assembly-line production, 99–102
development as fast food, 92–96
farming issues, 96–98, 255
pounds eaten per year, 96
special taste of McDonald's,
102–3, 125–27
suppliers, 96–99
types, 99
U.S. history, 93–94

G

gardening, 250–53

gastric bypass surgery, 202–3, 205–7,
223–33

H

hamburger (meat). *See* health and
safety issues, hamburger and beef;
meat used in fast food
hamburger (sandwich), 13–15,
23–24, 36, 211–12
Hamburger Charlie, 13–15, 36
Hanna, Emily and Maggie, 156–60
health and safety issues
additives, 123–24, 165
being overweight, 134, 139, 215,
245 (*See also* obesity)
bomb protection, 241
bone strength, 220–21
Chicken McNuggets, 172–73
cleanliness of fast food, 18, 80
cooking oils, 103, 125
feedlots and slaughterhouses,
164–167, 183–91, 196–98,
241–44
food poisoning, 192–98
food safety laws, 184, 195–96,
242, 243
gastric bypass complications, 225,
226–27, 230–31
going hungry, 136–37
hamburger and beef, 15–17, 18,
165, 183–86, 192–98, 241–42
heart disease, 216, 217–19,
222–23, 227
mad cow disease, 241–42
overworked staff, 72, 82
poisons, 106, 123
tooth damage and soda, 55, 143,
145–50
toys, 195
heart disease, 216, 217–19, 222–23, 227
hyperactivity, 124

I

IBP, 186
Illinois, 204–5, 223, 228, 236
In-N-Out, 255–56
International Flavors & Fragrances
(IFF), 104–6, 117–19, 120
Internet, 52–53

J

J. R. Simplot Company, 98
The Jungle, 183–85
junk food, 57, 137–39, 219–20. *See
also* candy; fast food; soda pop

K

Kapsner, Mary, 151–53
Kentucky Fried Chicken, 27–29. *See
also* KFC
KFC
chicken suppliers, 178, 179
demonstrations against, 238, 240,
241
in other countries, 236
owned by Yum! Brands, 38
purchase of chicken, 172
sports promotion by, 61
Kroc, Ray
and Disney, 39, 44, 48, 62
early days at McDonald's, 29–34,
43–45, 228–29
early life, 39
French fry development, 92, 93, 95
leadership style, 40
restaurant location strategy, 67,
70, 132
and Ronald McDonald, 47

L

labeling, food, 112–14, 219–20
labor issues
child labor, 59–60, 86
discrimination, 86
immigrants, 186, 190–91
responsibly managed restaurants,
255–57
slaughterhouse workers, 181–82,
183–86, 244
unions, 85–91, 169, 185, 186, 190
work hours, 82
Lambert, Sadi, 82–83
Lamb Weston, 98–102
Langdon, Trajan, 147–48, 153
laws
food safety, 184, 195–96, 242,
243
need for better, 253–54
work hours, 82
liver damage, 221–22
logos
Burger King, 134
Golden Arches of McDonald's, 8,
24, 49
on vehicles, 141, 147, 151

M

mad cow disease, 241–42
marketing
the American Dream, 131
as brainwashing, 53
Coca-Cola ads, 53
creation of a world, 40, 48
by Disneyland, 41–43
early, 39–40, 45 (*See also* Disney,
Walt; Kroc, Ray)
global, 38–39, 126–27, 214–15,
234–42
growth of, 48–49
to schools, 133, 134, 137–42
to teenagers, 245–46
use of television, 46–47, 56, 61
use of the Internet, 52–53
workshop, 37–38
marketing research, 51–56, 117–20
marketing strategies

children's clubs, 51–52
cradle-to-grave, 38–39, 49, 110
jingles, 14
kids nagging parents, 49–50, 52, 58
product-linking, 41–43, 45, 48, 62
repetitive ads, 53
Saturday-morning time slot, 47
Martin Luther King Jr. Middle
    School, 248–53
McDonald, Richard and Maurice, 19,
    22–25, 29, 30–34, 45, 74–75
McDonaldland, 40, 48, 62
McDonald's Corporation
    advertising, 46–48, 61–62
    assembly-line production, 24, 29,
        30–34, 74–75
    beef suppliers, 161, 186, 197
    Buffalo Grove, Ill., 204, 205
    Chicken McNuggets, 169–73, 178,
        180, 182
    chicken suppliers, 162, 171–72,
        173–74, 175
    Coca-Cola in, 142, 211
    creation of a world (See
        McDonaldland)
    demonstrations against, 126, 238,
        239–40, 241
    and Disney, 39, 44, 48, 62
    E. coli outbreak, 193
    franchise system, 32, 36
    French fries, 92–103, 125–27
    Golden Arches, 8, 24, 49
    Hamburger University, 236
    Happy Meal, 48, 58–61
    headquarters, 228
    healthier choices, 244–46
    history, 19, 22–25, 30–34, 44–45,
        74, 92–95
    innovations in food preparation,
        23, 39

labor issues, 83–91
lawsuits against, 126, 127
location strategies, 35, 67, 70,
    132–35, 238
manual, 75
marketing and public relations, 25,
    38, 45, 46–48, 243–46 (See
    also Ronald McDonald)
number of restaurants, 7, 35, 57,
    90, 95, 236
in other countries, 83–91, 126–27,
    214–15, 236, 238, 239–40
power of the company, 7–8, 243,
    254
recipe development, 40, 127
sameness as a goal, 32–33, 93,
    95, 161, 194, 236
in schools, 132–35, 141
sports promotion by, 61
statistics on popularity, 7
toys, 58–61
and vegetarianism, 124–27
Web site, 52, 53, 127
McDuff, Pascal, 83–91
McJob, definition, 79
meat used in fast food
    bad reputation, 15–17, 160,
        241–42
    cattle feedlots, 163–69, 196,
        241–42
    cattle slaughterhouses, 182–91,
        194, 196–98, 199, 201, 241–43
    cattle suppliers, 156–63
    chicken farms and slaughterhouses,
        170, 171, 172, 173–82, 194,
        244
    chicken suppliers, 169–74
    contamination, 183, 192–98
    diseased, 197, 241–42
    growth hormones in, 165

meat used in fast food (cont.)
  healthy, 256
  pig factories and slaughterhouses,
    198–201, 244
  slaughterhouse escapees, 198–201
Mickey Mouse, 40, 41, 42, 51
milk shakes, 29, 113–14
mouthfeel, 116–17

N

Nebraska, Milford, 168–69
nutrition
  education about, 57, 245–53
  Native American, 128–32
  poor quality of fast food, 210,
    211, 219–20, 227, 245

O

obesity
  emotional costs, 206, 213
  fat cells, 209
  gastric bypass surgery, 202–3,
    205–7, 223–33
  other health problems due to, 206,
    213–14, 215–23, 227
  U.S. statistics, 139, 207, 213
Occupational Safety and Health
  Administration (OSHA), 186–87, 190
oil, cooking, 102–3, 125–27, 173
Oz, Dr. Mehmet, 216–22

P

parents
  influence of children over, 50, 52,
    58
  working, 48–49, 58, 81, 204
People for the Ethical Treatment of
  Animals (PETA), 243–44
pigs and pig farms, 198–201, 244
Pilgrim's Pride, 179–82
Pizza Hut
  assembly-line production, 74
  in other countries, 235, 238–39

owned by Yum! Brands, 38
in schools, 133, 141
sports promotion by, 61
political issues, 253–54
pop. See Coca-Cola; soda pop
portion sizes, 75, 142, 211–12
power
  of the consumer, 254, 257–58
  of large corporations, 7–8,
    161–63, 243, 254
processed foods, 104, 112. See also
  additives
public relations, 21, 25, 45, 75,
  243–46

R

ranching, cattle, 156–61, 162–63
research
  chicken breeding, 172, 177
  Chicken McNuggets, 170, 171,
    172–73
  eating only fast food, 18, 221–22
  flavor additives, 103, 104–6,
    111–20
  fragrance, 106, 111, 112
  French fry, 94
  for marketing purposes (See
    marketing research)
  obesity, 213, 216–19
  sense of taste, 108–9
restaurants. See fast-food restaurants
Ronald McDonald, 46–47, 52, 53,
  126, 133, 245

S

salary issues, 21, 77–78, 85, 164,
  255
Salvino, Dr., 224–25, 227, 229–30,
  232
Sanders, Harland, 27–29
schools, 10, 131, 132–42, 144,
  150–53, 250–53

Shah, Hitesh, 124–25
Simplot, J. R., 92, 93–95, 96–97.
    See also J. R. Simplot Company
slaughterhouses, 163–69, 178–91,
    194, 196–98, 199
slow food, 247–48
smell, sense of, 106, 109–10, 112–13.
    See also additives, fragrance
Smith, Norah, 175–76, 177
soda pop
    caffeine in, 143
    drinking volume statistics, 143, 146
    drunk by toddlers, 143–44
    flavor additives in, 113
    impacts on Yupik culture, 145–50,
        151–55
    marketing overseas, 237
    and osteoporosis, 220–21
    in schools, 138, 141–42, 144,
        150–53
    teeth damage from, 55, 143,
        145–50
Speedee Service System, 24, 29,
    30–34, 74–75
Spurlock, Morgan, 221–22
staff at fast-food restaurants
    assistant managers, 72
    at early restaurants, 20–22, 25
    Employee of the Month, 84
    franchise owners, 33
    labor unions for, 85–91
    lack of power, 73, 76, 78, 86–87
    little skill necessary, 23, 73, 76
    long hours and low pay, 76–83
    management, 72, 78–79, 84, 255
    salaries, 21, 77, 78, 85, 255
    strict rules for, 75
    team spirit, 79
    teenagers, 70–73
    turnover, 76

Subway, 27, 133, 235
sugar, 120, 140, 143, 161, 211
Super Size Me, 221–22
Swift and Company, 161, 162, 165

T

Taco Bell, 26, 38, 61, 74
taste
    additives to create (*See* additives,
        flavor)
    comfort foods, 110
    and cooking oil, 102–3, 125–27
    sameness for fast food
        beef, 161
        French fries, 93, 95, 97, 102,
            127
        as a goal, 32–33, 76 (*See also*
            under McDonald's)
    the sense of, 106–8, 110, 122
taste testers, 117–20
teenagers
    gastric bypass surgery, 227
    heart disease, 222
    long work hours, 72, 79–83
    marketing to, 245–46
    popular jobs, 79–80
    as staff, 70–79
teeth damage, 55, 143, 145–50
television
    ads, 42–43, 46–47, 56, 57, 61,
        140–42
    Channel One in schools, 140–42
    hours watched per week, 56–57
    impacts on Yupik culture, 131
toddlers, 57–58, 143–44, 207
toys with fast-food meals, 58–62,
    195, 257
trans fats, 219–20
trusts, 161–62, 184
Turner, Fred, 75, 170
Ty, Teenie Beanie Baby, 60–61

Tyson Foods, 162, 171–72, 173–74, 175, 190

U

unions, 85–91, 169, 185, 186, 190
urban landscape
   effects of strip malls, 63–70, 205
   sameness in the, 36, 65, 66, 236
U.S. Department of Agriculture (USDA), 131, 137, 138, 195
U.S. Food and Drug Administration (FDA), 243

V

vegetarianism, 124–27

W

Walt Disney Studios and Company, 40–41, 48, 62
Waters, Alice, 246–53
weight. *See* obesity
Wendy's, 26, 61, 211
West Virginia, Martinsburg, 63–67, 68–69
White Castle, 18
WISH Center, 223, 227–28, 231, 232

Y

Yum! Brands, Inc., 38
Yupik Eskimos, 128–32, 145–50, 151–55